The Road to Reconciliation

Keith R. Wilson

CONTENTS

Introduction: Start at the Beginning   Page 1

1   Assess the Damage   Page 7
2   How to Keep From Cracking Up   Page 27
3   Feelings   Page 62
4   The Big Picture   Page 87
5   The Chasm of Culpability   Page 100
6   The Steps of Reparation   Page 114
7   Seeking Justice   Page 157
8   When Problems Take Over   Page 195
9   When Reconciliation Is Impossible   Page 227
     Acknowledgements   Page 262

INTRODUCTION: START AT THE BEGINNING

If you're the victim

You're wounded and angry. Someone close to you, who should love you, hurt you instead. This person might be a parent, a sibling, a child, a friend, a partner, or a spouse. Whoever it is; where you once had trust, you now have fear. You were attracted; now you are apprehensive. You had love, but now you have loathing. You don't know what to do. Should you stay or should you go? Put up with it or give it right back to them? Retaliate or bury your feelings? If neither choice seems good, it's because neither choice is good. You wish there was another way. Some way that affirmed your experience as a victim but didn't leave you weak and vulnerable. A way that facilitated change and showed mercy without opening you up to more disappointment. Some way to be firm but not rigid.

Luckily, there's a way. The road out of here can be a long, long road, often not well marked, and the choices are confusing, but there's a way.

If you're the offender

You've done something wrong. You hurt someone you love, someone who deserves better from you. This person might be a parent, a sibling, a child, a friend, a partner, or a spouse. Whoever it is; where you were once trusted, you're now under suspicion. You were close, but now you're distant. Loved, but now there's disgust. You want to do better, but you don't know how. You've apologized, maybe a hundred times, but can't get past it. You know your action, even though it was wrong, was not the whole story. There were precipitating factors. It's complicated, you'd like to explain, but you can't talk about it without sounding like you're making excuses. You wish there were another way between groveling and pride. You'd like to learn from your mistakes without losing your dignity and voice.

There's a way for you too—a way to repair what was damaged.

If you don't know what you are

So much has happened that you don't even know who's at fault. You've been caught in a cycle of injury and reprisal so long you don't remember how it started. It was once a loving relationship with a parent, a sibling, a child, a friend, a partner, or a spouse. Now you don't know what it is anymore. It's a bait you must take, a trap you can't escape. You've gone to years of therapy with dozens of marriage counselors and read a shelf full of self-help books, but you can't change. You'd like to, but it takes two, and you both can't seem to get it together at the same time. You wish there was another way, a way that was simple, clear, and direct.

I wish there was another way too, but there's not. There is no simple way. There's not a way without some pitfalls, temptations, blind alleys, and complications. The Road to Reconciliation is not easy, but it's easier than the way you've been going.

How to get going

We tend to divide people into perpetrators and victims and assume they have very different characters. But in reality, we are all both victims and perpetrators. It's not like the hurt person and the guilty one take different paths to reconciliation that start with them far apart and end with them meeting in the middle. Both sets of people are alike and travel the same path before they can come together. In all cases, whether it seems like you were harmed or the one doing the harm, the road to reconciliation begins with coming to terms with being a victim.

You might be surprised by this. When someone has done us harm, we usually want to start by convincing them they were wrong and getting them to admit they were at fault. We're looking for a confession, before repentance begins. We want them to be sorry, to take responsibility—if not grovel—pleading for forgiveness. But you don't need to start there; you may not make meaningful progress if you start there; you may not start at all if you try to start there. It goes better to start where they are. Often that's not at the conviction of sin, but at the conviction of injury.Being a victim puts you in a perilous position. It's hard to get justice. You'll often act out and harm someone, either someone you believe caused the pain or anyone close at hand.[1] Loved ones get the worst of it. Then, when your partner feels harmed, they may harm you right back. Around and around it goes. You could avoid all that by dealing directly with your feelings before you seek justice, so you don't need to act out and injure anyone else.Everyone is a victim, somehow. There are enough bad parents; bad neighborhoods; bad teachers and schools; nuns with rulers; thugs with guns; ruthless terrorists; selfish boyfriends; narcissistic girlfriends; vicious trolls; sexual predators; reckless drivers; treasonous spouses; ungrateful children; exploitive bosses; racist cops; corrupt, lying, demagogic politicians; and cantankerous elders to go around. These people and their actions don't bring out the best in you. When you don't know what to do with the harm they cause, you become someone who does harm. Before anyone becomes an offender, they were a victim first. They were a nail that became a hammer.

This is even true for those who seem to always get the breaks. People born with a silver spoon in their mouths can still complain that they never had to struggle, so they never learned how to cope with the little trouble they do have. Their complaints don't have to be justified or reasonable for these individuals to act on them; they just have to have them. If, in their eyes, they're harmed, that's enough to make them become the cause of harm themselves.

If you're a victim, you may resent that I ask you to open your ranks and let perpetrators of all kinds march with you. Why should you feel sorry for cheating spouses, self-absorbed parents, bullying siblings, alcoholic girlfriends, and drug-dealing, woman-beating boyfriends as well as child abusers, rapists, murderers, and criminals of all kinds? You may see it as yet another indignity visited upon you—you, who deserve to be called victim—that I permit sympathy for their kind. What am I, a soft, bleeding-hearted fool?

As you read on, I think you'll see I'm not. In fact, you'll find me up-front, plain-speaking, straight-talking, and unreserved. As a matter of fact, I'm going to start now by pointing out that this whole mess begins when a victim starts believing some people are more deserving of sympathy, care, and respect than others. That's when a victim crosses the line and becomes a perpetrator. So, cut it out. You don't have to feel sorry for the selfish prick who's blubbering that he's had it so hard; but you have to acknowledge that if that's where he's at, that's where he has to start.

The exception to the rule

I expect most readers will get the most out of the book if they begin with part I, assessing the harm done, and read it in order. The exception might be if you're feeling guilty for something you've done and believe you need to move fast to mend your ways because your partner is ready to give up on you. If you believe that if you dwell too much on how you were wronged, it'll sound like you're making excuses. If that's the case, then go immediately to part V, and proceed through the sections on culpability and work through the steps of reparation. I would never want to stop someone who is ready to accept responsibility. However, I would urge you to turn back later and come to terms with your being a victim. It is only by confronting your weaknesses and vulnerabilities that you'll understand why you did the things you did and acquire the tools to stop them.

You each have your own work to do

Just because both the offender and the offended travel the same road, it doesn't mean they can do it together. No victim wants to hear about how their persecutor was persecuted. You're just going to need to come to terms with it yourself before you can work jointly. You each have an individual part to play before you can play together.

There are a few waypoints on the Road to Reconciliation that are important to watch for. The first is where you're no longer limited to understanding how only you were harmed. You've climbed the long way out of feeling like a victim and can see the big picture. You understand your part in it and how your pursuit of justice made you lose your way. This is the Mountaintop Moment. From there you descend the Chasm of Culpability, ready to make amends. This leaves you able to enter a beautiful valley I call Personal Peace. It is only then that you are ready to work together toward Reconciliation.

Not everyone makes it all the way to Reconciliation. Your counterpart will not be ready for reconciliation exactly when you are. They may never be ready at all. In fact, if you have been hurt enough, you might not even want to go to a place called Reconciliation. Seeing the person who hurt you and interacting with them may already be a few steps too far. Well, relax; you don't have to reconcile if you don't want to, but I think you'll agree that you can use some personal peace.

Total, genuine reconciliation with the other person requires a collaborative effort that some people cannot undertake—cannot or will not. Both parties have to take responsibility for their share of the solution. If you have a counterpart who won't do their share, you will not make it all the way to Reconciliation. Luckily, you can make it far down the road without their help. You can make it all the way to Personal Peace, which is a kind of reconciliation with yourself. Personal Peace is a pretty nice place.

So, let's begin, not by reconciling, for reconciliation with the other is still a long way off, and maybe you'll never get there. Your initial objective is coming to peace with what happened. You get there by first going in what seems to be the other direction. You've got to get angry first or, at least, know your feelings about what happened.

1

ASSESS THE DAMAGE

Estimating Hurt

If you were in a car accident and sued the person at fault, you'd go to court and describe the accident to establish culpability; but at some point, the judge would ask you what it cost to fix your car. The judge is asking for a monetary figure, so she can fix an amount that would make it better. Any court I ever knew about requires that there be damages if you are trying to sue.

This is not a court and there is no judge, but if you were hurt by someone close to you and then want to settle, you would have to assess the damages. How would you know how to settle it if you didn't? Assessing the damages might lead you to conclude that no harm was done. The matter might be easy to settle then. If there was harm, establishing just what it was may help you in deciding how the person can make amends. So, what is the nature of the suffering you have had to endure?

Objective losses

For example, there's your wife, the compulsive gambler who ran up thousands of dollars in high-interest debt that both of you had to pay off. Or the violent man who broke your nose five times. Or the father who hocked your Christmas presents to buy dope. Then there's the promiscuous girlfriend who brought you an STD.

Maybe you had medical bills, heavy debts, lost time from work, missed payments, or repairs you had to make. In that case, the loss is right there in black and white. Maybe you've got bruises, broken bones, a ruptured spleen, or head trauma from too many blows to the brain; the damage is in black and blue. Maybe you can point to the damage in the form of scars, crooked fingers, or an x-ray showing bulging disks. If that's the case, then the harm done is physical, concrete, and unmistakable.

Emotional abuse

It may be harder to assess if the damage is less direct as it is when you suffer emotional harm. Let's take, for example, the mother who resented you for being born because you always reminded her of her no-good ex. She always said you were an idiot like your father. She never bought you books, never read to you, and never took an interest in your accomplishments, because she didn't think there was a point. You grew up convinced you would never amount to anything because she said so.

It's not too hard to imagine that, if this was your mother, you might suffer from low self-esteem. Maybe you never got good grades and now you can barely read and are lucky to get a minimum wage job. If that's the case, then it probably is her fault—but that's a harder case to prove. We may never know whether you failed academically because of her discouragement or if she was right about you all along.

For now, you don't have to prove anything. For our purposes, just make a claim, as you would in court. Later we'll sort it out.

What if you had a mother like that, but despite her lack of encouragement, you succeeded in school anyway? You don't have poor grades you can point to as evidence of damages. In fact, maybe her abuse even inspired you to prove her wrong. A case might be made that you have her to thank; I won't make it, but some might. Do you have any damages then? Well, I don't know; but I know a very successful person who, when he leaves his business, where he's the CEO, passes by scores of admirers, drives off in his BMW, glances at his Rolex to see if he's running late, arrives at my office, and—every time—confesses that he has a little voice in his head that warns him that, one of these days, everyone will find out what a fraud he is. I ask whose voice this is. It's his mother's. This CEO, you see, had a mother like the one I've been describing.

What can this CEO claim as damages? His therapist's bills, that's what.

Lost opportunity costs

While you're making your list, don't forget to assess the lost opportunity costs. That is, all the things you might have possessed, experienced, or accomplished if you hadn't been dealing with this thing you had to deal with, for instance, that drug-using boyfriend you've been hanging on to for three years. Maybe there haven't been any direct costs in terms of bills or broken bones. He might've treated you well and maybe he hasn't been abusive. Maybe all he's done is waste your time, time that might have been better spent looking for someone else. Your biological clock might've run out while you were with him, and you lost your chance to have children. Include that as a lost opportunity cost.

Injured feelings

You could go through this exercise and discover that there is no long-term cost, no bruises or bills, and no lost opportunities. Maybe you were worried because he didn't text; you got frustrated or disappointed. You lost trust in him.

Maybe the only consequence was your feelings were hurt. Well, jot that down if that's all there was. It's still important. We'll figure out what to do with those injured feelings later. For now, it's important that everything is acknowledged.

Assessing the damage can be tricky. Often, the damage is not directly apparent. I've had many clients in my office suffering from PTSD who were surprised to learn of all the problems (and strengths) that can arise out of the experience of trauma. They didn't know about that and, perhaps, didn't want to think about it. You often need a good therapist to recognize the links, and even then, it's speculative. Also, a lot of the problems don't emerge until later on. If your girlfriend cheated on you, you might think you're fine, now that you have broken up with her, until you get a new girlfriend and find you have a hard time trusting her. You never were suspicious about women before, but you are after experiencing that betrayal. That kind of damage is like a computer virus that sneaks into your software and causes it to crash some time later when you least expect it.

Counting up the damage can be a very emotional experience. It can drive home the reality of the loss you suffered, make real the pain. Having to total up the damage can seem like yet another awful thing you have to experience. But it can also be cathartic. It can affirm in black and white, and maybe blue, what you've been thinking all along.

If you were in court, suing for that traffic accident, all these expenses along with your pain and suffering would be converted into a figure in dollars and cents. That's just what courts do because they don't know how else to settle it. You don't have to do that unless you want. You don't have to establish that your lost trust is worth a hundred thousand, that your self-esteem can be bought for a million, that your worries go five for a dollar. Eventually, you'll have to think about what would settle the matter—what would make it right—but for now, just assess the damage so you have something to start with. Go ahead, made a list and add to it as you think of more.

Once you have your list, do I want you to hand it over to the person who harmed you? Do I want you to say, here, this is what you caused? No, not yet. If you do that now, I guarantee you'll be disappointed with the response. They'll say you padded it with self-inflected injuries.

As we go on, I'll write about further additions to make to the list and then we'll discuss whether there's anything you can remove. So, don't show it yet to the person who harmed you. There's more work to do before you are ready to call anyone into account. For now, make the list.

Has the Hurt Ended?

The wind stopped blowing and the sky looks nice, but if this is a hurricane, you may be passing through the eye of the storm. The earthquake has struck, but watch for aftershocks. You've had a minor stroke, but is a major one coming along? If your loved one hurt you and you have assessed the damage, there's another thing to take into account. Is he still doing it?

Many damages go on wreaking havoc long after the precipitating event. They're like ripples in a pond after a stone is thrown. The compulsive gambler who put you both in hock may have created a situation that may take years, or decades, to pay off. The guy who broke your nose might ruin your chance for a modeling career long afterward. The cruel and hurtful thing your parent said when you were young is a gift that keeps on giving. Therefore, if you're assessing the damages, don't forget to include not only what you have already suffered but what you're likely to suffer in the future. If you added up all the years of therapy you've needed so far, don't forget to include all the years you will need before you're done.

Eventually, most consequences of hurt will end. The debt your gambler accrued may well be eventually paid off. As a general rule, the first hurts we suffer are the longest lasting. Those cruel and hurtful things your parents said can continue to resonate long after you've forgotten what they were. They are built into your foundation and determine who you are.

Persistent harm

The next thing to consider is whether the damages will go on because the precipitating events persist. Is someone still chucking stones in your pond? If the compulsive gambler goes on gambling after you've restructured your debt, you'll never get out from behind the eight ball. Don't believe her when she claims her next big win will pay it off. The guy who broke your nose may break it again, or worse. That behavior tends to escalate over time because, once you have broken your girlfriend's nose once, you'll think you've got to do more to get her attention. If your elderly parent has verbally abused you all your life, she's not likely to stop now, even as you visit her daily at the nursing home.

Therefore, before you finish with your list of damages, make another list of future damages that are likely to occur if the behavior is not in check.

When it's not in check

Before I go on, I should stop and explain what I mean by *in check*. Many people believe the behavior is in check if the person goes into therapy. That's not what I mean. In check is when the behavior is stopped, permanently stopped, not stopped because people are looking, not stopped while he's sleeping on the couch because he wants you to let him in the bed, not stopped because she went to rehab; I mean stopped for good. Therapy is just maybe the beginning of the checking procedure. Most problematic behavior persists after therapy has begun, and by most, I mean all. It doesn't mean therapy ain't working; it means it takes time, it's a process, and it hasn't worked yet.

How you can minimize the damage

Some of these future damages may, perhaps, be ameliorated

by something you can do. You might be able to insulate yourself from the effects of the persistent problematic behavior. That's what separate bank accounts are for; that's what separate bedrooms, separate houses, and separated spouses are for. That's why people get divorced. The guy who broke your nose may go on breaking noses, but not yours, if you get an order of protection against him. Your old mother who can't stop talking shit about you may go on doing so, but you don't have to visit her every day at the nursing home and hear it. That's what I mean by insulating yourself.

I also mean another thing; there's another way of insulating yourself from most of the emotional abuse that people can dish out. It's called not letting them get into your head. Easier said than done, but possible if you are a mature, self-assured adult, especially if you know who you are and don't let others define you. It's impossible if you're a child and don't possess the resource of a thick, thick skin.

So, when you account for everything that was wrecked by the loved one who hurt and may well go on hurting you, take everything into account: the injuries of the past, the continued injuries of the present, and the projected ones of the future.

How to Tell If Nothing Has Changed

You'll never come to peace with the awful things that have happened if they're still happening. Nor should you. The most important thing is to protect yourself.

Maybe he's stopped doing that thing that hurt you: drinking, drugging, gambling, beating you up, whoring around, or whatever. The problem seems to have gone away.

Has it, really?

You'll be the last person to believe it's disappeared. Everyone else will celebrate her recovery while you're still waiting for the next shoe to drop. There's a reason for your skepticism. You have the most to lose.

There's another reason. Drinking, drugging, gambling, violence, and whoring can take on a life of their own, becoming what I call *the problem*. The problem takes cover sometimes when it feels threatened. It'll hide in the bushes and come roaring out when you least suspect it. Make no mistake; these things are cunning, baffling, and very patient. While your partner has been collecting key rings at his NA meeting, the problem has been doing pushups in the parking lot.

Problems prefer the dark. They like to perform their dirty deeds in secret. The night belongs to Michelob. However, the problem is rarely ever a real secret. It's kidding itself when it believes it leaves no trace. You can tell when the problem is still afoot if you are willing to read the signs.

Your partner declares everything has changed

Your partner is not the one to judge whether anything has changed. Everyone is prone to their own kind of problem. For some it's addiction, for others it's rage, and so on. Each is prone to their own kind of problem because that's the kind that sneaks up in their blind spot, impersonating, to them, something else. When it fools anyone, it fools them first.

Your partner hasn't done the things promised

If the problem behavior is gone, but he still hasn't been to see a therapist, attended meetings, written that letter of apology, changed associates, or done any of the things he promised, then the problem is just hoping you won't notice.

The behavioral changes have been minor

The longer the problem has been part of the relationship or the more serious it's has been, the more excited everyone will be when there has been a minor improvement.

She was drinking every day; now you're thrilled that she has cut down to once a week. He used to gamble away his entire paycheck; now he only buys a few scratch-offs. He used to beat you; now he only puts holes in the wall. The underlying attitudes toward drinking, gambling, or violence have not changed; the only thing changed is the frequency or severity.

When gardeners trim bushes back a little, they call it pruning. It doesn't destroy the bush; it makes it grow more. The same thing happens when only minor changes are accomplished. You wouldn't be satisfied if your surgeon left some cancer behind, so don't be fooled by minor behavioral changes.

Other problems have arisen

Sometimes the underlying problem plays whack-a-mole by extinguishing one problem behavior only to develop another. We see this often with addicts who will use one drug until the heat is on and then switch to a different drug. Instead of scoring heroin on the street and using dirty needles, they get their narcotics from a doctor. You'll think that's an improvement, until they start to abuse those pills too. The underlying problem remains.

Thinking has not changed

If the rationalizations that have justified the bad behavior are still in evidence, then the problem has not gone away. He used to say he needed to drink, so he drank. Now, he doesn't drink, but he still says he needs to. Guess what? He'll drink again. If he was truly in recovery, he'd no longer believe he needs it.

No fence has been built

When the government has something they want no one to get to, like a nuclear bomb, they build a fence around it. Then, at some distance, they put up another fence, and another, so no one can get anywhere near it.

It is not enough just to change the problem behavior to eradicate a problem. You also have to know the route that the problem takes before it arrives. You need to put up a fence and shut out behavior that, in itself, is not problematic but leads up to the problem.

Problems come masquerading as something harmless so you will not see them coming. Pedophiles start off by making friends with a child. There's nothing wrong with making friends with a child, right? But, then they gradually groom the child to accept more sexual behavior. We protect children from pedophiles by not permitting them to live near schools. This is not because it's bad to live near a school, but it's bad for pedophiles to live near schools.

Authentic recovery means you and your counterpart can see through the disguises and stop the problem while it's still en route.

History is minimized

If the story your partner tells about the problem differs significantly from your own, then the problem is still lurking about. If she talks about her gambling problem only in terms of her suffering and leaves out how it affected others, then she has not incorporated your point of view into her own. Her limited perspective is still all she has. She incompletely appreciates the costs of her choices. She should be able to tell your side of the story as well as her own.

Your partner is withdrawn

If your partner is virtually unreachable, emotionally inaccessible, or sexually uninterested, then the problem may be in hiding. It doesn't want you to ask too many questions, know too much, or get too close.

Your partner always seems to be angry with you

He may be blaming you for calling it out and challenging him. He may be using anger as a way to keep you away, off balance, and uninformed. Your partner may still be taking sides with the problem, against you.

You're working harder at recovery than your partner is

You've been on your partner like white on rice. Ever since he had that affair, you've been monitoring his phone, checking his whereabouts, scanning his e-mails, opening his letters. You've met all his female acquaintances and given them the stink eye. You've scrutinized his expression when every waitress approaches, tried every new position he wanted to reawaken your sex life. You've found a therapist for him, set up the appointment, gone to every session, paid, and done the homework assignments. You are working harder than he is.

If he has not taken responsibility for change, then he will not make the right choices the moment your back is turned. The recovery is yours, not his. He is still chummy with the problem.

You're careful not to upset your partner

If you still feel like you're walking on eggshells, then maybe you're picking up on something. You're still getting bad vibes—not bad enough to talk about but just enough to make you uncomfortable.

Your partner says to move on and not get stuck in the past

That's the problem talking, trying to convince you to not learn from the past. Truly recovering people remind themselves of the past regularly, so they'll not repeat it.

Your partner wants credit for improvements

An adult straightens the house every day. He scrubs the toilets when they need it and mops the floor when it's dirty. He doesn't expect a medal for it. He does it because it needs doing.

A toddler tickles the furniture with a feather duster once in a while and everyone will fall all over him, saying he was very helpful. That's what you do for a child. Is your partner a child?

When the problem takes over: the less you do, the more credit you think you deserve.

In a healthy world: you don't earn special points for doing what you should have been doing all along.

It's still all about him (or her)

You ought to be happy, but you're not. There still seems to be something wrong. Not only has your partner stopped the problematic behavior, but she's been going to therapy, attending AA, writing in her journal, and getting in touch with her feelings. These are all good things, but she's still as self-involved as ever.

Real change means taking action to being more loving, generous, caring, and empathetic toward others.

There are no signs

You looked over this list and you did not find a single thing that shows the problem may be lurking. There seem to be no signs. Well, that's your sign. If you are not seeing signs, then you may be fooling yourself. Look for the signs before you say there are no signs.

The road to recovery is the same as the road to ruin; you're just traveling in a different direction. You pass by the same markers as when you were heading to ruin. You should be seeing them now and recognizing them for what they are. You should also be seeing some signs that indicate you are heading in the right direction, coming upon meaningful change.

If you are not, you are still as subject to getting hurt as you were before. There is no way in hell you're going to feel at peace with what happened, nor should you. In order for you to come to peace, protect yourself.

Protecting yourself can take many forms. Maybe you have to leave and live somewhere else. Perhaps it's enough to just have separate banking accounts. It could be the only way to protect yourself is to press charges and put him in jail or apply for that order of protection. Possibly, you just need to speak up and say you will not take it anymore. The point is to recognize when you are at risk and take steps against it. No personal peace, much less reconciliation, is possible while you are still being hurt.

What Can't Be Hurt

If you're hurt by someone you love, it's important to get real about the injury and account for all the damages inflicted: your money the compulsive gambler spent, the trust the adulterer squandered, the confidence the abusive parent wrecked. It's equally important to note the damages that were not done, the parts of you that are untouched by your misfortune, and qualities of yours that may even have been strengthened.

I hope there's a lot that has been untouched. You may, to a greater or lesser degree, still have your health, friends, family, job, savings and credit, education, home, and many other *external goods*, as we might call them. Go ahead and take inventory, but now I primarily want to call your attention to a property of yours that no one can take away. One which may have been made perfect by adversity.

What is this thing that no one can take away and that may be strengthened by adversity? It goes by many names, all of them vague. The ancient Greeks called it *prohairesis*.[2] In English it's been translated as dignity, self-respect, the unconquerable will, the unquenchable human spirit, free choice, and moral purpose. This is a quality possessed by everyone, and it's always within reach. It outshines all differences of circumstance, accidents of fate, and actions of others, making them trivial. It's all you need to live a life you can be proud of. It may have been the very thing most lacking in your loved one that led to whatever he did to you.

Prohairesis

Prohairesis is the choice you have in giving in or resisting external forces. If someone calls you out on something, it's up to you whether you believe it. If someone has done something irritating, it's you who decides to be irritated. If someone strikes you, they may break a bone, but they don't have to break your spirit. The idea behind the concept is that, while you have no control over what others do to you or what fate does to you, you have control over what you do with it. The name for that control is prohairesis.

Let me explain prohairesis by metaphor. Two people walk into a bank. One has a great credit score, the other a bad one. They both ask for a loan. The banker may decide that she won't lend money to the one who has good credit and she may decide to give a chance and lend money to the other with bad credit. The banker is free to choose. The name for that choice is prohairesis. In the same way, regardless of whether your loved one is trustworthy, you are free to choose whether to trust him.

Another way to get at the concept of prohairesis is to think of a person who has triumphed over adversity—a survivor, rather than a victim. There are plenty of examples. A boy, born to poverty, who picked himself up by his bootstraps. A Pakistani woman, her face disfigured by acid, speaking out for the education of girls despite the reprisal. A girl, raped and pregnant at fourteen, who goes on to become Oprah. A divorced mother, writing at her kitchen table, collecting rejection slips, creating *Harry Potter*. A Black South African, imprisoned for decades, who gets out and leads his country into justice and reconciliation. A teenaged girl hiding from the Nazis in her attic, who, nonetheless, believes in the essential goodness of all. A religious teacher dying a slow death who enjoins God's forgiveness. A tired seamstress who won't give up her seat on the bus.

The list goes on and on, but it's not limited to extraordinary people. It includes a myriad of anonymous individuals who represent the triumph of will over hardship.

The roofer who works in the sun, the cook who works in the heat, the postal worker who delivers the mail in the wind and rain. The new dad, abandoned by his father, determined to be there for his children. The mother who gets up in the night even though she's tired.

Strength made perfect in weakness

Prohairesis is found more in conditions of weakness and vulnerability than in strength. You see it at physical therapy where stroke victims learn to walk all over again. You find it in rehab where addicts are determined to change. I witness prohairesis in my office when a depressed or agoraphobic person leaves her home to attend a session. It's there when you are patient with fools, kind to strangers, and whenever you refuse to stoop to the level of someone mistreating you. Prohairesis is really so common it's ordinary, except that it ennobles people to do extraordinary things every day.

Maybe prohairesis is a miraculous thing. Maybe it's the higher power the AA people speak of that empowers people to do what they couldn't do before. I could buy that, with the stipulation that if you get it by God's grace, then it's given to everyone, good and bad, all the time, like the sunshine and not doled out on special occasions only to the people who qualify.

How to exercise prohairesis

You exercise prohairesis by taking responsibility, not of everything, but only of the things you are responsible for: yourself and what you do. You deplete it by engaging in self-pity and feeling sorry for yourself. Taking inventory of the damage done, as we have been doing, could drain your tank of prohairesis if you stopped there, if you do not acknowledge you have something to say about how you live your life. The good thing is, no matter how much prohairesis you have let go, there's always more. You always have an opportunity to take charge.

I can tell you what hasn't been taken away. The answer is your dignity, self-respect, unconquerable will, unquenchable human spirit, free choice, and moral purpose. You may have misplaced it or never known it existed; you may have given it away; but you can always get more prohairesis.

Looking at the Flip Side

If you've been hurt by the one you love, don't forget to look at the flip side. That's the other side of the coin, the positives, the reason you've been with the person in the first place. It's only fair, but don't do it because it's fair. Do it because the flip side says as much about you as it does about him.

In the same way you were honest about how much he hurt you, now be honest about how he's good to you. Don't throw the baby out with the bathwater. Look at the flip side if you want to know what's going on, to get a full inventory. You can't judge a person only by the worst things he did; you also have to look at the best to get a complete picture.

Practice gratitude

You can probably think of one thing to be grateful for regarding this person. That's a start. Tomorrow, think of another. In fact, every day, identify one new thing you are thankful for regarding her. This can be her behavior, her characteristics, or anything she brings to the table. Schedule a reminder in your phone to think of a daily appreciation. It won't take long before you've covered the usual things and you'll have to dig. Digging's good. Don't make stuff up; just notice things you wouldn't normally have.

It's human nature to focus on the negative, especially after you've been together for a while. The problems, the hurts, and the disappointments are always much more noticeable while the benefits get taken for granted. Do something deliberate to counter the tendency to just see the bad.

This exercise works even better when you actually tell the person how much you are indebted to him. Just watch him melt. Observe just how much more frequently she makes your favorite macaroni and cheese when you express gratitude before shoveling it in.

If you can't even come up with one good thing you're thankful for, then take stock of the positive memories you made together. What were the things that attracted you to her? It can be super sad to think about the promise you had as a couple, especially given what has transpired since then; but it's important to take note that you saw something in him.

What your gratitude says about you

How does looking at the flip side tell you something about you? Whatever attracted you to her may well be the very thing that later drives you crazy about her. You liked him because he was fun loving; now he seems irresponsible. She was the person who could keep you organized; now you feel suffocated by her need for order. He was a rock, but now he's rigid.

This is where you went wrong. You looked for a partner who made up for qualities deficient in yourself. You were attracted to the fun-loving guy because you tend to be pretty serious; he helped you have fun. You needed an organized person in your life because you weren't. You were a pushover with your kids, but he could make them listen. Finding someone who complemented you looked like a match made in heaven until it wasn't. Now it's a match made in hell.

If you really thought being fun-loving was the way to go, why weren't you fun-loving yourself, so you wouldn't need anyone to loosen you up? If you thought it was important to be organized, why didn't you get organized, so you wouldn't need someone to organize you? If you really believed the kids needed a firm hand, you could've learned to be strict, rather than outsource all the discipline to someone else and then fight with him because he's so mean.

You don't share the same values. You joined with someone different from you because she was different, then you tried to make her just like you.

Here's another way that looking at the flip side teaches you something about yourself. Look at those things you are grateful for. Her blonde hair, his warm smile, that macaroni and cheese. The way she lets you sleep late in the morning, his love for the kids, the vacations you took together. What do they say about you? The fact that you like such things. These things teach you and affirm your values.

Your values are your moral compass. They tell you what is important. They keep you from getting lost. Showing gratitude is another method of finding your way and keeping you from getting distracted by all the hurt and pain you experience.

Meaningful Suffering

While you're looking at the flip side, look at this: the hurt you are experiencing may be providing the meaning and purpose to your life.

Your life needs meaning and purpose. It makes your life worthwhile; it indicates your existence matters. That's important. Sometimes, it's the only thing that keeps you going. It's something you can be proud of.

Meaning and purpose will organize your life. You know what you have to do when you wake up in the morning. It dictates the things you do during the day. It determines the choices you make and makes those choices easy. You find meaning and purpose by doing things that are worthwhile: raising children, taking care of sick people, providing for those in need, pursuing social justice. The harder these things are, the more meaning and purpose you get out of them.

Letting a homeless person move in with you is more meaningful than giving a dollar to one on the street. You find the most meaning by trying to do impossible, or nearly impossible, things.

Living with someone who beats you up while trying to rehabilitate him is an impossible thing.

Trying to keep a marriage together for the sake of the children while your partner is doing everything he can to blow it up is impossible. Being patient with an elderly parent who never was patient with you is impossible. Trying to earn money faster than a compulsive gambler can lose it, or a compulsive shopper can spend it, or a drug addict can smoke it, or an alcoholic can drink it is impossible. If they are not impossible, they are certainly really hard.

You get a lot of credit for trying to do impossible things. Not everyone has the pluck, the grit, and the intestinal fortitude to attempt the impossible. Riding with the six hundred into the valley of death[3] ennobles you. Keeping your head when all about you are losing theirs makes you a man, my son.[4] You become a hero, and your suffering, heroic suffering.

I use the word *hero* in the most complimentary, non-sarcastic way, and I don't mean the sandwich. Being a hero is the whole idea of looking for meaning and purpose. Heroic suffering grinds you down while it dignifies the sacrifices you make. You forget yourself, put your own needs on the back burner, and do whatever is necessary. Heroic suffering will kill you and you know it. It wouldn't be heroic if it didn't.

Your friends will see how trying to do the impossible is grinding you down and they won't like it. They'll try to warn you and say you're crazy for trying it. They'll call you codependent,[5] but they don't understand this is what you do to have a meaningful life. They'll go on about how impossible your partner is, thinking it'll convince you to leave, but it'll only make you more heroic and more attached. They'll say they want to see you happy, but you don't want to be happy—it's not about being happy. It's all about doing something that matters.

Let no one talk you out of trying the impossible. You may need to take a stab at the impossible. Lord knows, there are many impossible things that turn out to be possible once people try them. But if you try to do the impossible, keep a lookout for what the impossible is doing to you. Trying to do the impossible might turn you into an impossible person.

How to become impossible

You start to become impossible as the impossible wears you out. You secretly resent the sacrifices you make. You have your days when you're infuriated that you get nothing in return, feeling entitled to collect on kindness. You start belittling and disparaging any attempts your partner has toward growth, and you feel threatened if your partner doesn't need you. You create desires that only you can fill. You so need to be needed, you meddle, hover, and guilt, and call it love.

When you start thinking you're indispensable, you're making things more impossible than they would be without you. Keep going and you become so intent in propping up the fiction that you're a hero, you can't see that your "self-denying heroism" is manipulative and self-serving. You won't understand how domineering and coercive you can be. You're no longer part of the solution; you're part of the problem.

Try to do the impossible, but please don't turn into someone impossible while you do it.

Turning into an impossible person because you are trying to do the impossible is only one of many ways that being hurt by someone you love can change you for the worse. It's important to not stay victimized for long and get on the Road to Reconciliation or, at least, Personal Peace, before the experience deforms you. Becoming an Impossible Martyr is not the only malformation that occurs when people spend too long a victim. In the next section, we'll look at others.

2

HOW TO KEEP FROM CRACKING UP

Wreckage on the Road to Reconciliation

Spend any time with people who have been victimized and
you'll see a lot who are stuck. Not only are they not making it
to Reconciliation; they are nowhere near any kind of Personal
Peace. They are the wrecks that have gone off the road and
camped out rather than repairing and moving on. They are
those who try to take shortcuts, get caught in loops, and
travel far, getting nowhere. The Impossible Martyrs we saw in
the last part. There are the People Who Can't Steer. There are
whole tribes of other inbreds, settled into villages in the back
country: the Deniers, the Discount Pardoners, the Helpless,
the Big Babies, the Ax Grinders, the Righteous Idiots, the
Scab Pickers, the Retraumatized, and the Ones Who Can't
Admit They've Done Anything Wrong. Beware the traveling
troupes of thespians who specialize in playing the victim but
are really just a band of bandits. They are the strongest
reasons there are for getting on the way to Reconciliation.

Spend too much time feeling victimized and you'll be at
risk for becoming one of them. The Road to Reconciliation,
or even Personal Peace, is so difficult, poorly marked, and
treacherous that few people travel it without losing their way.
Remain in this radioactive country for long and it'll deform
you. Loiter in the Land of the Victims and your own mother

won't recognize you. You'll go from being a victim to becoming an offender. You'll become a monster who eats children to satisfy your insatiable hunger for vindication.

Let's go on a tour and study the people who have settled down, rather than progressing on the Road to Reconciliation. I'm sure you'll recognize something of yourself in many of them. If you do, then that's a good sign. It shows that you're willing to be open minded. Then you can be safe as you pass through. If you don't think you could possibly be any of them and are offended that I even suggest it, then it's already too late; you have already been altered. A vampire has bitten you, and you have become one of them.

Following our tour of the people you might become, we'll talk about emotions that threaten to take you over. There are many hazards on the Road to Reconciliation. Woe to anyone who tries to go that way without a guide.

The Deniers

One type you'll see on the side of the Road to Reconciliation are the Deniers. You'll see them, but they won't see you. They're blind, deaf, and insensible to touch. They only know what they want to know, what's convenient to them, what fits in the worldview they feel they must have. If the evidence threatens their ideas, they discard the evidence. They are the deniers who, although they are hurt by the ones they love, will never admit it.

You might have thought it's only offenders who engage in denial. Well, they do it best. They'll disavow everything if they can get away with it. They'll have a million excuses why they must do the things they do. But victims will engage in denial too if they can't accept that they've been hurt or want to avoid doing anything about it.

You might have done this in the first flush of love when the excitement of being in a new relationship was so great you missed all the red flags. If he had abusive language, you called it love talk. If he roughed you up, you thought it was affection. If he was insanely jealous, you thought he cared a lot about you. You could be excused from making that mistake the first time, before you saw how it all played out, especially if you've been indoctrinated into believing it's supposed to be that way. But if you're still believing it after he rapes you, then you have slipped into the state of denial. Still believe it after he rapes you again, and you're a full-fledged citizen. Go on believing it after he goes after your children, and the people of Denial will be ready to elect you president.

I want to distinguish between the Deniers and the Impossible Martyrs, who we saw before. The Impossible Martyrs know they're suffering. In fact, suffering is the point. They're willing to endure temporary hardship for the sake of a meaningful long-term gain. There is nothing wrong with that, so long as the gain really is meaningful, and they don't become impossible to live with.

What could motivate someone to act against their own self-interests and deny to themselves the true knowledge that someone is hurting them? They simply do not like conflict. Generally, the offender is also in denial and they want to agree with her.

Denial can be tricky. There's the most primitive kind, denial of fact, that we all can recognize when we have the facts. But when denial of fact doesn't cut it, denial retreats and hunkers down in a new position. There are six arguments denial can make before it has to give up and admit the truth.

Denial of fact

The first way is the most obvious. You simply don't admit something happened. You got that black eye by falling on a doorknob. She was home by eleven o'clock. His gambling has not begun to eat into your savings. They're just really good friends. You had a great childhood.

Similar to the denial of fact is minimization: denying some facts but not others. He only hit you once. She only parties like that now and then. He only bets on good horses.

You're fine as long as she doesn't flaunt it. Your parents may have forgotten about you a few times, but they were great when they didn't.

Minimization is misdirected. The bottom line is not how many times he hit you, how late she stays out, how much he bet on what horse, whether she has sex with that man or just prefers to spend time with him rather than you, or how many times your parents forgot you. The real question is this: Can you trust? Facts don't settle issues of trust. If you don't trust someone, you don't trust them. Why would you talk yourself into trusting them when you don't?

If the facts are on your side, then nothing beats denial of fact; why would you need any other method? But, if the facts contradict you, then denial of fact is a dangerous game. Facts are trying to tell you something, but you won't listen.

If a Denier can't get past the facts, then she has five more methods at her disposal.

Denial of responsibility

When you use denial of responsibility, you admit the fact of the misdeed but not the intention. You claim the person who hurt you was not a free agent. She did not have a will of her own.

He gave you that black eye, but you made him do it. Her friends kept buying her drinks. He's a gambler because his father was a gambler. The man seduced her. You had a terrible childhood, but your parents did the best they could.

Yes, as we will discuss, it's important to see the context of your loved one's hurtful actions. It's essential for you to accept your share of responsibility. But it's not like they have no will of their own. Remember prohairesis, the part of you that cannot be touched and can be made stronger by adversity? Your loved one has his prohairesis too. You might have been mean to him, but he still made the decision to hit you. Just because they're buying her drinks, it doesn't mean she has to drink them. If he can't afford to bet on the horses, he shouldn't bet on them. No matter how seductive he was, unless it was rape, she still had a choice. No matter how frazzled your parents were, how hard was it count their children before they left on vacation?

Denial of awareness

When you use denial of awareness, you're saying the deed was out of your loved one's conscious control. Something must have come over him when he hit you. She must have lost track of time. He gets triggered every time he passes an OTB. She has a passionate nature. If you didn't want to be left home, you could have spoken up.

Denial of awareness just kicks the can down the road a little way. Even if it's true they didn't know what they were doing, they're still responsible for not knowing what they're doing. Even if you let them off the hook for what they do when they're drunk, asleep, or unaware, they're still responsible for being drunk, asleep, or unaware and they have to accept the consequences that come with it.

Denial of impact

In denial of impact, you are admitting the deed, but there was no injury or basis of complaint. It was a victimless crime. The tree fell in the forest, but it didn't hit you.

It's just a black eye; a little makeup will make it look better. It doesn't matter that she didn't come home; you were asleep anyway. You can always earn more money. Some people have an open marriage and they're okay. You might have had a rotten childhood, but you turned out fine.

Have you carefully assessed the damage? Did you really estimate the hurt that was caused, or did you skim that chapter? Are there signs that the hurt has or will continue? Did you only look at the flip side, the positives, without noting the negatives?

The purpose of cutting through denial—in all its forms, yours and his—is not to humiliate, blame, or make your partner responsible for everything. The purpose is to see things clearly.

Denial of pattern

Nothing just happens by itself. There's always a context. No one goes from zero to sixty without going through all the steps between. There is always a pattern. You can be excused if you don't know it, but are you willing to see it?

Patterns can be hard to distinguish if you're not paying attention. Detecting a true pattern can be a tremendous benefit. It shows you how big the problem is, informs you of warning signs, and gives you a chance to get a jump on things. It lets you intervene on a problem before it gets too big. But to detect a pattern, be open minded about what it might be.

When you see the pattern, you'll know that after he hits you, he'll be full of remorse and nice to you for a while; but after he starts to resent you, he'll hit you again, and it'll be worse. You'll predict that every time she goes out with these friends, she won't come home till morning, and then she'll be hung over the next day. You'll realize that the worst thing that could happen would be for him to win at the races; he would use that to justify losing three times as much afterward. You'll recognize that she just does what she wants and never thinks about what it means to you. You'll admit that your parents didn't have a problem making promises, but they seldom followed through.

Denial of the need for help

He hit you, but he's sorry and it taught him not to do it again. She got so sick last night she never wants to see another Peppermint Schnapps. He just needs to stay away from the betting parlor and he'll be fine. She gave you access to her phone, so you can keep an eye on her. Your parents were awful, but now you're grown.

It might be no one's business what happened to you; however, if you agree to the facts, place responsibility and awareness where they belong, and see the impact and the pattern but will let no one help you, you're placing a bet you can handle it all by yourself. That's great if you can; maybe you will. But what exactly is on the line? Is his violence getting worse? Did she try to drive home drunk yet? Are the loan sharks looking for payment? Has she brought home a disease? Are you catching yourself acting like your parents did? Maybe you can deal with the consequences if you fail, but are you thinking about how it will affect others?

There are many kinds of help you may need: the police, a shrink, a marriage counselor, Al-Anon, a doctor, a lawyer, a trustworthy friend, clergy, or someone to stay with in an emergency. Your trouble is not everyone's business, but some have businesses devoted to helping people like you.

So, there you have the six strategies Deniers use to pull the wool over their own eyes. How about you? Have you blinded yourself from seeing what you need to see? Are you prepared to do something about it?

The Helpless

I'm glad I didn't decide to be an experimental psychologist. If I had, I might've had to lock dogs up in cages and shock them for the sake of science. As it is, others can do it and we can benefit from the things they learned by doing so.[6]

There was a classic experiment where they locked dogs up in cages. They rang a bell a few seconds before they administered an electric shock through the metal of the cage. The dogs quickly learned to go limp and flop when they heard the bell. I guess relaxing like that made the shock hurt less. Then the researchers did something very interesting. They would ring the bell and open the door of the cage before administering the shock. The dogs could easily escape, but they failed to do so. They were too busy flopping. Consequently, they would receive the shock, as before, but had no good reason to do so.

We call this learned helplessness. The dogs had learned to be helpless as an effective way of coping with something they, at first, could not avoid. The problem was they learned to be helpless too well and could not distinguish a situation in which helplessness made sense from a situation where it was unnecessary.

You, too, might have learned helplessness. If you have been stuck in an abusive relationship, then you probably have learned not to care too much, not to try things that would just add to the pain. You learned to put up and make do. You settled. That's fine. I get it. You didn't have a choice.

But maybe at one point you had a choice. Maybe a door that has not been previously open is open now. You might not have gotten out as soon you could have. You might not have spoken up when you could. The moment help became available, you might have dithered and said you'd be fine.

Look for the open door.

The Discount Pardoners

Once you've acknowledged that someone you love has hurt you, next comes the difficult decision of what to do about it. Some of the people you meet in the Road to Reconciliation think they've found a short cut. They give pardon away cheaply, believing then everything can just go back to normal.

Most of what passes for forgiveness is actually a cut-rate imitation, an easy, breezy amnesty you extend not because it's earned but because you don't want to deal with it. It preserves the connection you have with the person who offended you. You don't have to fight, express your feelings, or watch anyone squirm. You don't have to prolong the awkward scene of the offender down on his knees asking forgiveness or the equally uncomfortable situation of having to explain how you are hurt to someone who is clueless, defensive, and in her own denial.

You might feel good about yourself for offering grace at discount prices or think you turned the other cheek, gave the shirt off your back, and welcomed the prodigal sinner. You did what you thought you were supposed to do.[7] The problem is, because the process was rushed, neither you nor the offending party took the opportunity to fully assess the situation. You may not have defined the problem, acknowledged the injury, or confronted your own complicity. You wiped the slate clean before anyone got to read what was written.

Cheap pardon may seem to preserve the relationship, but it prevents you from achieving a more intimate bond. Magic happens when partners see each other naked, in all their ugliness, and decide to love anyway. That is very different from turning away from the ugliness or pretending it's not there.

Easy forgiveness lets the offender off the hook, while you still have to deal with the offense. It's a self-inflicted injury on top of an injury. It gives him a green light while you are still waiting at red.

An alcoholic who's serious about his recovery in AA, for instance, does not need cheap pardon. It hurts him. Right in the middle of the Twelve Steps[8] are seven that have to do with taking a moral inventory, admitting wrongs, and being ready to make amends and remove shortcomings. A recovering alcoholic working his program goes through those steps slowly, carefully, and thoroughly. When you let your alcoholic rush through them, he's skipping important aspects of his recovery. Don't be surprised then if he fails to stay sober or, even if he does abstain, remains the same selfish son-of-a-bitch he was back when he was drinking. You're not at fault, but you haven't helped the matter by letting him off the hook.

How do you know when the forgiveness you are offering is too easy? How do you set a price for pardon? I'll go into this in much more detail in the section on seeking justice, but for now, ask yourself the following questions:

- Do I deny the violation when others see it clearly?
- Do I beat myself up and blame myself when he mistreats me?
- Do I make excuses for the offender before she gets a chance to?
- Do I accept apologies without restitution?
- Do I say I forgive an incident but get angry or bring up that incident again?
- Do I reflexively repair relationships despite how I feel?
- Do I even know how I feel?

It's easy to get into the habit of granting cheap pardon. If you know someone, anyone, long enough, a million things will come along that annoy you or concern you or make you uncomfortable. Learning to live together involves learning to overlook things, to go with the flow, to not make a big deal about nothing. However, when you find that you are alienated from yourself, don't know your own feelings, or continuously act against your own interests, you're not properly learning to live together; you are chopping off pieces of yourself to make room for him.

We all know people whose feelings are easily hurt, who wear their hearts on their sleeves, who are enraged when others don't follow their agenda, and who are hypersensitive to anything that wounds their pride. These people continuously feel injured. They're always looking for apologies so they can get others under their control. You don't want to be like that. You're afraid that if you don't grant cheap pardon, you'll turn into that guy: narcissistic, entitled, and embittered. Therefore, you grant amnesty easily, sometimes before it's even requested.

The thing is, even if you are a person who is easily wounded, cheap pardon would still not be the way to go. It's enough that you feel hurt, that your girlfriends say you're hurt, that your best buddy doesn't believe the things she's done to you. Whenever there is any indication of harm, no matter how ill-founded it may be, you still need to get on the difficult road to real reconciliation and not take the shortcut of cheap pardon. As with many things, the journey is as important as the destination.

Stay on the Road

To stay on the Road to Reconciliation, and not drive off over the cliffs on either side, you first have to acknowledge your hurt and then set it aside. You must recognize that you were a victim, but don't play the victim. Avoid forgiving cheaply, but don't be such a fool that you never forgive. So, which is it, you wonder. Which way do you go?

Stay on the Road to Reconciliation.

Here's the thing about roads. You can drive off a road on either side. To get anywhere, you've got to keep moving. As you move, the road changes. When you fail to recognize the changes, you go off the road, over a cliff, and stop.

Here's another type who won't be getting out of the Land of Victims anytime soon: the People Who Can't Steer and just keep going in one direction, no matter what. There are lots of ways of making that error. One way is by sticking with an official story.

The official story

As any conspiracy theorist can tell you, there's a big difference between the official story and the real one. The official story is the public relations bullshit that's repeated so many times it begins to pass for truth. It's designed to tidy up the mess, reassure the public, establish the narrative, and maintain the status quo. It's what you tell your mother after a hot date or the explanation given to a prospective employer after you walked out on your last job. It's often not an outright lie, just a highly varnished truth. It contains elements of the truth, but it's not the truth. The truth is usually much more awkward. The official story is meant to be the last word. It's something people tell not to answer questions but to stop questions from being asked.

It's not just corporations, the government, frisky teenagers, or disgruntled workers who employ official stories. The person who injured you does it too. You've heard them. He hit you because you made him so mad. He hit you, but you hit him first. He couldn't help but hit you because his father did it to him too. He hit you, but he's sorry and it taught him not to do it again. These may have all been true. What makes them official stories is when they are meant to be the last word. When they are used to shut you up.

As the victim, you have your own official story. You may have adopted one of his and have been perfectly content to admit that you made him so mad he hit you, or he hit you because you hit him first. You might want to let him off the hook and say that he only did what his father did. You might accept a premature apology, only so you don't have to deal with the whole thing anymore.

Or maybe your official story is that you're a victim, subject to a paternalistic tradition, without rights, resources, or recourse. You may be correct in this, but it's an official story if you stop there and make it the last word. If you look at what happened and examine its context, then you can see the cracks and patches in the official story. You see that the official story, no matter what it is, glosses over significant exceptions and inconsistencies. No official story is the whole story. Even a genuine truth is not the whole truth or the only truth.

It's complicated

You're not just the victim and he's not just the perpetrator. In fact, the word *just* should no longer be in your vocabulary, at least not used in a reductionistic manner that conceals the details. Remember that while you'll want to hold the offender accountable, you'll also want to avoid getting stuck in just being a victim. There's more to you than that.

There's something about us humans that makes us want to take vibrant life and engrave it in stone. We do it so we can handle it, manage it, put it in a box, and carry it without dropping it. We fixate it and then we fixate on it, trying to keep it fixed on a pin. But life is not like that. You are not like that. Life is meant to be, well, lively. So, keep it moving and be suspicious of the last word on anything.

Let me say one more thing and it'll be the last word on having the last word. I promise.

How to eat a Cheerio

Go to your cupboard and find a single piece of simple food: a Cheerio, say. Before you pop it in your mouth, think about what it took to bring that single Cheerio to you—the context of the Cheerio, in order words. There are farmers, truckers, warehouse workers, and grocers as well as the tractor manufacturers, fertilizer salesmen, oil rig workers, agribusiness executives, box makers, etc., that support them. Then there are the parents, the partners, and the children of those farmers, truckers, warehouse workers, grocers, tractor manufacturers, fertilizer salesmen, oil rig workers, agribusiness executives, and cardboard box makers as well as their teachers, doctors, lawyers, barbers, and accountants. And those are only the people involved in the Cheerio. Don't let me get started on the chemical properties of the cereal and the history of the elements involved. Get the point? It's infinite. You could spend all day looking at the context of a single Cheerio, and it's just a Cheerio.

The official story is it's just a Cheerio. Well, if there's a lot to a Cheerio, then imagine what there might be regarding you, the loved one who hurt you, and an incident between you.

Don't let it get too complicated

As you can imagine, it could take you all day to eat a single Cheerio. Similarly, you could spend the rest of your life thoroughly appreciating the context of any incident between you and your loved one; you'd never be any closer to the end. That's no good, either. Life goes on. Seeing the context is a good thing, but at some point, you've got to chew and swallow the damn thing. There are lots of ways of getting stuck on this road. One way is by thinking too much and never settling on anything.

So, there it goes again. You need to see the context and be open to multiple interpretations but also figure things out and close around some conclusions and resolutions. Be decisive, but willing to change your mind. Which is it? You ask. Which way do I go?

Stay on the road. When you start veering over too far to one side, veer over to the other.

Playing the Victim

So far, you've been bearing right on the Road to Reconciliation. There's a good reason for this. To the left are all the hazards that come from not taking your injuries seriously enough: becoming an Impossible Martyr, a Denier, or a Discount Pardoner. You have gotten in touch with your hurt and insisted your partner do better than he has. Now, if you continue the way you're going, you'll head over a sheer cliff. You'll go from being someone speaking out against injustice to someone who is playing the victim.

You're playing the victim when you fabricate or exaggerate your suffering so that you can cope, seek attention, or justify abusing and manipulating others. You deserve an Academy Award if you act like you played absolutely no part in what happened to you. You're being a drama queen if you use your injury to extract unfair concessions. Go down this Playing the Victim road far enough and you will perpetrate your own wrongdoings.

Sometimes I ask people who have been victimized by something: Who would you rather be, the person who suffered the injury or the person who committed it? No one wants to suffer the injury, but in the aftermath, practically everyone would rather be the victim than have to live with themselves after having committed some crime or betrayal. This motivates people to play the victim.

41

People play the victim the same way other roles are played. Certain traits are emphasized and inconvenient contradictions ignored. You become histrionic and dramatic, possibly operatic. You're certain that your version of events is the only possible version and everything else is lies and cling to your script and don't know what to do when the footlights are off. You assign blame and forget that when you point a single finger at someone else, three more are surreptitiously pointed at you. You so strongly believe in a convenient fiction that you have lost touch with the truth.

Early on the Road to Reconciliation, it is necessary to get a clear picture of the damage done by the person who hurt you. You've become familiar with the pitfalls of cheap pardon and losing touch with your self-interests. It's necessary to acknowledge the hurt and speak out against oppression. The problem comes when you believe your rhetoric too much or become too strident in an effort to be heard.

People might falsely accuse you of playing the victim if they don't want to hear what you have to say. How can you tell if they're right? Have you've gone too far?

How to play the victim

There are four signs you are playing the victim. Four signs that result in at least four negative consequences.

• You accept no meaningful restitution

You don't have to accept any halfhearted apology; it's just that you can't complain about something without giving the person a chance to make it right. She can never meet your terms for reconciliation because you have elevated them to an unattainable level. You require a down payment no one can afford when you expect someone to accept all the blame.

• You don't acknowledge your power

One consequence of playing the victim is that you end up feeling powerless because you refuse to see the extent to which you have power. This powerlessness is incompatible with being able to take action on your own behalf. You fail to recognize your own efficacy. You victimize yourself through inaction and indecisiveness.

• You lose your humility

You lose your humility if you fail to admit that there is often a very fine distinction between the abuser and the abused, between the perpetrator and the injured party. You forget that, if not for the grace of God or random circumstances, you could've been him.

Let's take a marital argument, for instance, an ugly confrontation that results in yelling, name calling, throwing dishes, slamming doors, and sore feelings for days afterward. Someone started it, someone yelled first, called the first name, threw the first dish, and slammed the first door. One person held on to their hurt feelings longer than the other. It's seldom the same person who escalates or de-escalates things at each step. The person who called the first name may not have been the one who slammed the first door. It's often hard to say who started it or even when it started. When one person throws a dish, we'll never know whether, if she hadn't, the other might have thrown a dish a minute later.

• You're impersonating a victim

The fourth sign is hard to explain. Imagine going to a restaurant and getting a waiter[9] who is so attentive, so obsequious, so unctuous, so over-the-top in his waiter-like flourishes that he seems to be a caricature of a waiter. When he praises you for the entree you selected from the menu, you wonder if he's being sarcastic. You don't trust him because he doesn't seem real. He actually is a waiter, but he still seems to be playing a part. There is something inauthentic about him, something that seems faked or forced, something of bad faith.

So, the fourth sign that you are playing the victim is when you are more intent with keeping up the part you play than in just being yourself. You've got a mask on so no one can see who you really are.

It comes down to this: you don't need to play the victim if you are the victim, but you might end up doing so anyway. You then lose touch with yourself, your feelings, and values—again. You have confused yourself with the part you are playing.

In some cases, when you stop playing the victim and get real about your contribution to the problem, you may just find that you're really an offender, all along, and all your complaints were just distractions for the harm you have done. This can be disconcerting, to say the least. No one wants to admit they behaved badly, much less that they are guilty of covering it up. However, when you stop playing the victim, then you are able to see the problem clearly and do something about it.

So, get real and avoid playing the victim. Don't take yourself so seriously that you lose yourself in the process.

How to Tell If You're Just Being a Big Baby

At some point since you were first victimized, someone said, or maybe you just thought: *You're just being a big baby.* Let's take a look and see if that's really the case.

There goes that word *just*. Be suspicious whenever anyone uses the word *just*. But even if we get rid of that word, we're still left with the question. *Are you being a big baby?*

You're a big baby when your birth certificate documents you're an adult, but you're not acting like one. Five-foot-six, but it's like your legs can barely reach the floor. You vote, drive, smoke cigarettes, drink, cuss, and have a bank account, two hundred thousand in mortgage debt, a job, four kids, and a wife; your skin is starting to wrinkle and sag, but you might as well be wearing diapers and sucking on a pacifier. You're a big baby when you should've learned something by now, but you haven't.

There are five signs of true adulthood.[10] Five indications you can stand on your own two feet and take care of yourself: responsibility, composure, civility, perseverance, and wisdom. Five things to look for; if they're missing, you know you're being a big baby.

Responsibility

Adults make their own decisions and accept responsibility for them. Babies have to be told what to do and cannot be blamed. When babies make a mess, Mommy and Daddy are there to clean it up.

You know you're an adult when you realize that real people get hurt, or helped, by the actions you take. What you do has an effect. You're willing to admit your responsibility, even if it goes badly. You're willing to accept the consequences and you don't manipulate others into cleaning up your messes. You clean up your side of the fence even if the other guy hasn't cleaned up his.

You're a big baby when you avoid responsibility by maneuvering others into making decisions for you; when you provoke someone into throwing the first punch and then say it's all his fault; or when you devalue your marriage and then pout she divorced you. You know that, when it looks as though you're not deciding, you're still making a decision; deciding not to decide. You can be decisive when called for or await further study, if that's what's needed. An adult is the author of her own life, the originator of her own emotions. She doesn't blame others for making her feel a certain way and she doesn't make them responsible for feeling different. He doesn't look for someone else to swoop in and save the day. You're the one who swoops in and saves the day for others who cannot be expected to help themselves.

Being a responsible grownup enables you get close to others. Others can trust you, so they want you around. You get put in charge. They listen to your opinion because you are willing to stand by it.

Other people are not so powerful when you're an adult. You are their equals. You can say no. You can seek advice and let yourself be influenced by others because the final decision is yours anyway. You can change your mind when warranted. You can be flexible without losing your identity.

If you have trouble accepting responsibility, you'll feel like a victim, you'll be playing the victim. You'll be angry that others don't pick up your share. You'll be hurt that they don't seem to care for you. Everyone will seem so mean.

Composure

A baby needs to be soothed and comforted because he can't do it on his own. Every setback is the end of the world. A baby cannot see the big picture or know that all things will, in time, pass. To a baby, there is no time; there is only now, and when now sucks, it sucks big time.

An adult soothes her own hurts and regulates her own anxieties; she doesn't depend on other people or on some substance to do this for her. She's able to sit with her feelings, cope with her pain, and even moderate her triumph if there's a reason to do so.

You're an adult to the degree that you're a rock—firm, steady, and sure of yourself—but not so much a rock that you're rigid. When you bend gracefully, take the bad with the good, and live to fight another day but don't bow down at every bully or blowhard that comes your way. Adults understand and practice moderation. They take the middle way. You know you're an adult when you have feelings, but your feelings don't run your show. You have disappointments but not despair. You get angry but not violent. You have fear, but you are brave.

When you can compose yourself, you may be able to enjoy alcohol, marijuana, or even the harder stuff without needing it too much. You can appreciate but don't require coffee to get you up in the morning, or cigarettes or pills to get you through the day. We don't let babies use any of those substances because they can't handle them.

When you can regulate your own feelings and anxieties, you don't have to be dependent on others to make you feel good. You can just enjoy people for who they are. Not needing people sets you free to love them, and they don't have to be afraid to love you. You're low maintenance. Furthermore, when others have a bad day, you don't have to. You can empathize with them because their feelings will not be too much for you. You can be with anyone and go anywhere. Even the most difficult, toxic people will not be too much for you.

If you do not have composure, you are easily hurt. It's like you have no skin on your body. Any little thing gets to you, people see right into you, you've always got your guts hanging out. If you don't have composure, you're constantly the victim and never get anywhere down the Road to Reconciliation because even the pebbles on the road bother your feet. No one can ever make amends to you without inflicting a hundred other cuts in the process.

Civility

Babies cry a lot, over the least little thing. They scream bloody murder when there is no need to. They throw themselves on the floor and have temper tantrums. They have unreasonable demands. They piss in their pants and shit everywhere. They can't sit still in church, make a mess in restaurants, and just got to touch every fragile figurine. They can't have nice things and you can't bring them anywhere because you never know what they're going to do.

Adults may cry, they may ask for help, they might even get frustrated, but they avoid overreacting. They can follow the rules, control their bladders, shut their sphincters, practice patience, and pay respect to others.

When you're acting like an adult, your responses to others' behavior is proportionate. You don't go off the deep end. You deal with the matter at hand. You don't bring up old wounds. You don't have something to prove. You're not always yelling. You don't go to pieces over little things. There's not nearly as much drama.

When you make a mistake—for instance, when you've trusted someone too much—you don't overcorrect by not trusting at all. You avoid flying off into extremes. When others act poorly, you don't have to. You remember that their feelings are their feelings and not yours. You practice moderation.

You're careful about what you say and avoid hyperbole. Letting it all out scares people, and the hurtful words you say cannot be retracted, so you're careful about catharsis. You have no need to vent or blow off steam because things don't come to a boil in the first place. You're careful about how you act because what you do matters.

A baby will freeze, wrap her arms around her mother's legs, and fail to act when needed.
You're not acting like a grown up if you fail to react or take action when necessary. An adult can be decisive when it's needed.

When you're civil, other people want to be with you. They don't have to be afraid to bring you bad news. They'll try to solve problems with you because you'll work with them; you won't cause more problems. You can focus on objectives and not get distracted. Moreover, others won't have to run when they see you coming; they don't get sick of hearing you complain.

When you're not civil, you'll often feel victimized because you're always getting into fights. You bring out the worst in people. Nothing is ever easy with you. If they try to make it up to you, you just blow up at them, again, and you can never get past it.

Perseverance
A baby can't wait for anything. When he wants something, he wants it now. He requires instant gratification. He doesn't

understand the concept of sacrificing a little now to save for later.

An adult accepts temporary hardships for the sake of worthwhile objectives. It's natural to seek pleasure and avoid pain, but sometimes brief discomfort must be tolerated to attain better things. An adult possesses grit, determination, and endurance. She understands meaningful suffering.

People who can defer gratification do better, all the way around. They have more education and make more money. Their marriages are more stable, and they have happier children. Their health is better, they have more friends, and are more successful in sports. They invest more for their retirement.[11] They are more adult.

When you practice perseverance, people will respect you, even if the objective is not important to them, but because it's important to you.

When you fail to persevere, you will feel victimized because you cannot take the long route to reconciliation. You pardon people easily or you bail from the relationship at the least sign of trouble.

Wisdom

A baby has only ever been a baby; she has never been anything else. An adult once was a baby and still has vestiges of the baby she once was. A baby has no other point of view than a baby's. He can only see things one way, his way; nothing else makes sense. An adult can entertain multiple points of view; he can walk a mile in another's shoes. He knows that if there are ten people in a room, there will be ten ways of doing things and they will all, to their way of thinking, be right. You are acting like a big baby if you think there's only one right way.

A baby can only do a few things: eat, sleep, shit, and cry. An adult can do many things. She has skills that a baby can't imagine. If an adult doesn't like the view in one place, she can get up and walk to another. A baby is stuck where she is, like a plant. You're acting like a big baby if you don't do what you can do.

A baby can't say what she wants; she has to cry. Crying is the only way a baby has to communicate. An adult can say what she wants. You're acting like a big baby if you don't use your words.

When you're wise, people will respect you for knowing what to do, what to say, and when to keep quiet. They will go to you for your discernment and trust your discretion. You'll know a lot, but you'll also know enough to know what you don't know.

If you have wisdom, when you read this part, you'll see many ways that you've acted like a big baby. When you admit it, you're acting like an adult, no matter how childish you once have been. The wise person knows there's a big baby in him, but the wise person takes care of the baby in him so the baby doesn't always run the show.

When you have wisdom, you don't put a baby in charge of things he can't handle: you wouldn't have a baby drive a car, conduct surgery, negotiate a deal, talk serious matters over with a spouse, handle delicate issues, or take care of the sick and dependent. No, these are matters for an adult; you wouldn't put the baby in you in charge of these things either.

There are things babies are good at, which adults have forgotten: babies are open, playful, and eager to learn; they smile well, understand the necessity of touch, and are so gosh-darn cute. Therefore, when any of those qualities are needed, a wise adult lets her inner baby lead the way. A wise adult has many options and knows when to choose each one.

When you lack wisdom, you get victimized out of naiveté and misplaced trust. You disregard red flags and fool yourself into believing things that aren't true. You don't see things coming. You're your own worst enemy.

So, there you are; the five signs of true adulthood: responsibility, composure, civility, perseverance, and wisdom. How did you do? I bet you found many ways that you've been an adult, but I bet you also found many ways you've been a big baby. Remember, though: babies, even big babies, can grow up to be adults. The only difference between the two is what they've learned. Therefore, let this experience, the experience of getting hurt by someone you love, be a learning experience. Recognize and take charge of the baby in you.

Renounce Revenge

Once you've gotten in touch with your feelings and values, you realize that you are hurt. The next step, if you took the path toward healing, is to renounce revenge. If you don't, you are at risk of becoming the next specimen in our menagerie of people stuck on the Road to Reconciliation: the Ax Grinders.

Revenge comes in a variety of colors and flavors, all of them dark and bitter. There's the kind, practiced by mafia chieftains who cannot afford to appear soft, who hunt down and punish the wrongdoer with extreme prejudice. There's the Hatfield-and-McCoy, Montague-and-Capulet, Israeli-and-Palestinian type of vendetta that never seems to end. There's the tit-for-tat, eye-for-an-eye variety, practiced by couples who commit adultery in response to the other sleeping around. Subtle digs, where you never let your partner forget anything, are popular. So's passive aggression, where your partner may not even know what you're doing to get even. Revenge is codified and legitimized by courts in systems of retributive justice. Punish the offender enough, it is thought, and they will have paid the price of crime.

Revenge is said to feel good, but I have my doubts. I remember when Osama Bin Laden met his end. There was some satisfaction to see that happen, but it didn't help me forget 9/11. Does revenge work? Does it ensure that crimes will not be repeated? Does it deter misbehavior, right wrongs, or enforce order? When you bring someone to justice, is justice created, or is injustice given a new lease?

I have my opinion on these questions, and you may have yours. But the urge to commit revenge can be very strong and it's hard to believe it has no evolutionary justification. Besides, while it's one thing to preach love and forgiveness in church, a hippie commune, or an academic conference, it's quite another to do so in the ghetto or Iraq, where the questions come up most frequently.

If, after listening to your feelings and reengaging with your values, you believe revenge is the way to go, I suppose there's nothing I can do to convince you otherwise. I think it's strange to practice revenge on the people closest to you, to insist on a pound of flesh from your own flesh and blood; but I'm not you, I guess. I wouldn't want to be either a Hatfield or a McCoy. It might be cool to be a mafia chieftain and order my enemies killed while dining on veal saltimbocca, but it would be a bummer to be interrupted by a guy with a violin case before dessert arrived.

I will say that, if you are serious about reconciliation, or even personal peace, you will not get to it by seeking revenge. You can't get there that way. You will have to renounce revenge if you're going to get anywhere down the path to reconciliation. The reason why may become clearer as we go on, but for now I think you will agree that spending your time plotting revenge is incompatible with putting the injury behind you.

Does renouncing revenge mean that you can't ask anything of the offender before you can reconcile? Absolutely not. You can achieve personal peace without getting the offender involved, but to be reconciled, she has to do something too. It'll be hard for her. She'll have to hear you speak about your hurt and its effects. She'll have to take responsibility, make restitution, and change her ways. You'll have to insist on it. That's your revenge.

I've worked with many criminals over the years: thieves, murderers, rapists, and child molesters, to name a few. Almost all of them would much rather do jail time than look their victims in the eye and acknowledge what they've done. Most would choose solitary confinement before accepting responsibility. Some might even elect the electric chair over meaningful change. You're not letting them off easy by offering reconciliation.

So, don't be an Ax Grinder; renounce revenge, if only because it'll make you a better person than the one who hurt you. Like someone said once, living a good life is the best revenge.

The Righteous Idiots

The addiction, the madness, the lying, the cheating, and the selfishness have just done too much damage. Your relationship is crippled and you're not sure whether it will ever be the same again. You've heard enough apologies, forgiven too much. You can't forget all the things that have happened. You've hardened your heart, dug in, and started to hate.

I will not argue against the justice of your cause. Yes, she did things that were unwarranted, things that hurt. Bad behavior wrecks things and some of those things are your feelings. You probably can't even count the number of disappointments. It's your right. Your cause is just, but don't be an idiot. Don't be one of those people who think just because they are right, they can afford to be stupid.

The most idiotic thing you can do

The supremely stupidest thing would be to harden your heart and refuse any attempt at reconciliation while you continue to live with your partner. You've seen couples like that, who live together in a home, protected by force fields of hate. Their sadness is disguised as hardness. They pass in the hall, throwing invisible daggers at each other. They eat in shifts, have their own dens, their own TVs, their own unapproachable sides of the bed. They communicate through their children, who are caught in the middle. Every couple endures moments like this, maybe days, following a fight, when all they give each other is the cold shoulder. Image a lifetime.

The people who live like that imagine that their resentment preserves them from harm; their hate is a cold castle wall of safety. They're afraid that, if they forgive, they'll forget, and they'll let it all happen again. They fear that any warmth will just encourage the offending party. They're partly right. When forgiveness is given away cheaply or when you are still at risk, it'll do just that; but when the opportunity to earn genuine reconciliation is extended and taken, it's a welcome rain on a dry day.

What hate is trying to say

Hate is an idiot light in your car that's glowing red. I guess it would be like the low oil pressure light, because when there's low oil pressure, there's too much friction between the moving parts. What hate is trying to say is this: pull over, because there's an incompatibility between the relationship and your values. Either clear up the incompatibility, abandon your values, or get the hell out of the relationship. Reconciliation is where you clear up the incompatibility. People who continue to hate and do nothing about it are like people who drive for miles with a glowing idiot light in their car.

Other idiotic things you could do

The next stupidest thing is to take the opposite tack, to grant cheap pardon, to rush forgiveness just because you don't want to deal with your own feelings. Cheap pardon is when you abandon your values, just to preserve peace. We talked about that, already.

It might not be a bad idea to move out, before any more hurt can happen, while you work toward reconciliation. If you're in mortal danger, then you should move out right away. However, provided you are not in mortal danger, I would urge you to pause before you pack your bags for good. Moving out doesn't change everything. There's really no such option of getting completely out of a relationship.

Relationships are forever

It's important to remember that, once you're in a relationship with someone, you will always be in a relationship with that person. It's like the Hotel California: you can move out, but you can never leave. Even if you never speak to her again, move to the other side of the world, put up a dartboard with her face on it, refer to her only as *the bitch,* you will always be in relationship. There will always be a corner of your brain—I dare say, a corner of your heart—that has her name on it.

This is doubly true if you're in photos in Facebook together. This is triply true if she met your parents. It's quadruply true if you were married. It's doubly, triply, quadruply true if you have kids together. You're hitched.

Love may not be eternal, but relationship is. The legal end of a marriage is not the end of a relationship.

Relationship, at its minimal level, means that your partner rents space in your head. You think of him sometimes, happily or unhappily, with fondness or regret. He's part of your story and you're part of his. You have to account for him if you're honest. You'll be flooded with memories, good or bad, after the most trivial cues. He'll affect the way you relate to anyone else. He'll be an item for comparison and for contrast.

Former relationships rarely exist at this minimal level. Usually there are more feelings. Many more. You might continue to hate her, but there will still be feelings. At some point, time and time again, for the rest of your life, after the right buttons are pushed, you will be transported by your passions for the person.

You've seen this in others. You've had beers with the man who, at the mere mention of his ex, goes on a ten-minute tirade about the shrew. You've drained a bottle of wine with a friend who combs over every detail of her ex's pervasive perfidy. These are people still in relationship even though their divorces are final.

By the way, love and hate are not that far apart. They are both intense. They are both very, very far away from indifference. You'll never be indifferent about a former partner, no matter how hard you try to fake it.

If you agree that you will always be in relationship, then the question is: What kind of relationship will it be? Which road will you take? You have three choices: grant cheap pardon, extend everlasting enmity, or work toward genuine, but rewarding, reconciliation. You have these choices if you stay together, but you also have these choices if you're apart. Your address—whether it's where you sleep, where you call home, or where to get your mail—is irrelevant.

The Scab Pickers

By this point, you've come a long way toward peace with the things that have happened to you. You have connected with feelings you had previously turned away. You've recommitted to values. You're protecting yourself. You've renounced revenge in all its forms. You've decided not to be stupid and live in an atmosphere of toxic hate. What are these people squatting by the side of the road? They don't look too good. These are people who spend all their time and energy replaying the awful things that have happened. They're the Scab Pickers picking their scabs.

Imagine turning on your TV and looking at all the programs, movies, and sports available. You have cable, so you have thirty-four hundred channels to look through. You have Roku and subscriptions to Netflix, Hulu, and Amazon. There's also YouTube. Despite this bounty, there's one show you always watch, over and over again. Not just one show— one episode of one show. You could recite the lines and act out all the parts. You know what's going to happen, but you see the show to the end anyway. That's what it's like to be a Scab Picker. It's madness.

A Scab Picker will say, "I can't stop thinking about it."

Well, I'd answer, you just did. Right when you said you can't stop, you stopped long enough to say you can't stop. It's that easy.

Thoughts move

Human consciousness does not naturally think about
anything for long. It's always moving. It's like a flashlight in
the dark that does not settle on any one object. Good thing.
There's a lot to see. Human consciousness is like a TV set
that surfs channels on its own. If you want to watch your
program, you have to press the button on your remote that
brings you back to the last channel, that one episode of one
show you keep watching over and over. That's how crazy it is
to be preoccupied with something that happened.

If your thoughts moved on as they would do naturally,
then it would be inevitable that they would return to the
trauma. Okay, fine. If that happens, then move on again.

Let's take a closer look at what's going on when you say
you can't stop thinking about something. You know in your
heart that it's not an accurate statement; you do stop. On any
given day you've had a million thoughts, most of them having
nothing to do with what happened. You know it. Why then
do you say you can't stop?

I think you are engaging in hyperbole. You're
exaggerating for effect. You're trying to tell a story about how
hurt you are. You want to make a point.

If you're injured by something someone did, then it is
important to say so. You need to let the person know so that,
if they care, they won't do it again. If that person isn't
listening, you may need to say it again and again, till they hear.
You may need to let some third party know about the injury,
so they can intervene if they have a mind to. If they don't
listen, you may need to say it again. You also need to
acknowledge the hurt to yourself. After all, I asked you to get
in touch with your injuries, didn't I? If you aren't inclined to
assess the damage, the damage will mount till you hear.

However, there comes a point where raising the alarm
like this has exceeded its usefulness and is incompatible with
achieving personal peace. The time will come when you must

stop picking that scab, so it can heal and minimize the resulting scar.

How to stop scab picking

Here's how it works. You can't reduce the incidence of scab picking without first reducing the duration.

You know those people who walk through your neighborhood in pairs and knock on your door asking you to join their church? I get them in my neighborhood too. One day, I invited them in for coffee. I gave them donuts. We had a good talk, but I couldn't get them to leave. The next day they were back. I didn't want to be rude, so we had coffee again, and again, and again, and again. They were good people, but I wasn't going to join their church; I was already set in that regard. I was wasting their time and mine also. I couldn't stop. It was madness.

Then one day when they knocked, I made an excuse that I was painting the kitchen, so we couldn't have coffee. They were back a few minutes later in old clothes and offered to help me paint. Since I really wasn't really painting anything, I had to tell them the truth. Please don't knock on my door anymore. Goodbye.

The next day, they were back.

Eventually, I learned that even engaging with them in the doorway was a mistake. Whenever I heard the doorbell, I had to peer out a window. If it was them, I'd make like I was not home. Finally, they stopped coming.

Your bad memories are like that. So are your negative thoughts, anxieties, your cravings to use drugs, your unwarranted feelings, your paranoia, and your impulses to do what you'll regret. You can't stop these thoughts from knocking at the door, but you don't have to let them in.

When you notice you're picking the scab, that's the time to end it. Say to yourself, "Stop picking that scab," and the scab picking will stop the moment you say it. Seriously.

Oh, you'll be doing it again in, like, two seconds—so soon it'll seem like you never stopped. So, do it again. Say,

"Stop picking that scab," and it stops once more. Do this as many times as it takes. You will reduce the duration. Time spent watching that show will get shorter and shorter. You'll get better at doing this. It'll get easier for you to stop. Eventually, you'll learn to see it coming and, like me, pretend you're not home when it knocks.

I was complicit with my tormentors, but I didn't know it. I thought I had no choice. I gave them power over me when I let them in the door. I entertained them. I fed them. I sat with them and had coffee.

When you stop answering the door every time certain thoughts knock, you will see you were complicit too. The sooner you terminate your engagement with them, the sooner those thoughts lose power over you. They wither away, malnourished. You'll see.

How to Retraumatize Yourself

First, a bad thing happens. Rape, murder, combat, abuse. You don't have a lot of control over it. That's the point. Something happens way, way out of your control. You barely make it. Now you're left with the memories. That's the trauma.

Second, the memories come up. You don't have a lot of control over them either. They come up when you come across something you associate with the trauma. A plastic bag on the highway that looks as if it may be an IED. A dark alley like where you witnessed the murder. A program on TV similar to the incident. I knew someone who had a hard time every Saturday throughout her adulthood because, when she was a kid, her stepfather would creep into her room on Saturday nights. You find yourself caught up in the memory and start feeling as though it's happening all over again. It's like a trance you are in, a spell you are under.

You've learned to do things that'll break the spell. You found that a dramatic action will do it—the more outrageous, the better. It has to be extreme enough to compete and overpower that memory. You've got to drive fast, run hard, take a risk, get a stiff drink, or fuck the living daylights out of a stranger. You pick a fight, get some blow, or find a high, high place, hang your toes off, and flirt with death. Maybe, you don't go quite that far. Maybe you just go over the incident, again and again. Maybe you feel everything you had been feeling. Maybe you reenlist and return to the war zone, find another abusive man or return to the old one, one more time. Maybe you blame yourself for what was out of your control. Maybe you figure you deserved it.

Congratulations, you've just retraumatized yourself.

It gets to be that the original trauma is nothing; it's just the beginning. The bulk of the injury occurs over the years afterward. If, for instance, you were raped while walking through your college campus, that, in itself, is an evil thing. But, if for years afterward, every time it comes up in your mind, you feel terrible, then you are not only traumatized but retraumatized. If you can't have sex with your husband because you feel the shame and the terror of that rape, then you are not only traumatized but retraumatized every time you try to have sex. If you cannot be reminded of it without getting blind drunk, driving recklessly, shoplifting, yelling at your kids, or doing something regrettable just to break the spell, you are not only traumatized but retraumatized. If you watch *Law and Order - SVU* till you're numb, go to the scene of the crime, confront the rapist, sleep with a hundred men just to get over it, but feel that terror all over again, you are not only traumatized but retraumatized. It gets to be that the original trauma is just a small part of the pain you feel.

If you go to a therapist to get treatment for PTSD and tell the story, only to fall again into that pit of terror, you are not only traumatized but retraumatized.

It seems as if you can never get past it. It seems that every effort to straighten out the mess only ensnares you more thoroughly. It seems as though people are right when they try to deny it ever happened and avoid anything associated with it.

However, you can get past it. PTSD is one of the most readily treatable conditions there is. Plenty of people get past it. ONE STEP AT A TIME.

How to get past trauma

The first step is not to tell your story. Don't go into your therapist's office and get into the whole thing all at once without first considering what will happen when you are done. Oh, you have to say a little bit about it, just so your therapist knows the issue is there, but don't go into detail. Talk first about what happens when the issue comes up, how you have tried to cope with it so far.

For example, many traumatized people will turn to alcohol and drugs as a way to cope with their trauma. But if you're going to need a stiff drink or to shoot up after leaving your therapist's office, then nothing will be gained. You will only have succeeded in retraumatizing yourself by adding one more drink you don't need, one more relapse to the series of problems associated with this trauma.

Therefore, the first step is to take a look at the ways you have been retraumatized, not traumatized, and get control over that. Let's be sure what your reaction will be to dealing with the trauma, before we try to deal with it.

The second step is to tell your story, but maybe no second step will be necessary. It may never be essential that you go over the original injury. It's not like you're going to change what happened anyway, and it's not like you were responsible. What you want to change is how you respond to the triggers. That's something you can change. In the case of the woman raped on her college campus, she probably wants to be able to watch *Law and Order* without freaking out. She wants to be able to have sex with her husband, be free of nightmares, and see her daughter off to college. She doesn't want to have the need for all those crazy, dangerous, unhealthy behaviors that she used to turn to in order to break the spell. Really, all the important stuff is in step one. It's essential to end the retraumatization.

By the time you get to step two, you may want to tell your story anyway, if only because now you can. You are no longer silenced. You can speak out, testify, warn others, and join with those who've had the same experience. You no longer have to be alone with the secret because there is no longer the risk of retraumatization.

If you take step two and tell your story, then tell it in a place, at a time, and with a person who can contain it. You'll want to be able to leave the room in better shape than when you walked in. You let some feelings out as you tell the story; you may not be able to contain them within you, but we want to keep them contained in the room.

When you are done telling the story, the story is told. You, at last, may have been able to fit the pieces together in a way you haven't been able to do before. You couldn't complete the story because you were getting retraumatized. The hurt would start all over again, so you had to drop it. This left it unfinished and scattered in pieces all over. When you end the retraumatization, it becomes a story and not just fragments, jagged pieces of memory that don't seem to fit together.

Step three? Step three is up to you. Step three is living your life as you want to live it. Something awful still happened. You still have a memory, but it doesn't matter as much. You no longer are getting retraumatized; you no longer have to bear a secret, unless you chose to; and the story is complete. You've reached the end of trauma. Soon comes personal peace and maybe, if the offender is willing and able, reconciliation.

3

FEELINGS

Hitchhiking on the Road to Reconciliation

Here you are hurt and alone, plodding along the road from Hurt to Reconciliation. Powerful emotions keep passing by, giving you directions, offering you a ride. So, how about it? Can you trust these emotions and get onboard? Will they take you anywhere you want to go?

Anger and Rage

Anger and Rage are the first to pick you up. They drive an impressive muscle car, four-eighty under the hood and four on the floor. They tell you if you want Justice, they're heading that way and can take you there. "To get to Justice, go straight to the person who hurt you and hurt him back," they say. But Justice is not Happiness. The money he spent is still gone, the trust she squandered is still gone, the goodwill he pissed away, well, that's gone too. The person who hurt you made you feel small and now you made her small. In Justice, everyone is small together because that's only fair.

Sadness and Grief

Sadness and Grief come by too, driving a hearse. You climb on board and curl up in the back. The seats are soft, the lighting dim, the music in a minor key. There's a paradoxical comfort to Sadness and a goodness to Grief. You feel better after a good cry, but when you're in the middle of it, it's like being torn in two. Then you look out the tear-splattered window and realize you're not going anywhere. Sadness and Grief did nothing but acknowledge your loss and shelter you in place.

Contempt and Disgust

When you get out of Sadness, Contempt and Disgust are coming down the road in an Escalade. From a distance, they look a lot like Anger, but when you get in their car, you feel you're going to puke. You accept the ride anyway because at least they're going somewhere. "He doesn't deserve you," say Contempt and Disgust. "You're better than him." You ride high, looking down on everyone, feeling untouchable. After a while, that's the problem; you're untouchable and lonely in your superiority.

Despair

Contempt and Disgust leave you on the highway, gagging on their foul exhaust. "So long, sucker," they call. "You could've ridden in style; we'll beat you by a mile." The next thing you know, you're in a Pinto called Despair. There doesn't seem to be anyone at the wheel. The car is driving itself and you're heading over a cliff. You struggle to get out of Despair, but there doesn't seem to be any escape. Suddenly someone hits you. Shame hits you with its van and loads your broken body in the back.

Shame

Shame takes you to a bunker, ties you to a chair, and lashes you with what you could have done and who you could have been. You become Shame's slave. It rapes you, beats you, and calls you a pitiful loser. "You deserve everything you get," Shame says. "You make me do this to you. You make everyone hurt you." In time, Shame breaks you: then you're not even worth the trouble to mistreat anymore. It rips off your clothes and leaves you on the side of the road, naked and beaten.

Envy

Envy comes by and throws a cloak of sympathy over you. "You need to be taken seriously," it says. "Come with me and we'll show them." You go with Envy, driving the very car you always wished you had on an unrestrained spree of lawlessness. Every dirty thing anyone has done to you, you do it now, just to say you could do it too. If he gambled, you gamble; if she screwed around, you screw around; if he got high on drugs, you use the same drugs; you treat your children with the same abuse your parents subjected you to. You don't leave Envy until you see an ambulance coming down the road with its siren going and the driver leaning out of the window, screaming at you to get on board. This one is called Fear. You drop everything and go with it.

Fear

Fear drives fast but in no particular direction, just as long as it's away from the latest terror. You don't sleep, you don't eat, you don't even go to the bathroom because there are germs everywhere. Fear takes you right back to the one who mistreats you because you're afraid of being alone; then it takes you away because of fear of what he'll do to you. You finally give up on fear, not because you are not afraid, but because you're in Confusion and Exhaustion.

Confusion and Exhaustion

Confusion and Exhaustion don't take you anywhere. It's a rattletrap beater, broken down on the side of the road. The hood is up. The driver studies the engine, but he doesn't know what to do. A lot of other drivers stop and give advice, but they all contradict each other. A repair truck comes by, but Confusion and Exhaustion are just too heavy to tow away.

Guilt

When Guilt catches up to you, you almost don't get in the car. Guilt looks like Shame all over again. Guilt drives an old pickup truck; the shocks are shot, it has a punishing ride. "You're a good person," says Guilt, proving it's different than Shame, "but you did some wrong things and played a part in everything. Learn from your mistakes and do better. Try again."

As it turns out, Guilt gets you farther down the Road to Reconciliation than any of the others. It helps you see your part in the problem and your role in restitution. It hands you off to its friend, Compassion, who then takes you to meet the loved one who hurt you and teaches you his perspective on things. But you had to leave Guilt too. It has a regular route. After it stops at Compassion, it takes a trip back to Shame's bunker.

It turns out you can hitchhike on the Road to Reconciliation, but be careful from whom you accept a ride and how far you go with them.

What Are Feelings For?

If you're the victim, you make a lot of progress from hurt to reconciliation when you honor your feelings.

You've been putting up with a lot. This relationship is not what you thought it would be. There have been lots of problems; but, you say, there are problems in every relationship. You have to take the good with the bad, in sickness and in health, for richer or poorer. You're the type who, when the going gets tough, you get going. You put your head down and move on, don't make a big deal about things you can't change. Being hurt, you believe, is one of those things you can't change.

Now something has happened that you can't ignore. Maybe there's been a dramatic turn of events, the chickens have come home to roost, the things she's done to hurt you, she's doing to your children. Maybe it's you who has taken a turn for the worse; you've got bruises, you're falling apart, madness has come for you. Maybe your girlfriends have taken you aside and counseled you to leave the bum because they're worried about you. Something has happened that you can't ignore.

So, don't ignore it.

The first thing to do is to fight off the urge to grant a cheap pardon. You may think, in granting a premature amnesty, you're preserving peace. The truth is, you are putting up walls dividing yourself against yourself. You are turning aside your feelings.

What are feelings?

Feelings are like the idiot lights on your car. They're crude messages about your state of being. When the oil light goes on in your car, you know to check the oil. When you feel angry, you know there is a perceived injustice somewhere. You don't ignore the idiot light on your car, do you? Then don't ignore your feelings. Check them out to see what's causing them; and thank your feelings for alerting you to a potential danger.

I once knew a guy who had a check engine light that would not go off. He brought the car to the shop and they couldn't find a thing wrong. They offered to turn the light off, but it would cost a couple hundred dollars. He put tape over it, so he wouldn't have to see it. In doing so, he gave up any benefits having a functioning check engine light might offer.

People will often treat their feelings this way, especially people in demanding environments, with demanding people. The tendency is to tape over their feelings, put their heads down, and move on. Keep a stiff upper lip. Buck up. No one is interested in how they feel.

I think there are times when this kind of toughness is called for, but it is not the way out. It'll help you survive, but not thrive. It does not contribute to positive change. Not every hill is worth dying for, but some are. You'll live to fight another day, but one of these days, you'll have to fight.

By fight, of course, I mean confront the issues and create change. To do so, you'll have to welcome these strong, unpleasant feelings and honor them as the helpful allies they are. They're trying to protect you, warn you, and ready you for a struggle. They're also identifying and standing up for your values.

Feelings show values

Do this thing for yourself and your relationship now. Make a list of all the crap that has come your way because of his behavior. Take note of all the messes you've cleaned up, the anxious nights you stayed up, the blows you received, the lies you've heard, the money that's been wasted, the betrayals you've suffered. Just make a list, you don't have to act upon it. Go ahead, do it now. I'll wait.

There, done? Probably not. You will likely add to that list as you remember more and more. When you have something you're paying attention to, more comes up. When you remember it, take note.

Now, go to your list and jot down how those incidents make you feel now and how you felt at the time.

For example, let's say one of the items on your list was that you had to clean up his puke after he came home drunk and called Ralph all over the bathroom floor. What emotions might you feel? I might have felt concern when I heard him puking; anger when he left it to me; disgust at the smell; relief when he seemed to feel better; shame if there was anyone else around to see it. Those are just a few.

Once you're done doing that, see if you can spot the value that stands behind each emotion.

You felt concern because, despite everything, you love him. Anger because you believe in fairness. Disgust because puke can make you sick and you value your health. Relief because you value his health. Shame because you value your and his reputation.

You see how emotions stand in for and indicate values? If you didn't have emotions, you wouldn't know your ethics.

If you didn't have emotions, you would not be standing up for your standards. In fact, that is exactly the case when you deny your feelings, put your head down, and toughen yourself. You lose touch with what's important. You misplace your moral compass.

Once you have paid attention to your feelings and reaffirmed your values, their service is complete. They're like soldiers returning from war. They need to be demobilized, disarmed, and integrated back into polite society. To put it another way, they're idiot lights, not the driver. You're the driver. Your feelings should not be in charge. You should be in charge. Take note of your feelings. When they signal to you, investigate what they are trying to say, and then decide what to do about it. Don't make your feelings do more than they are meant to do; but pay attention and respect their intelligent design.

Action, Not Reaction

Once you get in touch with your feelings and allow them to speak to you, they can point you to what is important. They'll remind you of aspirations you've had since you were small, direct you toward life satisfaction, and give instructions for a meaningful life.

To the extent you've been victimized, your life has not been about growth, potential, aspiration, or mission. It's been about survival. You aren't your best when you're fighting back. You aren't standing for what you believe when you run away in fear. You aren't acting decisively when you're frozen in surprise. You've lost your integrity when you suck up to the enemy. You aren't taking action; it's all reaction.

Crisis makes us revert to primitive modes of behavior. Adrenaline awakens the animal in us. When things go from bad to worse, we're reduced to four options: fight, flight, freeze, or fawn. Our brains are designed to keep it simple when things get complicated. It's what gets us through, but it's not a way out.

Fight is when you strike back. You'd rather be a hammer than a nail. You might actually be violent, or your fight might be limited to emotional or verbal aggression. We shrinks call it identifying with the offender. It's the reason abused people can become abusers. Even though you're the victim in this case, you need to realize, if you don't already, that you can fight dirty. You can hurt others too; and when you're a victim lashing out, it'll feel good if you do so.

Flight is when you take off to avoid danger, make tracks to get out of Dodge. You might physically flee, withdraw emotionally, stonewall attempts to engage, dissociate from the here and now, or weasel out of any attempt to speak honestly. The funny guy who can't get serious is in flight. So is the gal who stays late at work to avoid going home. The bars and drug dens are filled with people fleeing. So are the ones binge watching Netflix all weekend and even those whose whole life is wrapped up with their children when their partner is right there, needing attention.

Freeze is when you have lost a will of your own. You can't make up your mind about what you want to do. You ruminate on your options until the cows come home, let others make the decisions for you, and ask a million people what they would do. You know you should leave, but you don't. You know you should get help but can't pick up the phone. Glaciers wonder when you will move. Moss grows on your shady side.

Fawn can be the most confusing. It's the Stockholm syndrome of responses to trauma. Fawn is when you are bonded to the person who abuses you because he abuses you, not despite it. You make nice, at first, so as not to provoke him. You ingratiate yourself so he thinks you're on his side. You know you can be the most convincing when you convince yourself, so you convince yourself to abandon your own interests. You start to believe you want this life, at first because you feel you have no choice, but then so thoroughly that when you have a choice, you miss your chance. The next thing you know, you're Patty Hearst, an heiress robbing a bank.

Fight, flight, freeze, and fawn keep you alive, but that's all they do. Sooner or later, you must take stock of the situation, how you really feel about it, and identify the things that are important to you. Then you must take a stand. You've got to serve something: either your ultimate values or the agenda of the person who mistreats you.

Emotions: Do You Have a Choice?

Anger, fear, sadness, hopelessness, joy, hope, gratitude, back to anger, fear, and sadness, in no particular order and sometimes all together at once. When your relationship is in trouble, you're on an emotional roller coaster. Let's take a step away and look at what emotions are and what, if anything, we can do about them.

The way you talk about emotions may reveal a misconception of how they work.[12]

You may say something like, "He makes me mad when he acts like a dick." As if the author of your emotion is him, in the way he acted. You had no choice but to be mad. He was the only one with a choice; he didn't need to act like a dick.

If you believe emotion works like that, the solution seems simple. He has to stop being a dick, then you can stop being mad. But it's not so simple. You can't get him to stop being a dick. You believe that by telling him off, you'll make him feel guilty. When he doesn't feel guilty, you think there's something wrong with him, but there's not. There's something wrong with your theory.

You go to see a therapist. If this is someone who specializes in cognitive behavioral therapy (CBT), she listens to your story and patiently explains, sorry, you're missing a step. Sure, maybe he's acting like a dick, but he didn't make you mad. You made yourself mad. You had a choice in the matter. You're the author of your feelings.

"How do I have a choice?" you ask. "I don't want to be mad."

She asks you, "When you say he's being a dick, what is he doing?"

"He's always correcting me in front of others. Then when he's wrong, he never admits it."

"I can imagine that can be annoying. Why is it annoying to you?"

"He's being disrespectful," you say, getting angrier.

"What else?"

"He's trying to make me look stupid." Getting even angrier.

"If that were true, if you were in a relationship with someone who tried to make you feel stupid, how would you feel?"

"I'd feel stupid, like I didn't see it coming."

"Well, you don't seem stupid. Is there another explanation?"

"He's acts like an English teacher, correcting my grammar all the time. Of course, he is an English teacher, that's what he does for a living, but he's not my English teacher."

"If he were to correct you in public and you said to yourself, there he goes, being an English teacher, would it make you as mad as if you thought he's being a dick, or disrespectful, or trying to make you look stupid?"

"No, I guess not. It's still annoying, but I guess I'd just roll my eyes and say, there he goes again, I guess he can't stop himself. Then, I guess he can't admit he's wrong 'cause he has this reputation of being an English teacher to hold up".

The idea implicit in CBT is that you can make yourself feel all sorts of things, depending on how you interpret an event. If you end up feeling angry or stupid, you interpreted the event in such a way that made you feel angry or stupid; but it could have been interpreted another way, a way that helped you understand, perhaps, or a way in which you could be patient.

Similarly, your boyfriend has a choice about how he feels; he can feel guilty when you're angry, like you want, or he can interpret your anger another way. He can say you're just being a bitch and not take your complaints seriously.

The ideas behind CBT are really nothing new. It's based on an ancient Roman philosophy called Stoicism. These ideas have been around for a long time because they work 90 percent of the time. Most minor emotional storms can be quieted this way, simply by reinterpreting the precipitating event. If you're angry all the time, about every little thing, or if you cry all the time or if you're always feeling hurt, then CBT, or Stoicism, is a great idea so you're not constantly buffeted about by your emotions. Take charge of your emotions so they don't take charge of you.

The limits of reason

CBT, or Stoicism, is one thing when you believe a stranger or distant associate has done something to you; it may be less appropriate when the offender is close to you. If you're on the bus and someone steps on your foot, it makes sense to give the person the benefit of the doubt and assume they meant no harm. If you were to go off on them, you'd be the one out of control. But when someone close to you does something that bothers you, it matters more because they're in a position to do it again. You have to address problems promptly before they get out of control. Therefore, if your boyfriend is being a dick, then it's important to say something because he might persist in his dickishness if he doesn't know it bothers you.

This doesn't mean you should complain all the time, about every little thing. There are good and bad times to bring up stuff and good and bad ways to bring it up. Here's where Stoicism is a good idea, even if you can't be a complete

Stoic. It can help you calm your emotional storm till you get a chance to have a discussion with your boyfriend about how he corrects you in public, then it can help you have that discussion without turning it into an attack.

There's another situation where CBT doesn't help; in fact, it's useless when you need it most: when the emotional storm has risen to a category five.

The next week, you have another appointment with your therapist. You sit down and immediately start to cry. Your boyfriend, the guy who you thought was a dick, died yesterday; he got in a car accident and was killed. You're beside yourself with grief, feeling guilty that you ever were angry, then angry at the guy who hit him, then scared about dealing with this alone.

No therapist, not even a CBT therapist, would ever say you have a choice not to feel those things. It sucks that your boyfriend died; there's no two ways about it. There are a few ancient Stoics who say it shouldn't matter when someone close to you dies—they say we shouldn't get close to anyone—but we can't take them seriously. In acute loss, you definitely feel you're in the grip of something you can't control no matter how hard you try to manage it.

Thoughts and emotions are often conceived as being in opposition to one another. Emotions are urgent and hot while rationality is cold and calculating. Strong emotions take you over. At such times, rationality can't touch them. If emotions are subservient to such cognitive operations as interpretation and judgment, if they are something you can choose or shape, then why do you suffer and lose yourself when you are in their grip? Why can't you handle them?

Thought's foundations

I'll tell you why. You can conceive of emotions not as being in opposition to thought but as old, foundational thoughts and decisions, upon which everything thing else is built. Take fear, for instance. If someone lets a tiger loose in a room in which you are sitting, you're going to feel fear, hopefully not disabling fear but fear that motivates you to arise out of your chair and run away. You don't want to have to think about it; you want to act first and ask questions later. Fear is there to take over the relatively slow way you normally make decisions and to make decisions for you—not because fear is an irrational force but because it is acting on instructions necessitated by a prior, foundational decision. A long time ago you decided it was better to remain alive.

You may not remember deciding to remain alive, but that doesn't mean you haven't done it. We call self-preservation instinctual, meaning, I think, that we were born with this decision already loaded in our software. Maybe, but it's a decision that can be countermanded anytime we choose, and many do; it's called suicide. Anytime you elect to remain alive, rather than commit suicide, you are reinforcing the decision to remain alive; you also do it when you chose to pay attention while you are driving rather than allow yourself to drift into the oncoming lane.

Love also is a decision. Yes, you may have been swept off your feet and fallen in love, but it's not like you didn't have any choice in the matter; you decided to go for it. Additionally, you already committed yourself to grieving when you chose to love. Grief was hidden in the fine print. You can't value someone without feeling terrible when he is gone.

There are other terms and conditions you also signed on to when you chose to love. You agreed to forgive. You can't be adding up all the good and bad points about your partner, or parent, or child according to how you feel every day. Everyone has their bad days; we love them no matter how annoying they can be. You would want him to forgive you, so, to be fair, you forgive him.

I'm not saying you have to put up with everything. I'm not saying you have to tolerate abuse or even persistent dickish behavior. All I'm saying is that's why divorce is so hard. It's supposed to be hard. Choosing to sever the bonds of love is like digging up the foundation of an old house and re-laying the stone to create a new footprint. You can do it, but it's not something to take lightly, even if you could.

The Help Page for Emotion

When you're having a strong emotion, it can seem as though you're being swept away by a power greater than yourself. It seems that way, but you're not.

Emotions are like a capability I have on my word processor. If I have a phrase that I type all the time, like *The Road to Reconciliation* and want to create a shortcut, I can go to system preferences > keyboard > text and set it up, so that, whenever I type *rr*, *The Road to Reconciliation* appears on the document. It's a handy little feature that saves keystrokes, but if I forget that I set it up, I might be surprised to see *The Road to Reconciliation* appear on my document every time I type *rr*.

You have emotions preprogrammed because there are some things that are so important or so foundational that you don't want to have to think about them every time before you act. Emotions speed up decision-making. (At least when emotions don't conflict with each other. When they do, you will freeze, just like your computer.) Emotions move you to action in a way that rational thought never can.

You may not remember programming your emotional shortcuts like I remember substituting *rr* for *The Road to Reconciliation*. That's because the process of learning the rules for emotions was also programmed, so you have a program automatically creating a program. You learned the rules for emotions when you were still very young by observing the emotions of people around you. Some aspects may have been programmed directly in you, genetically, in the same way that software engineers assumed I'd want certain shortcuts, like spell check, so they put them right in. The fact that emotions work outside your conscious awareness, both in the way they are set up and the way they operate, is proof of how well the system works. It frees your consciousness up for more important things that require your complete attention, like watching *Game of Thrones*.

Before you get any ideas, I must caution you against going into system preferences and rewriting the default settings for your emotions. They're embedded deep within your code and messing around with the way you feel may have many unintended consequences. Attempting to dampen or deny your emotions is a foolhardy venture. You have your emotions for a reason.

The anger program

Let's take a look at the shortcut you have set up called anger. Anger is a desire for retribution in response to a perceived insult.

Insult involves pain or hurt—actual physical pain or an injury to your ego, self-esteem, or social standing. So, the first phase of anger is feeling hurt. It's only after you perceive an insult that the desire for retribution gets going. The desire for retribution can be so intense that you might easily lose track of the fact that it began with an experience of fear, weakness, powerlessness, and vulnerability. An angry person looks like the most powerful one in the room, but he's actually the most fragile.

Not every injury ends in anger. If someone steps on your foot, you're not going to get angry unless you believe they did it deliberately or out of some carelessness. If someone has sex with your wife, and she with him, it's the perceived insult you're reacting to when you get angry. If you invited someone to have sex with your wife, and she with him, like if you were into swapping or threesomes, you wouldn't get angry because there would be no injury to your status. It might even elevate your status if you believed the desirability of your wife reflected on you.

Emotional rules vary from one person to another. Some people are quick to anger because they may not like to feel hurt. Some prefer to show their anger more than others. But the basics remain the same: anger is a desire for retribution in response to a perceived insult.

There are, of course, people who don't follow the rules, as you see when someone goes off when a person innocently steps on their foot. We call such a person crazy or irrational. We send them to anger management classes.

How to manage anger

If you don't like your anger, or if you are court ordered to learn to manage it better, there are things you can do to override the program. If *The Road to Reconciliation* appears on my document when I don't want it to, I can click on a little X and it will disappear. If you need to manage your anger, the first step is to reconsider whether the insult you perceived ever really happened.

Are you really hurt? Sure, the guy who stepped on your foot weighed as much as a hippopotamus, but you were okay with feeling pain when you played football. You even tolerate dental work and don't slug the dentist because you know it's for a good reason. It's the idea of physical pain that hurts more than pain itself.

If the injury is to your ego, self-esteem, or social status, you can ask yourself a few questions: Do people really give a shit? Will anyone in the movie theater really think about you for more than two seconds if someone steps on your foot and you don't deck him? Is your ego so delicate that you need to make a federal case if someone treads on your tootsies?

Did the person really mean to hurt you? People are often clueless and seldom belligerent. The guy who stepped on your foot probably didn't know your foot was there. Your wife and the guy who slept with her weren't thinking about you at the time; they were thinking of other things. You can still get angry that they weren't more careful, that your feelings weren't considered, but are you always careful about everything and do you always consider everyone?

If you've taken a good look at the perceived insult and concluded that it was real, the next thing to think about is the desire for retribution.

Retribution

Retribution can take many forms: you can hunt down and punish the offender or press charges and wait for the state to do it for you; you can give them a good tongue lashing or smile and complain about them behind their back; you can insist on a humiliating apology or inflict direct physical pain. There is no end to the forms that retribution can take, and people can be amazingly creative in executing it.

There's a case for retribution. It serves as a deterrent. If you get angry when someone steps on your foot at the movie theater, you can be sure the next person in line will be more careful. Also, if you're angry all the time, people will learn not to mess with you. They will give you a wide berth and won't try things that'll get your goat. Moreover, the person who stepped on your foot just might be more careful next time he goes to the movies with his big feet. This way, others benefit from you going apeshit. Going apeshit might be how you serve humanity.

Retribution can be the way to repair the injury to your social status. I think this is a bigger deal in some cultures than others. When I worked with people who'd been to prison, I learned that when someone disses you there, your main concern is who else saw it. You have to respond hard and fast so that others don't get the idea that they can do it too. It's dangerous to be seen as a punk in prison. In prison, when you succeed in retribution, it elevates your social status and makes you untouchable.

Anger promises to repair your injured ego or self-esteem. Even if nobody knows what was done to you, you can feel weak, powerless, and vulnerable. When you are filled with anger, you forget your powerlessness. If you succeed in retribution, you prove to yourself that you're the master of a situation.

Yes, retribution has some benefits. That's why we have anger; it's useful, to some degree. Hurt tells you there's been an injury to your body, ego, self-esteem, or social standing. Anger motivates you to do something about it. But if anger has gotten you into trouble, you have to reconsider whether retribution is such a good thing.

If you go a beat up the guy who slept with your wife, what does that change? You still have to deal with her. You could beat her up, but does that restore the loving feeling? Even deterrence is a questionable good. We catch more flies with honey than we deter with vinegar. If people give you a wide berth because you don't take any shit, won't that also prevent them from getting close enough to give you some love?

You can also, of course, feel a desire for retribution without taking any action. Being the bigger person and letting go of anger when you could've hurt someone could actually be a bigger boost to your self-esteem than any amount of havoc you could wreak. It's not the anger that's the problem; it's what you do with it.

So, you see, you can override your anger response at any time, just as easily as you can override spellcheck.

I know, it's not easy to override spellcheck if you're not paying attention.

You get my point. Pay attention.

Dismiss Disgust

If you need to be convinced that the feeling of disgust is a peculiarly powerful and primitive emotion, try this experiment. Get a clean glass. Spit in it. Now drink it.[13]

Even if you can drink the spit, you know what I'm talking about. You know there's nothing wrong with the spit. You swallow your own spit all the time, but by expelling it from your body, you make it an object of disgust, and disgust is not only powerful and primitive, it's also unreasonable.

Nonetheless, disgust is a useful emotion, as they all are. It patrols the boundaries of your body. It's your defense from imbibing something that is generally bad for you. Disgust keeps you from taking in spoiled food, stagnant water, and other things contaminated by feces, urine, or bacteria. Disgust is not foolproof. There are plenty of bad things that can still get past your nose, but for the most part, it has served you well and kept you alive.

Babies are not born with the sense of disgust; it's an acquired emotion. Babies are well known as being people who will put anything in their mouths; however, by the end of the first year, they'll start to wrinkle their noses at things, and by the time they become toddlers, they may become particularly fussy and squeamish eaters. Perhaps this brief window of disgust-free eating gives their parents the opportunity to introduce the foods of their culture.

Once the emotion of disgust sets it, the experience of disgust becomes particularly vivid. When you've been disgusted by something, you don't want to be disgusted by it again. You begin to erect fences around your disgust so that the very sight, the slightest smell, or even the briefest mention of it is enough to arouse your disgust. You are disgusted not only by the offending materials themselves but also by the things associated with it. This is how toilets, for instance, get imbued with all the disgust that properly belongs to shit and piss, even though they may be nothing more than clean, unoffending porcelain. Indeed, even the words *shit* and *piss* themselves take on the disgustingness belonging to the objects they refer to. You can even go so far as to say that the people associated with the objects connected to offending materials get marked by disgust. A garbage man, for example, becomes implicated because he handles garbage cans; a nurse, because she empties bedpans; and a janitor because he cleans toilets. In traditional India, you have a whole caste of people who handle disgusting objects consigned to being untouchables.

By the way, there's an interesting theory arising from the psychodynamic literature—from which many crazy, insightful theories originate—that misogyny, that irrational loathing many men have toward women and many women have toward themselves, comes from the fact that women are the receptors of semen. Semen, you see, comes out of the body and, even though it's the stuff of life, once it exits the body, it can be regarded as a disgusting fluid. To a misogynist, the people who receive any disgusting material become disgusting as well. This theory may also explain how homophobia originates and why male homosexuals, who are also the receptors of semen, get targeted with more homophobia than female homosexuals.

Exporting disgust

You can see how far we can take this. Disgust is such a powerful emotion that it travels well and arrives at a new place just as potent as when it left. People have used this property of disgust to make it do other work. The emotion originates from the need to protect the boundaries of the body from infection, but with a little bit of retooling, it can patrol morals as well. I don't think it's an accident that, when parents, religious leaders, and teachers indoctrinate children into morality, they use the language of disgust to make them regard evil as it were a spiritual pollutant. Raw disgust becomes refined by its importation into morality and is often called by different names: contempt, disdain, or superiority. It puts on priestly garb and busies itself with ritual purity, Levitical preoccupations, and separating the wheat from the tares and the sheep from the goats.

You don't have to listen to someone talk about right and wrong for long before you hear lots of words and images imported from the experience of disgust. Some behavior is said to be disgusting even though no contaminates are ever introduced to the body. Good behavior is clean living.

Innocence is pure. Evil is repulsive. When your husband comes home drunk for the hundredth time, you turn up your nose even before he pukes all over the living room carpet. If you find out that your wife has been lying to you, you may well be disgusted with her, but it's one step removed from the type of disgust you feel when you eat her cooking. Contempt is a metaphorical disgust that, from early indoctrination and frequent repetition, seems very real but, like any other metaphor, breaks down at some point.

Once disgust is exported into morality, it's easy for jingoistic leaders to use the language of disgust for whoever they single out for their hate. For example, Hitler, and many others, called Jews disgusting because of their vaunted control over the economy, making it an easy matter to deny them full human rights. History is full of examples of people having their stomachs turned by the mere mention of other, perfectly harmless, ethnic groups.

Morality shaped by disgust not only facilitates the division of people into those said to be clean and unclean but also unites sinners with their sins. When you find a hair in your salad, you reject the whole salad. The entire dish becomes tainted. A perfectly fine piece of lettuce, at the far edge of the dish from the offending strand, may turn your stomach. Indeed, the whole restaurant may fall under censure and you may never want to eat there again. Similarly, when you catch your wife in a lie, if you listen to disgust, she becomes a liar; any truth she tells may be questioned. If disgust has its way, you may never be able to trust her again.

Disgust is the driving force behind many an overreaction. It provides a script that, when used to protect you from bad food, works reasonably well but, when made to apply to morality, often throws the baby out with the disgusting bathwater.

It's disgust that gets in the way when you try to love the sinner while hating the sin. Disgust and the related emotion of contempt join the two. Disgust makes you say that the person is the problem and forget that the problem is the problem.

Overcoming disgust
Is there anything you can do to overcome disgust? Of course, there is; people do it all the time. There's even a word for it. The word is love.

Disgust is the border agent of the emotions, protecting you from invasion. Love is an invasion. It's probably no accident that the basic gesture of love is the kiss. The willingness to swap spit is a sure sign that disgust, and the need to patrol the boundaries of the body, has been suspended. Kissing paves the way for the sharing of other body fluids, but it doesn't stop there; it's also a symbol of trust, an agreement to regard the other person, his actions as well as his body, as a kind of extension of yourself.

No trip down the Road to Reconciliation is complete until you confront disgust, honor it for its services, and dismiss it. You don't need its services any longer. Disgust can still rise up when you find a hair in your food, but it has no place in a loving relationship. It's not the right tool for the task at hand. Disgust is incompatible with reconciliation.

Disgust Management
I have an idea for a new business opportunity for shrinks. You know how they have anger management classes that judges, employers, and spouses send people to when they keep losing their cool? Well, anger's not the only emotion that needs to go to class. There ought to be disgust management classes too.

Disgust is that feeling of revulsion you get when you come across anything gross, grody, ghastly, gruesome, creepy, hateful, horrible, nasty, nauseating, stinking, loathsome, objectionable, obnoxious, odious, hideous, beastly, detestable, distasteful, repugnant, repellent, rotten, vile, vulgar, cloying, foul, horrid, scuzzy, sleazy, noisome, offensive yucky, lousy, or icky. It's often accompanied by a narrowed brow, a curled lip, a wrinkled nose, and a tongue sticking out for all the world to see. You feel it in your stomach. It makes you want to hurl. It's closely related to hate, contempt, condescension, snootiness, and the reason bands of villagers go marching with torches and pitchforks.

Who would go to these classes? You've got people who've got to keep their peas and mashed potatoes separated and the kind who lay toilet paper on the seat. There are those who can't bear the sight of blood, won't do CPR, and are useless at an accident scene. You could send anyone who runs away whenever there's a spider, gets grossed out by handkerchiefs, or gets the shivers upon seeing nail clippings. If you can't keep down a perfectly good tapioca pudding, that's it; you're going to disgust management class.

It's not just the persnickety people who would be sent to disgust management. The emotion shows up anytime there's something different. Homophobes, transphobes, and xenophobes should apply, as well as anyone who can't bear the thought of Blacks and Whites marrying, if there's anyone left. If you can't ride in a subway car with a homeless person, it's disgust management for you. If you get all nervous and jerky when there are too many wheelchairs in the room, if you don't know what to say to someone who looks funny, then come to disgust management and tell us all about it. Whatever's your thing; maybe you can't stand Jews or Palestinians or Somalians or Syrians, or anyone with a turban on their head. If Indian food makes you retch, if the thought of Mexicans taking jobs away disgusts you, then I have a seat for you in disgust management class. If the thought of Donald Trump taking the oath of office turns your stomach, then there's a place for you too.

When the police pull up in their paddy wagons and get all the protesters off the street, they can take them right to disgust management class. Congress should go, both parties, and all the state legislators. You should have to graduate from disgust management before you get your own radio show, get a Twitter handle, or be permitted to comment on the Internet.

I can see people volunteering to attend disgust management. If it weren't for disgust, you could eat a whole plastic pumpkin full of Halloween candy without throwing up. No longer would creeps give you the creeps. If you wanted to, you could have sex all day, every day, with anyone in every way. Then, afterward, you could tolerate talking and cuddling and stay. The morning after would be like the night before.

You'd get along better with difficult people after disgust management class. There would be no eye rolling or lip curling to get you get in fights. You'd listen better, hug longer, and meet fascinating people. You'd have more friends on Facebook and actually stomach reading their posts. You'd get more news from more sources and have something positive to contribute.

If it weren't for disgust, dead people wouldn't be half as scary. You could make friends with a zombie, share a meal with a vampire, or go to a wake and actually look at the body. You could see your dying grandmother in her hospital bed and not have to run away. Bats would be nothing; rats would be fine; a Quentin Tarantino movie would be okay with you.

Disgust is a perfectly good emotion when kept in moderation. It keeps you from eating spoiled food and stepping in dog shit. But people go wild with it. They take it too far. Disgust gets imported into morality, theology, ethics, and politics. It shows up in things for which it was not designed, like arguments, seating arrangements, and public policy. You end up treating someone who disagrees with you the way you treat putrid vomit. What's meant for month-old fuzzy leftovers is used for people with skin darker than yours. There's nothing wrong with the emotion; it's what you do with it. If resentment is a poison you drink to hurt someone else, disgust is a poison you drink to keep from drinking a poison.

What would I do in this disgust management class? What is the treatment plan for disgust? Simple, I would ask you what disgusts you. I'd solicit your pet peeves. When I found out what gets you going, whether it be snot or spiders, creamed corn or cripples, people who speak a foreign language or someone who uses your language ~~wrong~~ incorrectly, I'd go get it and set it right there by you. Oh, not right away. Little by little. Enough to make you squirm, but not enough to make you barf. Enough to challenge, but not so much that you're running screaming from the room. It's called basic systematic desensitization coupled with progressive relaxation. I'm an expert in it. Relax, I'm like a doctor.

Love, respect, and civility suspend disgust. You'd have a whole group with you in my disgust management class, encouraging you, cheering you on to trust. Everyone knows where you're coming from, despite being disgusted by different things. Even if you are disgusted by me, well, I could be disgusted by you. We'll help each other get over our habit of disgust and have a party of disagreeable things. Dogs and cats sleeping together! A good time will be had by all.

What's that you say? We already have disgust management classes? They already exist?
I can't find them in the yellow pages. They're not called by that name. What do you call them?

A global economy, a multicultural democracy, a civil society, a diverse workplace, a heterogeneous classroom, a functioning military unit, a family, a marriage, taking care of someone. Any setting where different people come together is like a disgust management class. They all, if not one then the other, will put you right next to everything you detest. They provide social support to help you get over and manage your disgust.

Why aren't they working?

4

THE BIG PICTURE

See the Context

The world may have been created out of nothing, out of a nameless void, they say; but since then, anything that has happened has arisen out of something else. We call this context. If you want to come to some peace over something that has happened to you, then see the context from which it emerged.

Notice I carefully used the word *context*, not *reason*. Don't look for the reason something occurred. Many things just aren't reasonable. Much happens for no reason, or, at least, no good reason. Similarly, don't look for justifications; if anyone offers them, don't accept them. Justifications are closely related to explanations, rationalizations, and vindications. Stay away from all of them. They all contain too much of that quality by which we sort things out into good or bad, loving or hateful, healthy or unhealthy. Stick to the evidence without drawing too many conclusions about it. Just the facts, ma'am.

If you don't like the word *context*, then look for factors, conditions, background, or the scene. The point is to disengage the judging apparatus in your mind long enough that you can take in all the needed information. Remember to value your feelings as things that can tell you something is wrong. Then feelings can reconnect you to your values. Once feelings do that for you, their job is done and they should be quieted, in much the same way as, once you've been woken up and escaped a fire, you have no more use for a fire alarm.

Here's an example of looking at the context. Let's say your husband cheated on you. If you looked at the context, you might see, for instance, that he came from a broken home and married the first time when he was young. His first wife cheated on him, they split up, and he met you shortly thereafter. He quickly got a divorce and married you after you got pregnant. You love being a mother and had two more children in quick succession. They don't like to sleep alone, so, every night, at least one of them migrates to the bed you share with your husband. Needless to say, you barely have sex anymore. You actually seem to miss it more than he does. He says he doesn't like to ask because you always seem tired and distracted. He works in a large company with many women. He travels for business and it was on a trip that he began an affair with a colleague. They were out celebrating, having made an important deal, when one thing led to another.

I could have gone on and on, describing the context in which this affair occurred. Obviously, I just included factors that could be related somehow to his unfaithfulness. I could have also said that your eldest son won a competition at a science fair and your husband's best friend is battling cancer, but those facts are less likely related. Maybe not, though. Maybe his best friend having cancer reminded him that life is short, so he wanted to grab for all the gusto he could. Maybe your husband's ego was threatened by his son, who is very smart, so your husband wanted to prove he was desirable to someone. Sometimes it's hard to tell what factors are related. Motivations often come from unexpected directions.

Context, not cause

Notice, when I described the context, I tried to keep a neutral tone. I didn't say, for instance, it's no wonder your husband had an affair; you guys weren't having much sex. I also didn't say he came from a broken home and didn't have positive role models, so he didn't know how to be a good husband. We are looking for correlation, not causation; remember what I said about justifications, explanations, rationalizations, and vindications. We're not trying to say more than the evidence can bear.

If you really want to look for the cause of the affair, you can see, in my description of the imaginary husband, that there are a number of factors that could have contributed. He had poor marriage role models. He never had a chance to sow his wild oats. He was cheated on before, so he may have thought it was normal. Your marriage was almost accidental. He may feel left out of the alliance you have with the children. Then there's the lack of sex and privacy. He believes he cannot ask for what he wants. Paradoxically, you have poor communication because he tries to protect you or is afraid of rejection. He's around a lot of women, with some opportunities to be unfaithful. He may be able to be more open with them because there's less at stake. Presumably, there was alcohol involved when he and his colleague were celebrating, and the affair began under its influence.

You can see how all these factors might put a hapless husband on the path to being unfaithful. The context is quite powerful. However, there is one thing missing in our formulation. He made a choice. All of these factors could just as well have put him on guard, watching for that very thing. That's not what happened, though. He let down his guard and made a choice. That's why you want to stay away from causation, justification, explanation, rationalization, and vindication. All of them forget that there is a choice.

Dreams are context

Another thing to keep in mind when looking for the context is that not all the context resides in the past or present. Sometimes the most relevant context is the hopes and dreams the person has. Let's take this husband, for instance. He strikes me as a very isolated person, abandoned many times over, first by at least one parent and then by his first wife.

Even in his present family, he's the odd one out. He thinks he cannot express his desires to you because he fears he would be too demanding and would be rejected. It's not too much to believe that he desires affirmation, recognition, and respect and may have become embroiled in an affair in an attempt to get those things.

I admit that having an affair and imperiling his marriage, as well as his relationship to his children, is hardly the best way of gaining affirmation, recognition, and respect; but people adopt desperate, reckless measures when they are, well, desperate. Again, we're not looking for excuses; we're looking for context.

What is the value of looking at context? How can this help you? Let me tell you a story.

The Value of Context

I was walking around in Manhattan once. I turned the corner and saw a man with a gun, shooting another man. Blood spurted out everywhere and the victim fell. I reacted quickly, ducking behind a car before I got shot; but I was curious and peered out. Then I saw cameras, lights, microphones, and a director, sitting in one of those director's chairs. I had come upon a movie set, not an actual shooting.

When you see the context, you see more and understand more. Look at the context.

Get Out of the Middle of the Picture

One of the benefits of seeing the context is that everything ceases to be about you. That's a good thing; when it's not about you, you can relax.

Let's say you're deeply disappointed in your mother, who never was the mother you needed her to be when you were a child. You want to get past this because, after all, you're not a child anymore, right? The story, as you tell it, goes like this:

My mother divorced my father when I was young, and she had a series of relationships with men throughout my childhood. None of them were any good. They were drunken, violent louts. Nonetheless, she always chose them before me. She would do whatever they said and moved me in and out of different homes before she really knew any of them. None of these men wanted me around and I got the feeling my mother didn't either. I was just an inconvenience to her.

This is a heartbreaking story that is all too common. If this happened to you, the effects go deep and can persist a lifetime. You would really rather they didn't. What can you do to let it go?

Your mother is not just your mother

Here's a place to start. Stop calling her *my mother*. I don't mean you have to stop calling her *Mother*, or a variant such as *Mom* or *Ma*, to her face. Nor do you have to renounce her forever. She still is your mother. I mean when you tell the story, refer to her by name instead of title. If her name is Alice, call her Alice.

My mother is a being who came into existence when you did and exists only in relation to you. Alice was born long before you and has a life distinct from yours. *My mother* is so close to you that she's an extension of yourself and you're an extension of *my mother's* self. Alice is another person. You can connect as an equal to someone named Alice in a way you can never to *my mother*. When Alice chooses the company of men over you, it might hurt a little, but when *my mother* does it, it's catastrophic.

It was catastrophic when you were a child, but you're not a child anymore, so it doesn't have to be catastrophic anymore. Now it's as if someone named Alice did it.

Some people resist this exercise because calling their mother by name doesn't seem respectful. I think it's more respectful to understand someone as a whole person, independent of yourself, who is trying to play with the hand she is dealt.

The context of your mother

The second step is take a look at Alice's life, from the beginning to the end. Tell the story from her point of view—the whole story. How was Alice's childhood? What were her parents like? How might Alice have been shaped by her relationship with her first husband, George, whom you know as Dad? What were the social and economic forces of her early adulthood, the period when you were a child? What were Alice's dreams and aspirations?

I'm often amazed by how little adult children know about their parents, except the parts that directly pertain to them. You may be able to ask her to tell you these things. If not, then guess. You will probably be right. You probably know more than you think you do.

I'm going to go ahead and guess that Alice's dad, your grandfather Ted, was hard-working but emotionally unavailable. A lot of fathers were in those days. When she was a kid, Alice dreamt of going to college and traveling around the world, but she got pregnant in high school and married George, your dad. That's what people did in those days when they got pregnant. Shackled with a kid, little education, and a shotgun marriage, she didn't have a lot of choices. George had no respect for her, and when she never lost the weight she gained in her pregnancy, he ran off with his secretary, Mary. Now, she was really screwed economically and worried about raising her child without a male role model. She started to date, to find a man who would support her and her child. The prospects of an out-of-shape single mother in the marriage market were not good. She soon found herself scraping the bottom of the barrel. No matter how much she might have loved her child, she regretted ever getting pregnant.

See how different the two stories are when you are not in the center of it? You are seeing the context. You could conclude that she did the best she could. Maybe not. You could still be angry with her. That's your prerogative, but now it's an adult being angry with another adult, not a child being angry with his mother.

Your mother was not always the same as she is now

The third step is to calculate how old Alice was at the time in question. Let's just say she was twenty-five. Now, look around at the people you know who are twenty-five. How mature, wise, and together are they? Some are, granted, but most haven't got all the kinks worked out. Twenty-five-year-olds might actually be younger than you are right now. If that's the case, then remember how much maturity, wisdom, and know-how you had when you were that age. That's what Alice had to work with.

Now calculate how old you were at the time. Let's say eight. Look at eight-year-olds you know today. How much maturity, wisdom, and understanding have they? Do you really want to look at the situation only from an eight-year-old's point of view?

It's impossible to gain any of those insights about *my mother* but entirely possible with someone named Alice.

You can use this method with all the disappointing people who have titles in your life: husband, wife, sister, brother, friend, leader, colleague. When you are no longer at the center of the story, blocking the view, you are better able to see and, if appropriate, genuinely forgive.

The Mountaintop Moment

There comes a time, after you've climbed the mountaintop and gazed at the big picture, that you realize the part you played, and it hasn't been pretty. This doesn't mean that you were not victimized or you don't have valid claims for restitution. It doesn't mean that you weren't hurt or that someone didn't act like an ass. It doesn't mean that you deserve more or an equal proportion of blame; maybe she is still mostly to blame. It only means that you understand things better and can do something about them.

It's crucial that you go from thinking you're just a victim to knowing that you're a perpetrator, at least a partial perpetrator. If you can admit you've victimized others, sometimes including the one who hurt you, then you can proceed down the Road to Reconciliation. At that moment you can get real; you roll up your sleeves and take responsibility.

Let's say you caught your husband having an emotional affair with another woman. He didn't disclose it to you; you discovered it when you were looking at his phone. His culpability is obvious, but when you look at the context, the role you played also becomes evident. Maybe you haven't been there for him. You've been preoccupied with the baby. Since that baby, you haven't lost the weight you gained in your pregnancy. He doesn't seem to mind, but you do, so you've pulled away from him. There might be issues between you, disagreements you've not been able to resolve, so you avoid them because there's never been a good time to talk about them. When you avoid the issues, you avoid each other. He might have wanted to tell you about his growing friendship with this woman but had a valid fear you'd overreact.

I don't know what your part was; these are just some possibilities. When you're at this Mountaintop Moment, you see both sides of the problem. You're seeing the big picture. Your side doesn't absolve him of his, nor does his side absolve you of yours.

Here's the thing about seeing big pictures, though. You can't see everything at once. Your eyes travel around the big picture, first seeing how you were hurt and then seeing how you hurt him. Your feelings change with what you are looking at. You might feel like you are going mad or are frozen in indecision. Take your time. Take it all in. Once you absorb everything, it'll all make sense. Everything will come together.

This is a moment of decision or, perhaps, indecision. If you're saying, "Okay, I'll apologize to him if he apologizes to me; he has to go first." Stop it, just stop it. You'll never get anywhere that way. He's probably saying that too. If you both keep saying that, you will stand at this moment forever. You'll be another variety of people wrecked on the Road to Reconciliation, the Ones Who Can't Admit They've Done Anything Wrong.

Remember, everyone starts off feeling like a victim. Your husband did too. If he does any of the victim's work toward Reconciliation I've been describing, he'll be at his own Mountaintop Moment someday. Maybe he's already there and has been wondering what took you so long. How do things look from his perspective?

The view from the other side

Let's examine how it all looked from the husband's side of things. Let's trace where he has gone in his journey.

His wife caught him having an emotional affair with another woman. He didn't disclose it to her; she discovered it when she was looking at his phone. At that moment, she was angry with him, but she didn't see the context. The role his wife played is evident to him, but she's not having it. She hasn't been there for him. She's been too caught up with work and preoccupied with the baby. Since the baby, she's pulled away from him. She says she's ashamed of her weight, but he thinks she's beautiful. Nothing he says makes any impact of her. She never makes time to talk. She used to be his best friend, but they've become nothing more than roommates. Why is it surprising that, when another woman took an interest in him, he let down his guard? He wanted to tell his wife about the woman, but with her insecurities, he knew his wife would take it all wrong. She went snooping on his phone without his permission and found something she didn't understand. Then the shit hit the fan, making him look like the bad guy.

You see, both the victim and the perpetrator start at the same place. When the husband felt injured and ignored, he made choices that harmed his wife. Now she feels injured and may make choices that harm him as well. Around and around it goes. If the perpetrator found a way to deal with his injury, he wouldn't need to act out and injure anyone else.

When the husband stands at his own Mountaintop Moment, he'll realize that he wimped out, big time. With a new baby, he needed to suck it up. Women go through their own travail when they give birth; a father's labor pains come later, when he's feeling ignored. He was supposed to be okay with this because he's an adult. Instead, he found some other woman to mother him. That by itself may not have been so bad; everyone needs support. But when he didn't tell his wife about her, he guaranteed she'd go apeshit when she found out. So, get real, man; you're not just the victim here. There's a lot more to it. There's only one way to move on. Instead of claiming you're the victim, claim your share of responsibility.

Ideally, you and your partner will lay down your arms together. However, if your partner has not done so, you may have to show her how.

Taking Responsibility

What happens when you see the big picture and identify yourself as both offender and victim? You go through the same process of guilt, acknowledgement of shortcomings, and restitution as the person who hurt you would go through if he did the work of reconciliation.

If you're going to ask him to apologize for his shortcomings or to eradicate them, you have to do the same for yours. It's only fair. It also only makes sense. When you come to terms with the things you have done to harm others, only then do you have an appreciation of what's involved. You know how hard it is, so when you see someone do it authentically, you understand what they went through and won't dismiss it out of hand. If you see someone try to apologize unauthentically or make a half-assed attempt at restitution, you'll recognize that too and won't confuse cheap repentance for the real thing.

The choice you're making at the Mountaintop Moment is between moving on and not, between a sophisticated understanding of the problem and a simple one, between doing what you can about the problem and waiting for your partner to solve the problem for you.

It would be nice if others could solve problems for you. If only she behaved better, you'd be happy. If he wasn't such a prick, you wouldn't be angry all the time. If she were more trustworthy, you'd be able to trust her. It's nice when that happens, but you don't have to wait for it to happen. You play a part in how you feel. Actually, you play a bigger part than anyone else.

Let's go back to the situation of the last section, of the husband who had an emotional affair. You confront him, and he admits it. He promises to end it. He says he'll never talk to her again. You demand access to his phone and his computer at random intervals, so you can check on him. For a few months you do just that; but if that's all you do, a funny thing happens with your feelings: nothing. You continue to be just as suspicious as when you started. How do you know he isn't just deleting the correspondence? How do you know he doesn't have another e-mail account or a second phone or another laptop stashed away? How do you know they're not carrying on in a motel room, so they have no need to text or e-mail one another? You don't, and that's the point. Your feelings are your feelings and there's only so much he can do about them.

To really change the situation, you have to confront the circumstances that created it. If you had been ignoring him, you created the conditions under which he chose to have this affair. It's true he could have chosen differently, but you could have too. Taking on the underlying problem will do more to restore your trust in him than any amount of surveillance ever will.

The Mountaintop Moment is when you've waited for the other person long enough. You're ready to get started. Well, get started. Maybe he's done everything he can do to restore trust, but the rest is up to you. Maybe he'll never take a single step on the Road to Reconciliation; but if you fail to do your part, if you fail to admit your faults and begin to work toward restitution, that's something you're going to have to answer to.

The truth is we never know how reconciliation is going to go. Maybe you'll succeed in getting back together, stronger and better than you were before, or maybe you won't. Either way, you could use the experience to become a better person, to have learned from the experience and evolved so that if you do break up, you don't make the same mistakes in any new relationships.

So, what does it mean to come to the mountaintop and identify yourself as both offender and victim? It means you accept your part of the blame. You change the conditions under which your offender offended you. You don't just put all the responsibility for change on him; you take responsibility for yourself.

What's the difference between responsibility and blame?
Not everything is your fault. In fact, most things are not your fault; you had nothing to do with them. You didn't ask to be born to these parents or at this time or this place, at least so far as we know. You didn't invent the language you speak. You didn't have a choice about your genetics, nor your early childhood experiences, nor 99 percent of the experiences you have now. You might have chosen the person you married, but you chose him from a very limited field of possibilities. Unless you adopted and are remarkably prescient, you didn't choose your children.

You don't know all the consequences your actions will bring before you set them into motion. If you didn't have that second cup of coffee and left your house ten minutes earlier, you might have been hit by that truck that barrel-assed through an intersection with no brakes. If you had a third cup and left twenty minutes later, you wouldn't have been caught in traffic caused by the accident and would have gotten to work on time. There is no such thing as a fully informed choice.

Because of all this, many people say we don't have free will. They claim everything is completely determined by neurochemicals and the accidents of particularity. Well, maybe they're right. It could be that you're entirely blameless. Even if you're the biggest jerk on the planet, it's not your fault, it's your genes'. But, here's the thing:

You may be blameless, but you're still responsible.

Response-able

Take the word, *responsible,* break it apart, and you'll see why. *Response-able.* You have the ability to respond. In fact, because you have the ability, you're obligated to respond. People are waiting.

You're obligated to respond because you can't not respond. Even if you say nothing or do nothing, that's a response. It may be a piss-poor response, but it's a response. Actually, nobody is waiting—you've already responded—but they are waiting for you to claim responsibility.

Claiming responsibility means admitting that you have the ability to respond. It's called getting real.

You didn't choose your parents or the time, place, and circumstances of your birth, but it's your job to do something with it. You didn't choose the cards, but you play them. You didn't choose your genotype, but your phenotype is a more complex matter.

You didn't choose the life you were born into, but as you age, you begin to get the life you deserve.[14]

5

THE CHASM OF CULPABILITY

Culpability

I want to congratulate you for coming this far. You've avoided getting picked up and carried away by your emotions. You've managed to keep from cracking up on the Road to Reconciliation. Or, if you did get carried away or cracked up, you got back on track, arrived at the mountaintop, and saw the big picture. Everything is in context now. The part you played is there, but not everything is about you. That being the case, you can relax a little. You're halfway to Personal Peace.

How do you make it the rest of the way? Well, you're on a mountaintop, remember? The only way to get anywhere is down.

From this point, you can always go back down to feeling like a victim, or you can continue forward. Personal Peace is down below in a beautiful valley at the foot of this mountain. In order to get there from here, you must make a dangerous descent into what I call the Chasm of Culpability.

In other words, in the process of seeing the big picture, you've come to understand your own shortcomings. You've got to do something about them. Personal Peace is inaccessible without culpability.

These shortcomings could be anything. Maybe it was you who started all the trouble with your partner in the first place; all the things she did to you were in response to what you did to her. Or maybe you committed your wrongdoings by attempting to get justice for what he did to you. They are all mistakes, no matter who started it. If you got carried away by your feelings or became an Impossible Martyr, a Person Who Can't Steer, a Denier, a Discount Pardoner, Helpless, a Big Baby, an Ax Grinder, a Righteous Idiot, a Scab Picker, Retraumatized, or One Who Can't Admit They've Done Anything Wrong, then you have something to feel sorry about.

Making it right is going to take more than saying you're sorry. You'll need to acknowledge what you did wrong and why it seemed like a good idea at the time. Then you'll have to develop a plan to prevent it from happening again.

You are descending the Chasm of Culpability, a treacherous trail where you must pay attention. You are met by two guides who offer to direct you: one called Guilt and the other Shame. Beware—only one will take you to Personal Peace. The other will lead you over a cliff.

Guilt and Shame: Good and Bad Ways to Feel Bad

It's easy to confuse Guilt with Shame.[15] People refer to them interchangeably, like twins who are often mistaken. Along with embarrassment and pride, they both belong to the family of moral emotions. They pop up whenever you do something wrong. But other than that, they're very different, and if you discover that Shame has been your guide, you should ditch it as soon as possible and go the other way.

You can tell the difference by what they say. Guilt talks about something you did. Shame says the problem is who you are.[16] Guilt makes you sorry that you lied, stole, cheated, or betrayed. Shame calls you liar, thief, cheater, and traitor.

Let's say you've been to the track. You intended on gambling two hundred dollars on the horses. By the time you left, you were down a thousand dollars. If you go home and tell your wife the truth, subject yourself to her ire, and take your medicine, that's guilt. If you make up some story and cover it up, that's shame. The natural reaction to shame is to hide because you're embarrassed. You don't want anyone to know. Guilt moves you to repair. Guilt is a truth you tell. Shame is a lie you swallow.

Let's look at another example. You've been drinking much too much. You can't get through the day without at least two bottles of wine. Your husband is starting to look at you funny whenever you pour a glass. Guilt will help you admit you have a problem. Shame will cause you to deny. Guilt will propel you to get into counseling or, at least, into keeping the cork in. Shame will cause you to drink when he's not around. Remember, Shame wants you to hide, so you'll hide your drinking. Guilt puts it all in the open, so others can help.

How about this: your kids have their Legos all over the floor. It just drives you nuts. You ask them nicely to clean them up, but they blow you off. You yell. Your wife comes by and tells you you're yelling. Guilt tells you she's trying to help. Shame starts a war. Shame makes you argue back, and the whole thing turns into a knock-down drag-out fight. Guilt says you can do better than you've done. Shame says you're a yeller, so you yell some more. Shame is a threat to your self, so you defend yourself with everything you have. Guilt is open to suggestions.

One more. You're due to visit your elderly mother at her nursing home. She's not much fun to be around. She repeats herself, goes on forever about her aches and pains, and is unconcerned with anything you're doing except to the degree she might brag about you. You hate being around her and hate yourself for feeling that way. If you listen to Shame, you'll never visit. You'll make excuses to stay away. If Guilt is your guide, you'll find a way to make it good. Guilt leads you to empathy and compassion. Shame pulls you away.

Guilt identifies a problem and gives you a reason to change, so you'll do better next time. Shame prevents change. Guilt says you're better than that; shame says no, you aren't. Guilt is a surgical strike into the offending action; Shame is a carpet bomb. Guilt cuts out the tumor; Shame is like killing your cancer by killing yourself.

Four responses to Shame
Shame is such a powerful, toxic emotion that no one likes to feel it for long. You'll do anything to make it go away. There are four things people do. The first, the most natural, is to withdraw, hide, stonewall, or deny you ever did anything wrong. You convert your Shame to Fear.

Another method of dealing with Shame is to attack yourself, put yourself down, chew yourself out, tell yourself that you're a piece off crap. Of course you made a mistake, you tell yourself, what do you expect from someone who is obviously defective! Voila, your Shame is now self-loathing.

If that doesn't work, there's always avoidance. By this, I mean distracting yourself from the Shame. Drugs and alcohol are good for this. So is wild, promiscuous sex, shopping till you drop, or hours of mind-numbing TV. Where once there was Shame, there is now addiction. Then, if you feel shame about your addiction, well, there's always more addiction.

If you try those three methods and you still have Shame, then the last-ditch defense is to attack. You never did anything wrong, you say; it's the other guy. With Shame, you feel weak and defenseless; add a little bit of anger and, presto, you're now the scariest one around.

With Shame you're caught up with yourself; with Guilt you take the other person's perspective. Guilt makes you more empathic, compassionate, and patient. It's a spotlight that illuminates whatever you did wrong, rather than a blinding floodlight that makes everything about you look bad. Guilt is your new best friend. Condemn the sin, not the sinner. It's not the person who is the problem; the problem is the problem.

So, now that you are ready to accept responsibility, take a close look at how you feel. If your feelings move you toward others while making you more accepting of them and more willing to make repair, that's Guilt. It's safe for Guilt to be your guide. If you're tempted to hide, to lie, to argue, or to judge, then Shame is showing you the way. Get a new guide. Look for someone called Guilt.

How to Ditch Shame

I know, if you ditch shame you're afraid you'll go back to doing whatever you did.

How to ditch Shame without losing your scruples

It's not Shame you need. You need Guilt. Guilt addresses what you've done. Shame indicts who you are. Guilt makes you seek repair and pursue change. Shame makes you want to hide.

Shame says you're a hopeless loser, a chronic relapser, a dog who'll turn back and eat his own vomit. Shame says you'll never stop doing what you're doing. Shame says there's no way out; Guilt shows you the way. Guilt makes you think of the people you victimized; Shame makes you think of yourself. Shame keeps you from trying; Guilt urges you to admit your mistakes and make restitution.

Shame says you've always been like this; you'll never change. You've done the things you've done because that's the way you are. Guilt says you're better than that, you can do things differently, and the way you've always been is not the same as the way you'll be. Guilt points to the future; shame keeps you stuck in the past.

Shame says you don't deserve forgiveness. Sure, if you fail to follow Guilt and listen to Shame, then you won't admit your wrongs, make repair, and change. If all you do is blame others, wait for others, feel sorry, or even occasionally say you're sorry without changing anything, that wouldn't be deserving of forgiveness. On the other hand, if you accept responsibility, acknowledge the harm, make amends, and come out of it a different person, then that is deserving of forgiveness.

You may say you'll never be forgiven. The person you harmed will never let go of the harm you caused. They will hold it against you forever. If you're thinking that, those thoughts do not come from Shame or Guilt; they are just thoughts. They may be true. Past a certain point, forgiveness is out of your control. If you have done everything deserving of forgiveness and the person you harmed does not forgive you, then that's on them. Maybe they just aren't there yet. Maybe they'll never be. We don't know. We'll never know if you don't put yourself in the position to make it happen.

So, if Shame makes you want to hide, blame others, or castigate yourself, what does Guilt want you to do?

What Guilt wants
Guilt has a program designed to help you address the thing you did wrong.

1) Admit the exact nature of the wrong.
2) Acknowledge the effects that sprang from your wrong.
3) Be willing to make appropriate amends.
4) Follow through with making amends.
5) Permit the change that results in taking these steps to settle in and become part of you.

So, how do you ditch Shame? What makes Shame go away?

You think Shame will stick around while you do all that? If you listen to Guilt, you won't have to ditch Shame; Shame will ditch you.

Should You Feel Guilty?

Shame isn't the only thing that could stop you from doing what is right and getting down the Chasm of Culpability in one piece. Watch your step. There are many ways you can go wrong.

When your partner offers cheap pardon

You might have a partner who's not taking your misdeeds as seriously as you. You feel bad about them, but he says it's nothing, forget about it. Well, it's not nothing if you're concerned. Don't let a person in denial or a Discount Pardoner prevent you from being the best person you can be.

Your partner has his own reasons to offer you cheap grace. It might pass for forgiveness, but it's really a cut-rate imitation, an easy, breezy amnesty extended not because it's earned but because he doesn't want to deal with it.

He might feel good about himself, offering grace at discount prices. The problem is by rushing the process, neither one of you will have the opportunity to fully assess the situation. No one will define the problem, acknowledge the injury, or confront their own complicity. The slate will be wiped clean before anyone has a chance to read what was written.

It's important to call cheap pardon for what it is: an offer to collude. It may seem to preserve the relationship, but it prevents you both from achieving a more intimate bond. Magic happens when partners see each other naked, in all their ugliness, and decide to love anyway. That's very different from turning away from the ugliness or pretending it's not there.

Accepting easy forgiveness is a trap. You may think you got off Scott-free, but believe me, if you abandon Guilt and continue your nefarious ways, Guilt will come back. Your loved one will not forget that she easily forgave you before. She'll hold it against you that you failed to change when she didn't even ask you to.

When your partner's behavior is worse

Your partner's behavior may be worse than yours. She may be so evil and vindictive in reprisal for what you did to her at it overshadows your own wrongdoing. Being a victim doesn't bring out the best in people; it brings out the worse. She's been wrecked on the Road to Reconciliation. Don't be rubbernecking past this accident so much that you crack up yourself. Don't get so distracted by the malfeasance of others that you fail to improve yourself.

When others say you have nothing to feel guilty about

Well-meaning people might try to talk you out of feeling guilty because they want you to feel better. Saying you have nothing to feel guilty about is no different than saying you have nothing to cry over to someone who is crying or you have nothing to be sad about to a person who has just lost a loved one who had been sick for a long time. It's insensitive. It denies the validity of someone's feelings. True friends respect your feelings. You should too.

When you get caught in someone else's agenda

You're drinking late at a bar, look at your watch, and realize you promised your wife you'd be home an hour ago. Your buddy says, "Screw her, you deserve some fun. You shouldn't let her control her."

You made a promise. Why is he telling you not to feel guilty? Probably because he's doing the same things you are and he doesn't want to feel guilty.

When you have survivor's guilt

People will try to talk you out of feeling guilty if you have survivor's guilt. That's when you feel guilty that you survived. Accident survivors get it, witnesses of violence get it, combat veterans get it in spades, people who have been victimized get it when they think about how much worse it could have been. Folks have a hard time understanding survivor's guilt. They'll say it wasn't your fault that you survived, you had no choice, anyone would have done the same thing. They'll counsel you to not get caught up in the what-ifs. They'll warn you against 20/20 hindsight. They'll call you a Monday morning quarterback.

If you have survivor's guilt, you may be overestimating the amount of power you have, but you still have some. Whenever you feel guilt, look at what Guilt is trying to show you. It's trying to show that life is precious and the actions you take, even the little things, have impact.

When you're being scrupulous

People will try to talk you out of feeling guilty if they believe you are just being overly scrupulous. For instance, if you are beating yourself up for possibly breaking your mother's back when you stepped on a crack. This is a crazy thought that doesn't make any sense, but don't blame Guilt for it. The thought got manufactured elsewhere and loaded on Guilt's truck for delivery to you. Guilt is just showing you you're having those thoughts. Besides revealing that some of your thoughts are irrational, it's trying to tell you that you love your mother and, because she loves you, you can hurt her. Were you supposed to call her?

When you pay attention to the guide, not what the guide is showing you

Guilt is your guide toward self-improvement. You can't travel in a new country and expect not to get lost without a guide of some sort, be it a live human, or a guidebook, or signs by the side of the road.

Nevertheless, you don't travel just so you can meet a guide, stay with a guide, and look at nothing but the guide. No, you're interested in what the guide shows you. So, when I say that Guilt is a guide, I don't mean you have to stay with Guilt. I mean, look at what Guilt is showing you. It's showing you what your values are. It should get you to thinking whether things could be different.

Identifying what you could have done differently helps you get your power back. If you were a victim and feeling powerless, it shows you where you have power. If you did something wrong and felt you were powerless to stop yourself, it shows you had power after all. Guilt says you matter and the things you do make a difference.

Making Guilt Contingent on Forgiveness

Even if you do everything right and follow the suggestions of Guilt to the letter, your partner might be so stuck in being a victim that he won't see that you've changed. Or he might see it and not want to be with you anyway. If that's the case, why should you bother to make amends?

You're not doing this for him; you're doing it for you. You're doing it because you are caught in a Chasm of Culpability and need to get out. You're doing it so you won't have to be here again.

Whether or not she forgives you, may not even be about you. Let's go back to the banking metaphor from the "What Can't Be Hurt" section. Two people go to the bank. One has a good credit score, the other a bad one. One is clearly more creditworthy, or trustworthy, than the other, based on past behavior. One paid his loans on time; the other sometimes defaulted. These two see the same banker and ask her for a loan.

You may think you know the sensible thing for the banker to do. She's supposed to give the loan to the one with a good credit score and turn down the other with a bad credit score. But she doesn't have to do that; she can do what she wants. For instance, she could say the person with a good credit score can get a loan anywhere, so he doesn't need to get it from her. She could decide to give the one with a bad credit score a break. Having a good credit score does not dictate the banker's decision. She makes her own decision.

Say someone got caught up with cocaine and her partner is trying to decide whether to trust her again. She makes a complete turnaround. She goes to rehab, gets off the blow, and pisses clean for the next twelve months. She's made a complete moral inventory and admitted her shortcomings. Everyone else has forgiven her. They applaud her at her NA meeting. She's a changed person. Anyone would say that her credit score had been bad, but it's improving. Objectively, she may be more trustworthy now than people who never used cocaine at all and never had to deal with the dark side of themselves. That doesn't mean the partner has to trust her. Trusting is up to the partner.

Or, alternatively, say someone is still stuck in the same old behavior he was in before: fighting, cussing, carrying on. His partner never knows when he's coming home at night; she doesn't know whether he's coming home at all. He could be with anybody, doing anything. He could be in jail, in the hospital, or in bed with another woman. He could just be shooting pool with his buddies, blowing off her texts. The man, by any measure, is completely untrustworthy. Everyone says the partner should dump the loser. His credit score is zero. You know what? It's still up to the partner whether to trust him. She can do what she wants. It doesn't have to make sense.

What would cause a banker to ignore a low credit score and lend money anyway? She could be just a rank fool. She could be trying to lose her job. She could believe it's her job to save the most wretched. She could be a loan shark, offering a payday loan of trust and goodwill that will ruin the creditor in the end. Maybe trust is burning a hole in her pocket and she can't get rid of it fast enough. She could be a banker with so much money in her vault, so much goodwill, brimming with so much self-esteem, that she can take risks that others cannot.

What would cause a banker to ignore a good credit score and refuse the loan? Maybe she, too, is a rank fool. Maybe she's uncomfortable with success. Maybe she finds suspicion more compelling than grace. Maybe it's too boring, too safe to give trust to someone who deserves it. Maybe she's just a miser with her trust. There could be so little money in her vault, so little goodwill, so little self-esteem, that she's not willing to risk a dime.

The point is, it's up to the banker. If that banker is your loved one; if you did something to hurt him and have done everything you can do to regain trust, it's still up to him. You can't force him to trust you. If you're the banker, it's up to you.

Cleaning the Closet

Everyone's got a closet where they put whatever they don't want people to see.

There's good and bad stuff in the closet. There are things you're ashamed of. Memories of what you've done, words you've said, people you've hurt. You cram that closet full. It gets to be that you can't even open the door to cram anything more in. You also can't open the door to get anything out. You're afraid that when you open the door, the bowling ball you perched atop the pile will fall on your head. You're afraid if you open the door, you'll never be able to shut it again. It's too full, so you never open the door.

Most of the time you can live with that. So, you have closets that you never open, stuffed to the gills with junk you can't throw out. You have more than one closet filled like that. You might have garages, attics, cellars, extra rooms, all filled. Some of us have years of our past that we can't permit ourselves to remember but are unable to forget, entire regions of ourselves we don't want to let people see.

That's fine, until something happens.

Some other person could open the closet door by mistake, looking for the bathroom. The bowling ball, the wooden tennis racquets, the regrets, the disappointments, and the shame all come crashing to the floor. It's embarrassing. It all comes out and you can't cram it back in.

That's how it feels when someone brings up your hurt or confronts you with your behavior. An intervention feels this way. So does the kind of fight where your partner says all the things she's been meaning to say. It also feels this way when she leaves, when she's had enough and can't take it anymore. You're left alone with a closet full of recriminations cascading around you.

There could be something in that closet that's starting to smell. Maybe something's died in there. You may have to clean out the closet and go through everything until you find it.

That's what it's like when there's something evil growing in you, a rage, an addiction, a resentment, an anxiety, a trauma, a need. You may not even know what it is. You only know there must be something there. It is there, buried in your closet.

Maybe you want to move, trade up to a bigger or better house. Then it's time to clean out the old closet. You collect boxes, start with the books in the living room, move on to the kitchen, and save the closet for last, not because it's more efficient that way but because you're dreading it. You finally get to the closet and go through it, not because you want to but because you have to, so you can move on.

That's what it's like when you're ready to change, when you're tired of living the way you've been living. You're sick and tired of being sick and tired. You're ready to look at your past so that you can make sense of it. You decide it's time to move ahead, learn some lessons. If you had awful things happen to you, you might have put the memory away in this closet so that you could deal with it later, after you acquired the knowledge, skills, resources, coping mechanisms, and supports that you needed. Perhaps it's time, and you are ready.

Sometimes you clean out the closet because you have to, not because you want to; you can't shut the damn door anymore.

Once you decide to clean out the closet, there's nothing left to do but to buckle down and go through the junk. Sift through it and sort out what to keep, what to throw away, what to give away, and what to display on the coffee table.

You might be surprised. There could be stuff in that closet that you need, that you haven't been able to find. You could have put something in the closet to protect it, away from prying eyes, because it's so valuable you can't let it go.

That's what it's like when people look at their past, their regrets, and their losses and find capabilities they didn't know they had, choices they forgot they ever made, insights they never knew, feelings they thought they had lost. A sense of wonder that's been neglected, an ability to play that's been deserted. For buried under all that junk—the mistakes, the resentments, and the losses—is a child. That child is you, you as a child. You locked that child, with all her spontaneity and innocence, in the closet and buried her under stuff, partly to control her, partly to protect. When you clean the closet, you set the child in you free.

It may be time to clean out your closet. Let's begin.

6

THE STEPS OF REPARATION

Admit the Exact Nature of the Wrong

Now let's look at an essential part of the process of going from wrong to reconciliation, a part that many people, incredibly, try to pass over. What is this indispensable but neglected component?

Identifying what you did wrong.

People often want to pass right over this part to get to forgiveness, to argue their case, or to go right back to doing it again. Others disregard identifying what they did wrong and, instead, punish themselves for how they are wrong, without any recognition of what they did. This trick of Shame keeps them stuck and miserable while ensuring that they'll learn nothing from the mistake and go right back to doing it again, remaining under the thumb of Shame. Guilt, on the other hand, demands that you identify the exact nature of the wrong.[17]

So, let's get started.

Before you go to anyone to make an apology, you should first take a few minutes, or a few days, to sit down and write a statement of responsibility. This doesn't need to be long, but it does need to be thorough and accurate. It also needs to be *written*, not because you're necessarily going to have anyone read it but because you'll take more time and more care for something you write than something you just say or ponder.

115

You'll have fewer distractions than if you say it to someone. You won't get caught up in defending yourself, responding to someone's reaction, or otherwise losing track of what you set out to do. You'll have a written record of your accomplishment, indisputable documentation that you got real and honest, if only with yourself. Don't let a tendency to make spelling or grammar errors stop you. It doesn't matter if your handwriting is bad; no one else in the world needs to read it. You're doing this for you.

Let me give you an example, first, of how NOT to write a statement of responsibility and then of how to do it correctly. What follows is something someone might write on their first attempt. This is from a man who beat his child and, years later, wrote a letter to her in an attempt to reconcile. Please note, it's not necessary to address your letter of responsibility to the person you hurt, as he does, nor is it necessary to give it to them. We'll talk more about that later.

He wrote:

> "I'm sorry I hit you, but you were a bad kid, you never listened, and I was afraid that you'd grow up not having any respect for authority. My father used to hit us worse than that and it instilled discipline in me so that I was able to be successful in everything I did. I wanted that for you. I love you."

There's so much wrong with this statement, it's hard to know where to start. If you were ever on the receiving end of an apology like that, the only reason you would ever grant forgiveness is because you found it too frustrating or embarrassing to continue, so you just wanted the process to stop. I suppose if the writer had never acknowledged that he hit his child, it would be progress, but I think he can do a lot better than that.

Let's start at the beginning.

"I'm sorry."

It's not necessary in a statement of responsibility to apologize. Your focus at this point should be on identifying your behavior, not stating your feelings of sorrow. You can certainly say you're sorry later on, if you really feel that way, after you have stated what you need to be sorry for. Incidentally, I don't think this guy really is sorry for hitting his child; I think he's sorry he has to write a statement of responsibility.

"I hit you."

This is the best part of this man's statement. He's describing the offending behavior. It might be better if he gave more detail—if he said, for instance, whether he punched her in the face or spanked her on her bottom. If he gave that kind of detail, there certainly would be a clearer picture of the offense. He would not be hiding behind vagueness and obfuscation.

"But."

This word should not appear anywhere in a statement of responsibility. Avoids buts. Buts produce bullshit. Anything that comes after a but in a statement of responsibility should be flushed out of sight.

There may well be mitigating factors: you may well have had good intentions; you definitely had your reasons for doing what you did. However, a statement of responsibility is not the place for excuses. It's the place for a clear-eyed acknowledgement of the offense.

"You were a bad kid, you never listened."

Here the man totally abandoned the project of making a statement of responsibility in favor of making an accusation. He turned the victim into the offender and himself into the victim. He's playing the victim in a bald-faced attempt to garner sympathy or to weasel out of the wrongdoing.

Of course, there is a context surrounding every misdeed. You may be right to want to address the crimes committed against you too, but this is not the place for that. The statement of responsibility is the place to focus on your actions. You can hope that, in doing so, you'd be modeling the type of forthrightness that you would hope from anyone admitting offenses against you.

Besides, just as your crime was a response to their crime, their crime may have been a response to another one of yours. The victim in this example may have been a "bad kid" who "never listened," but how did she get that way? I think it's reasonable to believe that, before this guy ever hit his child, he was given to yelling. What happens when a father yells at his daughter? She doesn't have to work too hard to listen.

"I was afraid that you'd grow up not having any respect for authority."

Here this man is stating the intention he had for doing what he did. You could look at this two ways. On one hand, there's a place for confessing his fears and talking about his aspirations for his daughter. On the other hand, when people explain their intentions, they seldom fail to put some spin on it. It's always good intentions they disclose. We might believe the road to hell is paved with good intentions because no one ever mentions the bad ones. I think that if this man dug deep, he might come up with other intentions. He might say, for instance, "I was afraid I was losing my authority, and you had no respect for me. I decided that if you weren't going to respect me, I could at least make you fear me."

When you complete the first draft of your statement of responsibility, you should be suspect of anything that puts you in a positive light. Look closer at your motives. I'm not saying this because I believe you're a total dirt bag, incapable of doing anything good, or even anything bad for a good reason. I'm saying it because I know that good intentions are what comes to the surface; selfishness hides within. If you're honest with yourself, you'll find that a lot of things motivate you, and not all of them are pretty.

If you ever deliver your statement of responsibility, if you ever stand up and say it to the person you hurt, anything positive is going to sound like an excuse. They're not going to believe you're serious about your remorse and may conclude that you're doing it for show or other venal reasons.

"My father used to hit us worse than that and it instilled discipline in me so that I was able to be successful in everything I did. I want that for you."
I'd advise that this man imagine that he's a little boy again, the age of his daughter when he hit her. Visualize what it was like to be beaten when he was small, powerless, and utterly at the mercy of his attacker. I suspect he doesn't allow himself to go there. Instead, he's constructed a belief that it wasn't so bad and it was for his own good. This is what victims do to cope. It's a form of denial. While it's definitely possible for trauma to be used for growth, this is how people who've been abused grow up to be abusers. This first step is to forget the horror of it. The second step is to make yourself believe it was good. From there, it's easy to start abusing your own child. Traumatic growth does not happen when we forget; it happens when we remember.

If this man believes discipline has been so successfully instilled in himself; he should ask himself whether he was really disciplined when he beat his daughter. I suspect not. I suspect he had lost control of himself and was utterly undisciplined. If this man believes he's successful in everything he has done, why does he need to reconcile with his daughter?

"I love you."
Here the man is making an incongruous claim, totally at odds with the rest of his statement. He beats his child, calls her a bad kid, expects that she was going to grow up to be a monster, criticizes her for not doing as well as him, and then

wants her to believe that he loves her. Is this what love means to him?

Something's missing

Wait, there are more problems with this statement of responsibility. It's missing an account of the aftermath. After this man beat his child, what did he do then? Did he recognize he did something wrong and try to repair the damage to their relationship? Did he nurse her wounds, tenderly dry her tears, hug her, tell her he was wrong, and immediately apologize? Or did he leave her by herself, pretend it didn't happen, deny it happened, lie, or force her to lie? Did he keep her home from school the next day out of fear the teacher would see the bruises on her face and start asking questions? What did he tell her mother? Did he say he would beat her more if she ever told anyone? Did he even need to?

After working with hundreds, if not thousands, of trauma survivors, I've learned that what happens in the aftermath of an offense that does as much damage, if not more, than the wrong itself. It's not the crime; it's the coverup. The crimes of the coverup get charged to the initial offense because, if not for the crime, the coverup would never have existed; but there is a huge difference between a misdeed committed within the context of a loving, supportive, affirming environment and one that blames the victim and casts her out on her own.

Neglect, abandonment, and betrayal are more to be feared than actual abuse. Think about it. What would you rather get: a single slap in the face or a lie? A single beating, followed by remorse, or an ongoing terror threat? A wife who slipped and slept with someone, confessing immediately thereafter, or a wife with a double life? Even in the cases of the single slap, single beating, or single slip, a lot of the damage comes from the prospect of more, the possibility of a total dissolution of the relationship, the fear of being alone.

An improved statement of responsibility

So, what would a better statement look like? A statement of responsibility this man might write after a course of therapy and an honest look inside might look something like this.

> "When you were ten years old, and I was a full-grown man, I lost my temper, made a fist, and hit you three times in the face with all the force I could. I then sent you to your room. Later, I told your mother you fell and hit the coffee table. I went on pretending it didn't happen for years until you brought it up. You didn't deserve that kind of treatment. I was afraid I was losing my authority and you had no respect for me. I decided that, if you weren't going to respect me, I could at least make you fear me. I should have known better. I was beaten as a child too. I should've remembered what that was like and not bought into the lies that it was a good thing. I failed to love you like I should and want to learn to love you better.

Oh, another thing

What we have now is an improved statement of responsibility. But it could be better if the man looked at the incident from the eyes of his child and acknowledged a wrong he might not have thought of himself. A broken promise.

Broken Promises

While you're at it, while you're acknowledging the exact nature of your wrongs, don't forget one wrong you might've committed that is so central that it may overshadow all others and be key to this whole business of reconciliation.

Broken promises.

Embedded in every wrong is a broken promise—a promise either declared or implied, clearly pledged or vaguely expected, guaranteed or merely hoped for. Sometimes a broken promise is the only wrong. Sometimes that one wrong is enough.

Adultery, for instance, is a broken promise. When your husband finds out you've been having an affair, you may actually be surprised that he cares about those vows you made so long ago. You might not think they're so germane or vital. After all, you're the one who broke them. The person who breaks a promise is the one who hasn't been taking the promise as seriously.

Some promises were made so long ago, and there have been so many changes, you might think they've been revised. When you made your weddings vows, you might have been very young; things might've been very different then. Your husband couldn't keep his hands off you, he didn't have that belly, and he had some hair. You were both poorer, but his career was just taking off. Now, he's been passed over for promotion four times, he's grown balder and fatter, and you haven't had sex in three months. You might think you're the victim of a bait-and-switch scheme. You may think that he broke the vows first by becoming a fat, bald middle manager who hasn't gone down on you in years. You acted as though the deal was null and void.

If you really felt that way, it would have been better to say something than to just act as though the promise no longer applies. Sit down and say, "You're fat, bald, and boring, and I'm horny and need someone with more money. I want a divorce." I know, you wouldn't do that. You'd feel like a witch. Is it better to protect his feelings, say nothing, and have an affair?

Many promises are made in haste because you didn't want to talk. You agreed to clean out the garage that weekend because you didn't want to have to tell your wife you had plans to play golf. She's already pissed that you play so much golf and you didn't want to have that fight again when she asked you to clean out the garage. So, you made a promise and deferred the fight to this morning, when your buddy is in the driveway and you're loading up your clubs. When you get home, there's going to be hell to pay, not just because you didn't clean out the garage but because you broke a promise made in haste.

If you're not sure whether you broke a promise, just ask yourself if you've been getting a lot of nagging. The presence of nagging is a constant irritation that obscures, but indicates, a broken promise. If she's on your back all the time to clean out the garage, it's not because she's a nag—a shrew, a hypercritical, impossible-to-please woman—but because you promised to clean out the garage and didn't.

There are some promises that you're held to even though you never explicitly made them. This promise is assumed when you take on a role. When you climb into your car and drive down the highway, for instance, you don't raise your right hand and swear to drive considerately, to give others space to stop, to go promptly when the light turns green, and to signal your turns—but you should hear the reactions from others if you fail to do so. They have a reasonable expectation that you will drive as if you have your life in your hands, and theirs too.

Fatherhood is another example of an assumed promise. You never signed on the dotted line to become a father, you never stood up and recited vows, but the child and the mother of your child have some reasonable expectations of you. At the minimum, you owe child support, assistance in rearing, love and concern, and an assurance of safety.

In all those cases, you are held to a promise you never made because it's inherent in the role you took. Others have a reasonable expectation of you. What should you do in cases when the expectations of others are unreasonable?

Unreasonable expectations

Your husband expects you to drop everything, wait on him hand and foot, constantly be at his beck and call because that's what his mother did for his father. You never promised to be that kind of wife. In this day and age, he shouldn't expect that kind of wife. He shouldn't be angry that you don't have dinner on the table at exactly six o'clock when you don't get home until 5:30 after a long day's work. He shouldn't be angry, but he is.

In this case, it was his mother who made the promise for you. It's not fair, it won't hold up as a contractual obligation in court, but his mother's promise is something you're going to have to contend with. You're going to have to acknowledge that you broke the promise his mother made on your behalf if you're ever going to reconcile your differences.

You see, there are objective wrongs and subjective ones. The objective wrongs are those that everyone recognizes. Subjective wrongs rest in the feelings of the person who regards himself as the victim as your husband does in this case. They look unreasonable, they sound whiney, you believe the supposed victim is just being a big baby, and you could accuse him of playing the victim; but to the person who has the expectations, they're real.

What should you do when there are unreasonable expectations? Do you have to apologize? Is this something for which you have to make amends?

In a just world, it would be his mother apologizing and making amends to you for setting you up to fail, but you can't wait for justice if you want reconciliation. No, you're not to blame for failing to meet unreasonable expectations, but you are responsible—responsible in the sense that you are able to respond.

What is the best response to an unreasonable expectation?

"No."

That's it. You have to say no and follow it up with actions, like you mean it. If you haven't said no, or have said no ambiguously, then it's reasonable to assume you have accepted the expectation. Maybe that's what you have to apologize for: not saying no.

Why don't people say no when they need to? It's hard to say no. Saying no involves being honest and inviting conflict.

It puts the relationship at risk. But not saying no is the same as making a promise you can't keep.

So, if you have looked within and found a broken promise to add to the other wrongs you have committed, then you probably have found even more misdeeds: a failure to be honest and an avoidance of conflict.

The Effects of Your Actions

Once you have written your statement of responsibility, you're ready for the next step: imagining the effects of your actions.

Don't get hung up on expecting hard evidence that one thing was caused by another. We have hard evidence for some effects but not others. We have hard evidence that, if a man punches a child in the eye, the child will have a black eye, but we don't have hard evidence that the reason she failed in school that semester was because of it. There could have been a connection, but there's no way to prove it.

You can't prove it, nor do you have to. This is not a court of law. You're not treating cancer or building a highway or filing taxes, activities that require a higher level of certainty. You're using your imagination. Just to entertain the possibility that one thing may have been caused by another is sufficient.

It's also not necessary to say that your action—whether it was violence or addiction, cheating or lying, nagging or criticizing—was the only ingredient that led to a particular reaction. No one is saying you are to blame for everything. There are obviously lots of reasons things happen. Generally, it's a confluence of factors. A child may fail a semester of school for reasons besides the fact that she was getting beat up at home. She could have had a bad teacher, disruptive classmates, or any one of a number of other factors. She probably had a lot to do with the failing grades.

So, if you are willing to entertain possibilities that the things you do matter, then consider the following questions with respect to the thing you did, whatever it was.

Physical

What physical changes did you see in the person you hurt? Were there bruises, contusions, broken bones? Did the person get sick? Was there an alteration in consciousness?

Emotional

What emotions did you observe in the person after you hurt him? Anger, annoyance, contempt, disgust, irritation, embarrassment, fear, helplessness, powerlessness, worry, doubt, frustration, guilt, shame, despair, disappointment, hurt, or sadness? Was there a fight-or-flight response? Did he freeze?

Mental

Did the person develop a mental condition after the thing you did? Chronic anxiety, worry, panic attacks? Depression, despair, suicidality? Can she pay attention? Is memory impaired? Was there post-traumatic stress? Nightmares, flashbacks, irritability? Did you start to see more bottles of pills? Did he go out and buy a gun? Did she start to hallucinate?

Economic

How did the person's economic status change? Could he pay his bills after that thing you did? Were his savings toward retirement set back? Did he miss days of work? What was the dollar-and-cents cost to the person for the thing you did?

Social

Did that thing cost the person any friends? Did family members shun him? Were there things she wouldn't be able to tell anyone? Did you get between him and the people he loves?

Addiction

Did the person start to drink harder than before? Did drugs come into her life? Did he seem to go through cigarettes faster, start guzzling coffee, eat herself out of house and home?

Recreation

Was there a change in how he engaged in recreation? Did she abandon hobbies or quit going to the gym? Did he stop going to the movies? Did she sign up for classes in martial arts?

Housing

Did the thing you did cost the person his hearth and home? Is her room more of a mess? Has his house fallen into disrepair? Does she now spend more time cleaning than is humanly necessary?

Spiritual

How has this changed your person's view of God? Has she lost faith? Is the thing you did an example of evil and suffering in the world for which God gets the blame? Does he believe God to be mean and vindictive because that's how you treated him? Has she stopped going to church? Has he ceased studies for his bar mitzvah? Or, alternately, has she become more rigidly religious, more fundamentalist, more extreme in her behavior and beliefs? Is he now a Jihadist?

Relational

Finally, how has this person's relationship with you changed? Can she trust you now? Is he always critical? Is she forever rolling her eyes? Is she interested in sex? Does he want to cuddle? Are you getting your calls returned, your texts answered? Are you still getting invited to parties? Did she place an order of protection? Are you getting a divorce?

This is by no means a complete list of all the questions you could ask or all the effects people have when you do awful things to them, but if you answered those questions honestly and owned up to the influence you have on others, then you have come a long way in accepting responsibility for your actions.

Six Places Denial Likes to Hide

Remember denial? You read about it in the "Cracking Up" section in the context of denying you're a victim. Now let's turn the spotlight of you as an offender. There are six ways you can practice denial. However, just a word of caution: when you're trying to deny something that really happened, none of them work.

Denial of fact

The first way is the most obvious. You just don't admit something happened. Look them in the eye and say you didn't do it. You declare:

> *I never touched her. I was never near the place. I never said that. It's all a big misunderstanding. I did not have sexual relations with that woman. I never lied, not a single time, ever.*

Similar to the denial of fact is minimization—denying some facts but not others. You had two drinks, not seven. You went to the casino but only gambled one hundred dollars, not five. You smoked but never inhaled. You only kissed her. You're telling the truth this time, honest.

If you truly never did the thing you're accused of, then nothing beats denial of fact; why would you need any other method? But if you are guilty, then denial of fact is a dangerous game. Facts can be discovered. Truth can be exposed. There are often witnesses. There's GPS. Some disappointed Other Women have been known to come forth and contact the wife at home. Why, you might even slip up and forget which lie you told to whom and when. Moreover, you're putting your sanity at risk. Watch out when you start to believe your own bald-faced lies. You won't know the difference between up and down.

The other problem with denial of fact is that it's often misdirected. It's not the fact in question that's the real question. It often doesn't matter whether you had seven drinks or two; touched her or didn't touch her; said something or didn't say it; inhaled, told the truth, gambled, or whatever. The real question, a question that is seldom asked but always present is this: Can you be trusted? Facts don't settle issues of trust. It doesn't matter whether you can marshal documents, witnesses, or evidence to support your case; if he doesn't trust you, then he doesn't trust you.

If you have a loved one who has lost trust in you, then there are only a few things you can do about it. You can leave, or wait for the other person to leave, because if there is no trust, then what's the point of the relationship? You can be patient and wait for your loved one to forget she lost trust in you, like that's ever going to happen. Or you can be honest and tell him everything.

When you're honest about something you did, then at least you're being honest. She may not like what you are admitting, but at least you're honest about it.

If you do get caught in denial of fact, then you have five more methods of denial at your disposal.

Denial of responsibility

> *I did it, but it's not my fault. She wouldn't take no for an answer. They kept pressuring me. There were a lot of factors. It was going to happen anyway. I have a disease, an addiction, a weakness to temptation, I was pressured. I'm the victim here; why are you yelling at me? It's my wife's fault I cheated on her. If my husband didn't nag so much, I wouldn't need to drink so much. I didn't mean to do it. I was trying to win enough money to pay the rent. I have to drink so much because of my anxiety. I didn't go to work because of my depression. The devil made me do it. Mistakes were made.*

When you use denial of responsibility, you admit the fact of the misdeed but not the intention. You profess you're not the agent of change. You claim you did not have free will.

This is a good place for denial to hide. It's almost impossible for someone to prove an intention. You're the only one who knows what you intended. But what did you intend? Can you really, honestly say that you never planned the misdeed or allowed it to happen? Does it really matter if you intended it or not?

Lots of things happen that are not your intention. You could be a kind, considerate, mindful, pacifistic, and vegan, but on your way to yoga class, you could run over a squirrel. The squirrel would die a slow, excruciating death and its family would mourn, but you didn't mean to do it. Then you get to class and realize there was a meditation exercise you forgot to do. You didn't mean to forget, but you still promised to do it and failed to follow through. Then your teacher says your check for the classes bounced. You look at your checkbook and find a simple subtraction error. Again, you didn't intend on stiffing the guru, but you still have to pay the fees. Class begins. You're all doing the downward dog and out comes a massive fart. Everyone knows it was you. You apologize, but it's not like you meant to stink up the place.

It doesn't take long before using denial of responsibility makes you look like you have no will of your own. Is that what you want? Is it better to be flaky or forthright? Slippery or scrupulous? In bad faith or a bad ass? Your choice.

Denial of awareness

I didn't know what happened. It all happened so fast. I don't remember. I'm not sure. I just lost track of time. Things got away from me. I must have blacked out. I overslept. I have ADD. It just slipped out. I didn't know you cared about that.

When you use denial of awareness, you are still trying to evade responsibility by saying the deed was out of your conscious control. The vegan didn't see the squirrel he hit. He didn't write down the homework assignment. He hadn't balanced his checkbook in a long time. The fart snuck up on him.

Denial of awareness just kicks the can down the road a little way. Even if it's true that you didn't know what you were doing, you're still responsible for not knowing what you're doing. It's your mind, so it's up to you to use it. Even if you're not held responsible for what you do when you are drunk, asleep, or unaware, you are still responsible for being drunk, asleep, or unaware, and you have to accept the consequences that come with it.

Denial of impact

No harm was done. I'm just hurting myself. It doesn't need to be that big a deal. Everyone does it. There's no victim. Yeah, I ate some of the cake you baked for someone's birthday, but there's plenty left. This hurts me more than it hurts you. It's my body…money…house…life…etc., so I can do what I want with it.

In this case, you are admitting you did the deed, but there was no injury and no basis of complaint. You committed a victimless crime. The tree fell in the forest, but it didn't hit anyone.

Have you really carefully examined the effects of your actions? Are you listening to what people are saying about what you have done to them?

Let's take a woman who was raised by alcoholics. You're her husband. Things were awful when she was growing up because of the drinking. There were fights to dodge, puke to clean up, smaller siblings to watch when she'd rather just be a kid. She couldn't wait to leave home and be done with it all. Then she gets married to you. You drink. No, you don't drink too much; you don't fight, don't puke, and don't even have kids to neglect. In fact, you never drink more than two beers in a row. You could stop anytime you wanted if you had a good reason to do so. Your drinking causes absolutely no problems, except one. She gets uptight every time she sees a beer in your hand.

Does your drinking have an impact?

Of course, it does. It's a simple case of cause and effect. She sees the beer, and she gets uptight. It's true that, perhaps, she is reacting more to the events of the past than what is likely to happen now, but your beer is triggering her. Her parents loaded the gun, but you pull the trigger. It's true that, perhaps, she is being unfair to ask you to not drink because of her, but if you love her, isn't it enough to abstain because it makes her crazy? It's true that it might be better for her to deal with her past. You could even make an argument that seeing you drink responsibly could help her be less reactionary to alcohol, sort of like exposure therapy. All that could be so, but please call it as it is. That beer is having a detrimental impact.

The purpose of cutting through denial, in all its forms, is not to humiliate, or blame, or make you responsible for everything. The purpose is to sweep away all the complications, so you can see things as they are.

Denial of pattern

It just happened. No one could've seen it coming. I didn't set myself up. I didn't prepare myself. I didn't groom my victims. I didn't know I was going to do it until I did it. I go from zero to sixty before I know it. One minute, I'm in recovery; the next minute, I'm looking for drugs. I was just going to get water when I went into the bar. I don't have to change people, places, and things; I just have to stop using.

Nothing happens by itself. Every event is part of a pattern. There is always a context. No one goes from zero to sixty without going through all the steps between. There is always a pattern. You can be excused if you don't know it, but are you looking for it?

Patterns can be hard to distinguish if you're not paying attention. It's possible to think you see a false pattern, but that doesn't mean there's isn't a pattern. Detecting a true pattern can be a tremendous benefit. It informs you of warning signs. It gives you a chance to get a jump on things. It lets you intervene on a problem before it gets too big. But to detect a pattern, you have to be open minded about what it might be.

People often want to deny a pattern because, if they were to acknowledge it, that would mean they may have to give up some things that, by themselves, are not a problem. Take the woman who uses cocaine every time she goes to a particular bar. She admits that cocaine is a problem and wants to stop using it, but she likes the bar. The bar is cool, all of her friends are at the bar, and there is nothing bad about her drinking—except that when she goes to the bar, she uses blow. If she were to admit there's a pattern, she would have to admit that the bar is part of the problem.

Denial of the need for help

I can stop any time I want. I can do this on my own. I don't need to go to group…a therapist…see a doctor…stay in rehab; all they want is my money. There's nothing they can teach me. I've been there and learned it all already. I've got to just do it. I don't need to be punished; I'll never do it again. I learned my lesson. I don't need anyone on my case…on my back…being suspicious…reminding me of the past. I'll stop, cold turkey.

To a certain extent, if you deny the need for help, I like your spirit. At least you sound like you're taking responsibility for the solution to your problem. After all, even if you do accept help, it still comes down to you. You've got to want to change. You have to do it. No one is going to do it for you.

However, when you admit you did something wrong but won't get help for it, you're placing a bet that you can handle it all by yourself. That's great, if you can; maybe you will. But what are you betting? What exactly is on the line? Is your husband threatening to leave? Are you giving your wife black eyes? Are you squandering your children's future? Are you breaking your parents' hearts? Maybe you can deal with the consequences if you fail, but are you thinking about how a relapse will affect others? How does it sound to them, the people you have already harmed, when you say you're going to gamble with doing it all again? Is this how you think you can make it right with them, by disregarding their feelings?

There's another thing to think about when you decide whether to get help. Let's say you have a shopping addiction. You've run up credit card bills. Every day a new package comes from Amazon with something you don't need. You can't even walk in the spare bedroom because of all the crap you put in there. Your husband wants you to go to Shopaholics Anonymous. No, you say, you don't want to talk to strangers about your problem. You agree to cut up your credit cards. You let your husband change your Amazon password. You go for a run every time you get the urge to shop. You've got this. You don't need any more help. But there's just one thing.

Maybe it's your husband who needs the help.

Maybe he can't handle it on his own. Maybe he doesn't know what to do. If you go to Shopaholics Anonymous, you're helping him too. That way, he doesn't have to be the only one watching out for you. He's got a village. He has others on the team who can be more objective. He doesn't have to worry quite so much. He can trust you just a little more. It looks like you're taking his concerns seriously.

Maybe your husband needs a group of his own for spouses of shopaholics. That'll be good if such a thing exists, but it's not a substitute for his need for you to get help for yourself.

So, six places where denial hides. Did you find any of yours there?

Making Amends is Better than Making Apologies

No one is interested in your apologies unless you back them up with a change in behavior. Making amends repairs the damage; making apologies is only a promise to repair the damage. One is action; the other, words. One will cost you something; it might even bring about a transformation. The other is as cheap as spent air, blown out in such a way as to make noise with your lips. The word *amends* comes from the Middle French for reparation. The word *apology* comes from the Greek for justification. Let me ask you this: When you're hurt, what do you want more, reparation or justification?

I thought so. Save your apologies; work toward making amends.

Amends comes in two categories. There's direct restitution and there's indirect. Amends, or restitution, compensates the victim for the harm done. If you've inflicted physical injury, then pay the medical bills. If you lied, then tell the truth. If you were careless, then take care. If you've robbed them of their time, give of your time. If you broke faith, keep faith. If you've said horrible words, even if they were true, say uplifting ones that are also true. If you've neglected, pay attention. If you lost your temper, acquire self-discipline. If you frightened, protect. If you failed to keep your promises, don't make promises you can't keep; if you do make promises, keep them.

This is why you write a statement of responsibility and an account of how your actions harmed another. Look at every item and decide how you're going to make restitution. Let's take the father who punched his child in the face. He wrote in his statement of responsibility:

> "When you were ten years old, and I was a full-grown man, I lost my temper and made a fist and hit you three times in the face with all the force I could. I then sent you to your room. Later, I told your mother

you fell and hit the coffee table. I went on for years and pretended it didn't happen until you brought it up. You didn't deserve that kind of treatment. I was afraid I was losing my authority and you had no respect for me. I decided that if you weren't going to respect me, I could at least make you fear me. I should have known better. I was beaten as a child too. I should've remembered what that was like and not bought into the lies that it was a good thing. I failed to love you like I should and want to learn to love you better."

How can this man make restitution? When he lost his temper, he failed to model self-discipline to his daughter. To make restitution, he should show her self-discipline. Since he hit her and caused bruises, to make restitution he might apply ice to those bruises. Because he sent her to her room and isolated her, restitution would involve being available. When he lied to her mother, he caused the child and her mother to not know what to believe. From now on, he needs to tell the truth to both of them. Where once he made her fear him, now he can protect her. When he forgot what it was like to be beaten, he should be up-front and honest about how he was a small child once, totally at the mercy of someone who used him as a punching bag.

All this, as hard as it might be, can easily be done if the harm has just recently occurred and his daughter is still small, if the bruises have not faded. If years have gone by, as they have in this case, it's going to be impossible to make much direct restitution. He can still model self-discipline, be available if she wants him around, tell the truth, protect her if there's an opportunity, and be open about his experiences; but ice is not necessary, the damage to his child's development is already done, and she's already grown.

There are many situations in which direct amends are impossible. It could be too late. They could be unwanted. Some people you've hurt would rather not have anything to do with you. They may not feel safe around you. You might have an order of protection. The adult daughter in our example may very well have a distant relationship with the father who used to beat her and want to keep it that way. She's not going to have him babysit his grandchildren if he's shown that he cannot control his temper. If that's the case, then the only direct amends he can make would be to accept the consequence gracefully and not whine and complain that he doesn't have a grandchild to bounce on his knee.

You'll want to be careful that, in your eagerness to be rid of your guilt or achieve reconciliation, you don't cause more harm by attempting to make unwanted direct amends. Some victims don't want to be reminded of what happened. The nightmares have finally stopped. They've only just moved on with their lives. Just the thought of you is enough to give them the shudders. In that event, it's a profoundly selfish thing to show up at their door, unannounced, with flowers. Keep your flowers along with your apologies; give the flowers to someone else who could use them. That would be an example of indirect amends.

There are other cases in which the victim doesn't know they've been victimized. For instance, I often see spouses who've been cheating on their partners. They believe their partners don't know it. They fear that being honest about the affair will cause their spouses unnecessary anguish. It's better, they say, to quietly end the affair and devote themselves to be better partners than unburden themselves at the expense of their loved ones.

It's hard to know what to do in these cases. It's true they can do a lot to be better husbands without confessing they've strayed, but they can't make amends for lying by continuing to hide the truth. Furthermore, I often suspect that the spouse knows more than anyone says. People have a sense that tells them there's something wrong. Often, they can't put their finger on what, but they know something's not right. On the other hand, sometimes people just don't want to know. This is such a thorny problem, we may need another section to discuss it.

If you honestly find you cannot make all the direct amends you're called to make, then full reconciliation will be impossible, and you're left with indirect amends. Maybe someday the opportunity will arise for that man to embrace his alienated daughter, do the right things by her, and bounce his grandchild on his knee. It'll be a beautiful moment if he's ready for it. He can prepare by enacting a program of indirect amends.

Confession to a Neutral Party

Once you have written your statement of responsibility for wronging someone, it's time to put the show on the road. The essence of taking responsibility is to declare it to someone. It makes no sense to take responsibility in such a way that nobody hears it.[18] When this particular tree falls in the forest, if no one is around, it makes no sound.

It is time to put your show on the road, but you're not ready for the big time yet. The big time would be to read it to the person you harmed; that's the person who really matters. If you have a well-prepared statement of responsibility, properly delivered to the person you harmed, it could lead to reconciliation. If your statement still needs work, if it is defective in any way, it may set your reconciliation back and do more damage to your relationship. Sometimes, you only get one shot. Once you have completed your statement of responsibility, read it out loud—not to the person you harmed, but to a person you trust. You're ready for a dry run. Open your play in New Haven before you put it on Broadway.

The person who hears your statement of responsibility should be a person who is capable of listening. Don't pick that friend who can't stop talking about herself or the one who never takes anything seriously. If you have someone who always feels he must solve every problem, tell him this is not a problem to be solved; it's a story to be heard. Don't pick the friend who never thinks you can do wrong or the one who's fed up with everything you do. Sit down with someone in the middle range between automatic approval and default disdain. You want someone who, when it is time for them to react, can be honest and forthright, not dodging and dissembling—about halfway between kind and cruel.

If you have a friend or relative who is like this, you can confess to her, but she should not be someone who's involved. You don't want to compound your error by putting this person in an awkward position with the one you've harmed. Don't tell your wife's sister you've been sleeping around; she may need to tell your wife. Your confessor should not be party to the crime, like the woman you're having an affair with, or anyone who has an interest in the proceedings. It does you no good to confess your alcoholism to your favorite bartender or your drug addiction to your drug dealer. It should be a neutral third party. Someone who can be objective.

If you use clergy to hear your confession, you get the added bonus of getting someone who can put a good word in with your higher power, if you believe clergy can do that. They accept donations, but they will not send you a bill.

If you don't have anyone in your circle like this, you might have to hire one. That's where counselors come along. Any counselor with minimal training in listening can serve as your confessor; you don't need a specialist or a highly paid Park Avenue shrink. Just be sure they know you're hiring them to be objective and wise, not to cosign your bullshit.

The purpose of verbalizing your statement of responsibility is manifold. You need to hear how it sounds. You'll feel better once you get it off your chest. You're very likely to find that people won't think you're as loathsome as you think you are. Talking about what you did dispels shame. It gets your guilt in gear. It's a dress rehearsal for saying it to the person who most matters, the person you harmed.

The person you confess to may need a little direction. You might tell her that you don't need her to make you feel better; only you can make you feel better, you and the process of atonement. If your confessor doesn't back away slowly without turning around, with a horrified look on her face, after you tell her what you did, then she's doing well. She also needs to know that you're going to see whatever look she has on her face; therefore, if she is nauseated, there's no sense denying it. She will probably not be nauseated though, or run screaming from the room. You are probably harder on yourself than anyone else will be.

Your confessor can be most useful as a bullshit detector. Have him listen for hidden justifications. Have him look for spin. Urge him to see what you don't want to see and tell you what you don't want to hear. Coax him to consider how your statement may be received by the person you harmed. This is where having an honest and forthright confessor is invaluable, someone who can tell you if you're kidding yourself.

But for all I've said about your confessor being a bullshit detector, her job is not to judge or to point out your flaws but to be a mirror held up so you can see yourself. Think of her as someone you ask if spinach is caught in your teeth. You have to show her your teeth, and if you have some, she has to be truthful. But mostly she's someone who, when she tells you there's no spinach there, will give you the confidence to smile.

To Confess or Not to Confess, That Is the Question

No question about it: confess to yourself. If you can't be honest with yourself, who can you be honest with?

If you believe in God, then confess to God. He knows anyway.

If you have a neutral third party you can trust, then confess to her. Confession is cleansing. It's a double check for bullshit. It returns you to the land of the righteous.

The only time confession might be questionable is when your confession brings harm to the person you've already harmed.

The idea is that your confession should not be at the expense of the person you harmed, so you can feel better. That doesn't seem to be the route to reconciliation. That road heads the wrong way. On the other hand, you're cutting yourself off from a powerful source of healing, you are underestimating your victim's capacity for grace, and you're crawling even further in the doghouse than you belong.

The question comes up most when one partner has had some extramarital sexual activity and feels guilty about it. He comes to me, his therapist, and tells me all about it. I'm the neutral third party he can trust. He asks me the question, "Do I tell my wife?"

Some therapists have answers to that question. I don't. I just have more questions. Some therapists have firm opinions on what a marriage should be; they believe a marriage should be perfectly open and honest and that any marriage that is not is headed for trouble. I believe there are all kinds of successful marriages. I also believe being perfectly open and honest may be a quality to which to aspire, but it's not a status to achieve. No one knows their partner fully, and it may not be especially desirable if they did.

The question comes up in other cases too. The rapist should probably not seek out his victim to tell her he's sorry; he's likely to be misunderstood. It may be too late for the father who beat his daughter to bring it up now. She may have no stomach to review the past.

Like I said, I have no answers. I only have questions. Questions like:

Are you reluctant to confess because you want to avoid the consequences?

Be careful how you answer this question.

If you say you are reluctant to confess because you want to avoid the consequences, then you are not serious about change. You're just trying to get away with the thing you did. You're not ready for a confession anyway; it would just be worthless.

If you say you won't tell her because she'll call you a selfish prick, make you sleep on the couch, tell your mother what you did, and file for divorce, then grow some balls. You brought this on yourself. If you know now she'd react that way, you knew then. It was okay to risk your wife's ire when you were sleeping with that other woman; why is it not okay, now? You wouldn't walk out of a restaurant without paying; it's time to pay up now.

On the other hand, if she'll take a knife to your private parts or tell your children they're worthless because they came from you, then you might have a good reason not to confess. If you somehow know that she's going to hunt down the other woman and literally kill her, then I'd say keep it to yourself. You have my blessing, but I will wonder why you would risk that reaction by sleeping with the other woman in the first place.

You should anticipate consequences and, to some degree, be fearful of them. To claim otherwise is nonsense. However, if you decide not to confess, you should not be tainted by your fear of the repercussions, except in the extreme cases I mentioned. Your decision should be motivated completely out of a realistic concern for your victim.

How can you be sure your decision not to confess is not prompted by your desire to avoid the repercussions? Easy, there should be repercussions anyway. Even if you decide not to confess, you should still go ahead with making amends as if you did confess. These consequences, which you put on yourself, should be costly so that there's no question that you decided not to confess because you were avoiding the aftermath.

What kind of relationship with you does your victim want to have?

If your victim has an order of protection out on you, then you know what kind of relationship he wants to have. He wants you to keep your distance. If he wants a confession out of you, he'll ask for it.

What if there's no order of protection? That was the case with the father and the daughter he abused when she was small. In those situations, you can look to see whether your victim is trying to get close to you or whether she seems to want you to keep your distance. Is she is trying to make sense of her past, or would she rather pretend it never happened?

If you're still married to the person you hurt and there's no order of protection, then I think you can assume she still wants a relationship with you, on some level. She, at least partly, feels that way if you haven't gotten papers from a lawyer. In that case, does your partner want the kind of marriage where you tell each other everything or the kind that is compartmentalized, where secrets are expected? There are all kinds of marriages. In some of them, there is an understanding not to ask too many questions. Is this what she wants, or is this what she is settling for?

For that matter...

What kind of relationship do you want to have?

You've created the kind with secrets. Is this your idea of marriage?

If you don't know what kind of relationship she wants to have, or if it's not evident by her behavior, then that's a conversation to initiate before you consider confession. If the two of you want a different kind of marriage, then you have bigger problems than extramarital activity.

Here's another question for those in love relationships:

Who did your partner fall in love with, you or a perfect person you were pretending to be?

When you first started dating, you were probably on your best behavior; you were playing a perfect person. There's no way you could have kept that up. At some point, you did something that put him off; something horrifying, annoying, discomfiting, or just plain weird. If he stuck around and didn't reject you, that's how real love was formed. Love doesn't come from flowers, kisses, and sweet nothings but from acceptance following anger, embarrassment, and shame. It's a beautiful thing when it happens, even though it ain't pretty when it's made.

Here's a related question:

Who do you want your partner to love, you or this fiction you created?

Do you want him to love the real you, with your imperfections, or a statue that belongs in the town square covered by pigeons?

Not every client I see who confesses extramarital sexual activity asks me if he should tell his wife. Sometimes I have to ask him whether he will tell her. "Hell, no," some say. "It'll kill her... What she doesn't know can't hurt her... She doesn't want to know."

For them, I have more questions:

How do you know it'll kill her? How do you know she'll never forgive? How do you know she doesn't want to know?

You're staking a lot on how you believe she would take it. Maybe you know these things. Maybe you had a talk once. Maybe she said, "If you ever have an affair, don't tell me. I wouldn't want to know." But she probably didn't.

Once a relationship passes the initial fake perfect stage, you might think the couple would feel free to let it all hang out and be honest about everything. But, no; often that's not what happens. What happens is the relationship has now become so vital that you don't mess with it. You don't quite go back to your original position of putting an attractive face on everything because, like, who are you kidding, but you head in the direction of secrecy. You don't want to risk losing someone who knows you so well. Once your loved one has seen the bad and still loves you, you think you can never let her see anything like it again.

That is when couples stop communicating. That's when they stop being honest, not out of any malice but out of a desire to protect and preserve. That's when you start your extramarital activity with someone who doesn't matter.

To put it another way:

If your wife failed to know you well enough to suspect extramarital activity, then how can you be sure you know her well enough to know how she would react?

Here's another one:

How many chances are you willing to take?
When your cover is blown, and she finds out before you tell her, all hell will break loose for two reasons: the crime and the coverup. The coverup is worse.

If you are a risk taker and willing to take a chance on coverup, then…

Can you take a chance that confessing will be the very thing that changes your marriage for the better?
That happens sometimes, most of the time, actually—especially when the one doing the damage is serious about change. A marriage is one of those things: to keep it you have to be willing to lose it, not through extramarital activity but by putting weight on it and counting on your partner's trust and understanding to get you through.

If you've considered my questions and still believe you can't confess your wrong to the person you hurt, then go back to your written statement of responsibility and add the following.

"I could have confessed to you, but after consultation with an adviser, I carefully decided that a confession would just hurt you more. If I was wrong and have given you more reason not to trust me, then I acknowledge I was wrong to do this. I accept any consequence that comes of it and am committed to disclosing everything to you in the future if you want me to."

Date it, have your adviser witness it, and put it in a safe place, so you can take it out when the jig is up.

Ten Ways to Screw Up an Apology

If you've decided you can't apologize to the person you hurt because it would hurt him more, then go with God. If you've decided you can't apologize to the person you hurt because it would hurt **you** more, then see you in Hell. But if you've decided you **will** apologize to the person you hurt because it's the right thing to do, read on. There are still mistakes you could make.

You apologize without confessing

You might think it would be impossible to make an apology without admitting wrongdoing, but people sure try. They can't seem to resist saying *I'm sorry* without following it with the word *but* and all manner of justifications and rationalizations. You need to admit what you did wrong, acknowledge the harm you caused, and say what you're going to do to make it right.

The problem comes when you go beyond the simple acknowledgement of the deed and attempt to explain why you did it. There's a time and a place for that, just not now in your apology. To your victim's ears, explanation sounds like justification and excuses.

You may have had good reasons for doing what you did. The person you hurt may have harmed you in some way first before you harmed him, but to bring that up now obscures your own confession. It confuses things and makes it sound like you're not taking responsibility for your part of the problem.

You're vague

Saying, "I'm sorry I hurt you," is an apology in the same way that a moped is transportation. It's lame. A moped will get you where you're going, but not as memorably as a Ferrari. If you want to make a memorable impact on your relationship, make your apology into a Ferrari.

List the bad things you've done and the particular ways they had an effect on her. The more concrete you can be, the better your apology. "I lied," is better than, "I hurt you"; but, "I lied to you about what I was doing Tuesday night," is better than, "I lied."

If you're too vague, it sounds like you haven't done the work, you haven't gotten down and scrubbed out all the corners, and you tried to get by with passing a quick broom across it. There could even be confusion over what you're confessing. He could think you're confessing the lie you told on Friday night, when all you're talking about was Tuesday.

You only apologize when you're forced to

You get three points if you apologize after she's caught you in the act or when she confronts you. It's like telling her you love her after she says, "You don't tell me you love me anymore." It's the bare minimum. You score a touchdown when you tell her you love her without being asked. A good apology comes unprompted after full consideration.

If you are confronted or caught in the act, it's necessary to acknowledge the transgression right there and then, but you're not done yet. Sometime later, after you do the work, bring it up again on your own. This shows you're taking it seriously.

You don't show empathy

It's important to acknowledge in your apology the effect your actions had on him. This is to show you are taking his perspective. "I lied to you about what I was doing Tuesday night and now you can't trust me," shows you're putting yourself in his shoes.

You might find it hard to know just what the effects have been. That's okay. You don't have to be right; you just have to show that you've tried.

You ask for forgiveness

People screw up a perfectly good apology when they ask for forgiveness. Asking for forgiveness puts your victim on the spot. It requires her to do something at a time when she may be unprepared. Besides, she shouldn't be forgiving you just yet. You're not off the hook until you actually change.

Some victims will offer forgiveness without being asked. Sometimes this comes from a good place in them; sometimes they're just uncomfortable with receiving the confession and want it over with; sometimes they think it's what they're supposed to do. At any rate, when that happens, you should respectfully and graciously decline the gift or, rather, offer to pick it up later, after you've made amends.

This doesn't mean that things have to go on being tense like they may have been. You don't have to sleep on the couch. An apology is supposed to be a turning point. You've changed direction, but you're not there yet. You have not yet arrived at reconciliation.

You don't answer questions

Your apology is not over when you've delivered your statement of responsibility. You need to stay for questions. Answering questions ensures that you haven't missed anything or been too vague. It also shows that you're willing to stand under scrutiny.

Depending on the nature of your transgression, you may be tempted to say to him, "You don't want to know." This happens often in the confession of an affair when the cuckolded spouse thinks he wants details. You might very sincerely want to protect your partner from the knowledge of where and when and how you had sex with that other man. You know he's not going to want to have that image in his head. There's also the matter of what he's going to do with that information. Once he knows who you've been sleeping with, is that person going to be safe?

At times like this, when you don't believe your partner is asking the right questions, you, as a couple, need help. There's no good way out of this jam by yourselves. If you fail to answer the questions as asked, no matter how ill considered, it's going to look like you have something to hide. If you do answer them, you may have just hurt him more. You may not be able to complete your confession just then. This is the time to enlist someone objective, whom you both can trust. This person can help your partner frame his questions in such a way to help him move on.

Most, if not all, of the questions a partner has boil down to one thing: "Can I trust you?" At the time of the confession, the true answer, the answer you have to give if you are honest, is no. He can't trust you. You have to earn your trust back by making amends.

You want the whole thing over and done with and don't offer to make amends

Saying the words, "I'm sorry," is not a magical incantation that makes everything better; it has to be followed up with improvements. Nothing changes just because you admitted you did something wrong. People apologize over and over about the same thing all the time without doing anything differently.

You should commit to change. If you've done your work prior to the confession, you will have identified how you can make amends. If you've lied, then telling the truth will make it right. If you broke a promise, then keep your promises or don't make promises you can't keep in the first place. If you ran up the credit card bill without her knowing, then pay it off before buying anything for yourself again, and so on.

Making an apology is just the start of the process of reconciliation with your partner; it's not the end. It ain't over till it's over.

You confuse symbols with the real thing

Sometimes, when a contrite husband brings his wife flowers to apologize for something, she gets angry and throws them in the trash. That's what happens when the symbol of the apology and the real thing get confused.

The real part of the apology is the acknowledgement of the deed, its effects, and the way to make amends. The flowers serve as a reminder of the commitment to change. When you've done the actual work and made a true apology, the flowers don't get thrown in the trash. When you make the flowers do the work for you, it looks like you're trying to buy her off.

You don't listen

After you've admitted wrongdoing, the person you hurt may have something to say. He may have questions; he might want to point out how your actions impacted him; you may have missed something; he might have something else in mind about how you can make amends; maybe he has something he needs to get off his chest. Who knows, he may have a confession of his own to make. After you've made your apology, listen.

Listening, by the way, involves attending to more than just the words he says. You also have to pay attention to the way he says them. Note his body language, emotion, and inflection.

After you listen, summarize what he said in your own words. This lets him know it's sunk in so he doesn't have to keep saying it. If you get it wrong when you summarize, he'll let you know. This is important. Maybe you didn't hear him right. This could be a case of chronic miscommunication. If he does correct you, then summarize that until you have heard it correctly.

You don't document

After you've acknowledged the misdeed, its effects, and the way to make amends, write it all down so no one forgets. Date it and make yourself a reminder to pull it out and go over later. Then you'll see if you've followed through with making amends. If you have, that might be the time to ask forgiveness. If you haven't, then you have another apology to make and a whole lot more work to do.

You may not feel you need to do all of this if the misdeed is minor, like if you ate the last donut one morning. But if you're always eating the last donut or if there is a pervasive pattern of selfish and inconsiderate behavior and eating the last donut is only one example, then the full treatment is necessary.

The more pervasive the pattern of misbehavior, the harder it's going to be to change. You're going to need all the help you can get. Make your apology and do it right and you'll be less likely to need to do it again.

Making Your Apology Stick

All too many people apologize and promise to change but fail to follow it up. Not only do they fail to fulfill their promises, but they even fail to notice whether they've fulfilled them or not.

When you make your formal apology, admit your mistakes, work out how to make amends, and document the proceedings, you're still not done—not until you both open up your calendars and schedule a time to review your progress. You should meet again sooner rather than later, after a week or two or even after a few days, depending on how long it takes to enact the amends you have promised.

Some amends take longer to enact than others. Take amends for violence, for instance. If you're the kind of guy that scares the bejeebers out of your family by punching holes in walls, overturning furniture, cussing, and slamming doors, you probably don't do all that very often. Having a temper tantrum once every few years, or even once, is enough to scare people to their core and even hurt them, as well as get you in serious trouble. If you sincerely apologize for this behavior and promise to make amends by never doing it again, it may take years before anyone can recognize you've kept your promise. Twenty years could go by and they could still be expecting another meltdown.

The amends you promise should be something you can do right away, or even every day, and be related to the offense. Rather than promising never to put another hole in the wall, you can promise to talk about your feelings respectfully rather than acting on them. Pay attention to that and abstaining from making holes in the walls will take care of itself.

If you schedule your review session very soon, like after a day or two, and if your amends are the kind you can perform daily, your partner will probably report you've done very well. Anyone can do well for a day or two after they apologize. If you don't do well, maybe your amends need a tweak. You could need some help. The point is, the sooner you schedule a review, the sooner you notice if it's not working and the sooner you can prevent the problem from getting momentum again.

Let's say your husband has been concerned about your drinking. You apologized for puking all over his stamp collection and promised to make amends by replacing a rare Mauritanian dodo bird stamp and keeping your wine consumption under a glass a day. When you review on day three, you're able to say the stamp has been found and ordered, but you have to admit that, on day two, you got sloshed again. If you can't go three days without getting sloshed, you need help and may tweak your amends by adding that you'll attend AA or go see a counselor about the problem. You might even find it easier to not get into the wine at all rather than try to stop after one drink.

When people fail to schedule a review of progress, it's not like their progress is never noticed. It's noted when they relapse. What happens is that you go on limiting your drinking to one a day until three months later when you don't. Then the shit hits the fan, and you get told that you don't take it seriously when you really did very well, unnoticed, for three months.

Having frequent reviews can ensure that you get positive feedback when you're doing well. These sessions also give you an opportunity to gracefully perform the hardest operation in this whole apologizing business: addressing your partner's part in the problem. Right after he says, "Yes, you have been limiting your wine consumption to one glass a day and I appreciate the Mauritanian dodo stamp you got me." That's when you say, "Thank you. Now that I've been drinking less, I've noticed that you pay more attention to your stamp collection than you do me."

If you're like anyone who's gotten in trouble, you know you don't deserve 100 percent of the blame. You could have been drinking all that wine because you were feeling ignored and you had to silence yourself from disturbing your husband when he was preoccupied with his stamp collection. You've done well if you've restrained yourself from pointing fingers at him till after you've taken responsibility for your part, but if you go on feeling ignored without saying anything, that'll turn into one more thing to be sorry about.

Listen to Your Lookout

When you're finally done apologizing and making amends, you probably don't want to have to do that again. You'll want to keep those problems away. So, listen to your lookout. He'll tell you if they ever start coming around.

When the wheels start to come off, everyone is prone to develop their own kind of problem and make their own kind of mistakes. Some use substances, or gamble, or have sex with everyone, or can't stop shopping; others get controlling. Still others get depressed or anxious or angry or just withdraw into themselves. Some have a combination of several kinds of problems and mistakes. Everyone's got their thing. Your own type of problem and mistake is yours because it's the very thing that sneaks up in your blind spots. It fits you like a glove. When it fools anyone into thinking it's a good thing, it fools you first.

It takes hard work to eradicate problems and eternal vigilance to keep them away. Relapse can be expected. When we're talking about addiction, it takes an average of seven real attempts before recovery feels solid, and even then, you won't know if you're going to need eight. Mental illness also tends to be episodic, and each new episode tends to be worse than the last. People who have succumbed once to the temptations of violence, sexual recklessness, self-harm, suicide attempts, or self-pity are more likely to do it again. Moreover, problems will often go into hiding when they feel threatened, so what appears to be recovery is really a more pernicious hidden phase of the same problem that troubled you before.

If you're in a close relationship, you have a resource that others don't have. You have a lookout. Your problem was not custom made just for her. It doesn't sneak up in her blind spots. She observes it coming before you do. She can see through the deceptions more easily. She has a vested interest in keeping you safe from this problem. She could warn you that it's approaching if you'll only listen.

Paid professionals can help—they have the knowledge, they have the objectivity—but they don't have the access your partner has. They don't see you on the weekends and at night when problems often strike. They don't have as much at stake.

Far too many people fail to use their lookout. The lookout sees the problem coming and they argue with her, deny it's happening, and get defensive. This is a mistake. It's as if a lookout on a ship, up in the crow's nest, saw an iceberg up ahead and the captain yelled, "You're crazy, I'm not going to hit an iceberg. You never trust me. I'm going to do what I want. Get off my back." It would not be good if a captain did that.

To be sure, many lookouts don't understand their role too well. When they see problems coming, they often make accusations rather than observations. It's as if the lookout, up in the crow's nest, called out, "You're hitting an iceberg again! Don't you care about me?" They should just warn you that there's an iceberg. They seem so unreasonable, you might be tempted to dismiss their warnings as crazed paranoia. It would not be good if you, or any captain, did that.

However, you've got to realize that you've hit a few icebergs in your day and your lookout should be excused if she gets excited when she sees another one.

There are a few things you can expect from a good lookout. Don't be surprised when you see them.

A good lookout doesn't resign

If your partner comes down from the crow's nest and tells you that you've got to look out for your own problem, you can figure that next she'll be going off in a lifeboat. A true partner doesn't resign as lookout unless she's about to leave the relationship or she's damn fool. She has to be a lookout if only to guard her own interests.

A good lookout stays awake

He doesn't watch like a hawk in the beginning and then forget about it later on. If it's months or years since the problem last struck, don't be surprised if he's still on the lookout. He has to be. That's his job.

A good lookout scans the horizon

She doesn't keep looking in the same place. The main thing to look out for is the way the problem arrived in the past. It is likely to come that way again. If, for instance, you get snappy at Christmas time, then she should be especially on the lookout at Christmas time. But understand, snappiness can come wherever there is busyness, family contact, alcohol use, overeating, darkness, or an imperative to be merry.

A good lookout is not deceived

Problems arrive in disguise. No one starts off drinking three six-packs a day just to feel normal. No, they start off with a glass of wine at dinner, a beer during the game, or a shot with a friend. These things are all good things; there is nothing wrong with any of them in themselves. They are only evil because of where they lead. A good lookout sees through the disguises. He knows the masks that your problem wears.

A good lookout is jumpy

She's got to be vigilant. If you keep driving by that place where you used to score drugs, she should be seeing red flags. This may very well be the way the problem creeps up innocently.

A good lookout raises the alarm

If he sees the problem return, he should say something, not keep that information to himself. You need to know it. He may not want to do it—no one wants to be the bearer of bad news—but this is what lookouts are for. If the problem has given the two of you a lot of trouble in the past, he might not want to believe it's back. If the problem has already taken you over, he might get an argument.

A good lookout keeps her eye on the hazard

If your lookout spots the problem, she should keep her eye on it, even if you say it's nothing. In the case of chemical use, don't be surprised if she looks for confirmation in the form of a home drug or alcohol testing kit to eliminate suspicions. For this, or other kinds of problems, she may want to get a second opinion from a professional—sort of like calling in another lookout and asking what he sees.

A good lookout keeps himself safe

He shouldn't be so busy being a lookout, watching out for your problem that he gets overcome by his own. Yes, even your partner has his own kind of problem and makes his own characteristic mistakes.

A good lookout has someone looking out for her

Be your partner's lookout, just as she is yours. Watch each other's backs. You can see her problem more clearly than she can her own. If your partner has been dealing with your problem for a long time, she's probably worked very hard to keep herself strong. Someone in the house had to function. The laundry, the cooking, the kids, the relatives, the shopping, and going to work didn't get taken care of by themselves. She may not be accustomed to relying on you for anything; you just haven't been reliable. That's going to have to change. She needs a lookout too.

If you've ever complained that your partner doesn't trust you, let him be your lookout. This is how he learns to trust you again.

7

SEEKING JUSTICE

How to Demand an Apology

If you've been traveling the road to reconciliation this far,
then you've come a long way. You've avoided going off the
road or taking supposed shortcuts that don't take you
anywhere. You managed to not get carried away by your
emotions but, rather, use them to the purpose they were
designed for: to show you your values. You climbed a steep
path, saw the big picture, and grew able to admit that you
played a part in the problem. You then developed your own
statement of responsibility, your made your apologies, and
you are hard at work making amends.

You might be wondering, what about the harm that was
done to me? When will my partner take responsibility for
what he's done? Can't he and I travel this road to
reconciliation together?

Ideally, your partner has already taken the hint. She
noticed how well you apologized and the positive
transformation you have undergone and wants a little of that
for herself. You might have inspired her with your example
when you couldn't with your complaining. When you put
your defenses down, she put down hers because she could,
and that's all she really wanted all along.

Believe me, it usually works out this way. One person
starts doing the right thing and the other one follows. One

stops blaming the other and the other stops hitting the blame back like an angry and destructive game of ping pong. It usually works this way, but not always. Sometimes your partner is only too happy to see you accepting blame so he doesn't have to.

Modeling a new behavior, as you've been doing, is a very effective method of teaching, but sometimes people need a good swift kick in the ass, followed by step-by-step directions. It's a delicate matter to deliver a good swift kick in the ass without violating the humility and conscientiousness you have developed as a result of traveling this far down the road to reconciliation. You may need step-by-step instructions on how to give step-by-step instructions.

There's a reason you looked at your own guilt before asking for an apology. If you neglect that step, then you're no better than the guy who lets his partner do all the apologizing without admitting any regrets of his own. You're looking for a free ride. There ain't no free ride on the Road to Reconciliation. Everyone has got to pay the fare.

To put it another way, if you want to learn how to assert yourself and effectively deal with the people who misuse you, you can't do it just by learning how to complain. You have to travel this path and get in touch with your own power. You find your power right there next to your guilt.

There's another reason to examine your guilt before you demand an apology. You learn how to make an effective demand by first making an effective apology. An effective demand for an apology is a mirror of an effective apology.

1. In an effective apology, you admit the offense you're guilty of. In an effective demand, you describe the offense you suffered.
2. In an effective apology, you acknowledge how your offense impacted the other. In an effective demand, you declare how the offense impacted you.

3. In an effective apology, you promise how you will make amends. In an effective demand, you ask for what you want.

4. In an effective apology, you follow through with making amends and review your progress with your partner at regular, frequent intervals so that you can make adjustments as needed. In an effective demand, you remember the promises and review progress at regular, frequent intervals. You give credit due for progress and see failure as a need to make adjustments.

5. In an effective apology, you work toward change; eventually you change. In an effective demand, you work toward forgiveness. Eventually, you forgive.

If you've been traveling this Road to Reconciliation with me, then you're ready to seek justice. Let's look more closely at how.

What Do You Have to Complain About?

Some things are not worth complaining about, but many of the things that *are* aren't ever addressed. For every person who carps about every little thing, there's another person who stuffs his indignation. Sometimes it's the same person who carps and stuffs—complaining about a hundred little things that don't matter while he's silent about the things that do.

To help you decide what to complain about, here's a formula:

All the crap - All your crap - Your feelings + (Your values/2 x his promises) = Things to complain about.

All the crap

Let's say your husband sits in front of the TV watching sports and drinking beer seven nights out of the week. He's gained weight in the process, and where he once had a svelte, athletic figure, he now has a belly so big you don't even want to look at it or be seen standing next to it. He yells at the umpires and is crabby when his team loses. He snaps your head off when you walk in front of the set. When the game goes to extra innings, he falls asleep there, sometimes spilling beer in the process. You never do anything together anymore. You can't even talk about anything with him because all he knows is baseball. You feel lonely even though he's always around. You would miss sex if you weren't so disgusted by him. He snores. Then, in the morning, when he wakes up hung over, he's good for nothing.

All the crap, in this case is: watching baseball too much, yelling and being crabby, snapping at you, being embarrassing, not sleeping with you, snoring when he does sleep with you, spilling beer, being ignorant about everything but baseball, ignoring you, not having sex, being disgusting, getting hung over, and failing to do what he was supposed to do when he was hung over.

That's a lot of crap.

All your crap

If you've been traveling this Road to Reconciliation, you've already taken a look at your own part in this problem, so you have no problem with deducting your crap from his. You agree that you have more control over your own actions than you do over the actions of another. You decided that all your complaining just made the problem worse instead of better; it caused him to withdraw even more from you and watch his sports and drink his beer out of sheer spite. You admitted you walked in front of the TV just for spite too. So, you made amends by stopping the complaining, cooking him healthy food, getting him other things to try drinking, and developing more of an interest than you ever thought you would have in the St Louis Cards. He no longer snaps at you because you no longer passive-aggressively walk in front of the TV. When he yells at umpires and gets crabby, at least you know it's not about you. As for the loneliness, you took up a hobby, started regularly having dinner with friends, and got a second TV so you could watch your own shows in another room. You got a new wardrobe, changed your hair, and started to look not bad for your age. With all the changes you made, you're a better person. You like yourself more and have learned that filling yourself with loathing for him doesn't do you any good. But he's still sitting there every night, drinking beer, as if nothing had ever changed.

Even though he's done nothing to change, you are not nearly as much a victim as you used to be. You can be happy while he's miserable. You can be attractive while he's out of shape. You can have a full, vibrant life while he drinks himself numb, looking at shadows on a screen. But still, some offense remains. What is it? Why does his behavior matter?

Your feelings

You miss him, you're worried about him, you're ashamed of him, and you're disgusted.

If you've been traveling this Road to Reconciliation, you've learned that no one can make you feel anything. Your feelings are your feelings. You have control over them. Therefore, you can't complain about how you feel. You have to take your feelings out of the equation, except for one thing.

You've also learned that feelings show you your values.

Your values

What values are being expressed by your feelings?

You miss him because you value companionship. You're worried about him because you value health and a long life. You don't want to lose him. You value freedom, so you don't want to have to take care of an invalid. You're ashamed and disgusted because you value certain body shapes over others and certain smells and sounds over others.

Divided by two

If you knew you were marrying someone who doesn't value companionship, health, a long life, freedom, and certain body shapes, sounds, and smells precisely as much as you do, then you don't have much to complain about. Here's the thing: no one will value anything precisely as much as you do. If you take any two people and put them together, one will be more companionable, be healthier, live longer, and like certain aesthetics more than the other. That's the case for everything. There will also always be one partner who is hornier, cheaper, more permissive, messier, more social, harder working, and more religious than the other. If you didn't know that when you got married, you should have. At any rate, it's something you'll have to get used to.

You will never find anyone who perfectly matches your values. Your values are what make you special. If you ever find anyone who perfectly matches you, run the other way. First of all, it wouldn't be true; secondly, if it were true, why would you need two of you?

If you're asking him to be just like you, you're asking too much; but, if you're expecting him to be as open minded about your values as you are to his, then you know what marriage is for.

His promises
If he promised to go with you to the yarn store but then changed his mind in favor of watching baseball, then you have something to complain about. If you painstakingly extracted a vow to cut down his drinking, but he seems to have forgotten about it, then that's a broken promise. If he talks a good game about health and exercise but never takes steps in that direction, then you have a good reason to call him out on his failure.

What you have to complain about
You now know what is reasonable to complain about. Start with all the crap and deduct all your crap. Then write off your feelings but not the values they indicate. Divide your values by two because partnership is all about compromise. Multiply the sum by any promises he's made. That's what you have to complain about. Have at it. You're in a good position to

demand an apology because you've been fair and have given yourself the same treatment you're giving him.

If he never promised anything and if your crap exceeds his crap and if you're expecting him to learn from your values more than you learn from his, then maybe you owe him an apology. That would be a heck of a thing for a vibrant, attractive woman to be in debt to a drunken lout who never gets off the couch, but stranger things have happened.

If that's the case then, for your own sake, make your apology and think about setting both of you free. You, of having to change a man who doesn't want to change. And him, so he could go on watching his baseball and drinking his beer in peace.

What Kind of Justice Do You Want?

You caught your husband on the website Ashley Madison making arrangements to meet another woman. You're outraged. You want him to make it right. But what's right?

There are three ways of looking at justice, otherwise known as *what's right*. There's a fair share, fair play, and just desserts.

A fair share

Distributive justice is about fairness and equality. If you're concerned with there being a double standard—that he can run around on you but you can't run around on him—then you're concerned with distributive justice. If you don't think that you're getting your fair share of attention, or sex, or thoughtful gifts, then distributive justice is your thing. If it bothers you that other women enjoy the company of your husband without having to do his laundry, then there you go: distributive justice. In that case, your primary interest will be in getting what you think you deserve. Making amends for you would consist of making things equitable. Reconciliation is when the books are balanced, the playing field is leveled, and everyone starts at the same place.

The problem with seeking distributive justice is that not everyone puts in the same effort or has the same needs. The shirker gets the same rewards as the hard worker. When everyone gets the same portion at dinner, the teenage boys go hungry and the old women can't finish their meal.

In your case, if you caught your husband on Ashley Madison, you may not have any desire to be on Ashley Madison. For that matter, you may have lost your interest in him—his attention, his sex, and his gifts. And as for the laundry, well you're doing laundry anyway, so maybe a few more things don't matter. Also, having to dress up, put on makeup, and meet someone for a first date, like the women he's meeting have to do, seems like an awful lot of work. If you're asking for the same thing he or the other women are getting, be sure you want it.

Fair play

This is called procedural justice. If you're concerned that he broke his vows, told lies, did the whole thing in secret, and didn't allow you the chance to object, approve, or solve the problem he used to rationalize his adultery, then you're concerned with procedural justice. If he had just spoken up, you might have gone for an open marriage or an uncontested divorce. What burns your ass is that he disrespected you so much that he went behind your back. He could have just talked to you, but he didn't.

We're generally okay with an inequitable share when there has been a fair procedure to divide the shares. No one begrudges the victors of a sports contest the spoils of victory when the ref has been impartial. No one objects when hard workers live higher on the hog than those who sleep late and leave early. You know that there are times when your partner is needier than you and are okay with it because you're in this relationship for the long haul and things balance out over time.

There are some problems with seeking procedural justice in a relationship. First of all, few couples—and fewer parents and children, if that's the relationship in question—have a complete set of bylaws that govern their interactions. Much of what passes for procedure are vague, unspoken norms. He may not have known he could have talked to you or he might have thought you would have gone apeshit if he confessed he was attracted to other women. Furthermore, many relationships are built on a foundation of lies. In the beginning, you hide all your faults and he hides his; then, when you see them, your answer is to pretend they're not there. If you like strong men who take care of themselves without whining and complaining, then you can't blame him if he failed to come to you with problems.

Here's another thing. As long as there are only two people in a relationship, it's easy to come to an impasse. There's no referee to adjudicate disagreements and often no way to resolve differences. Intractable conflicts go on being intractable conflicts when there's no procedure to settle the dispute.

Finally, he can only be as honest with you as he is with himself. If he's fooling himself, then he can't help but try to fool you.

In many relationships, it's like you're in a court of law with no judge, no lawyers, no due process, and a litigant and a defendant who may be incapable of participating in their own defense. That's a funny place to ask for, much less expect, procedural justice.

Just desserts

The day you found out about his Ashley Madison account, you called him all sorts of names and made him sleep on the couch. You've been cold to him ever since. You made him hand over his cell phone and forbade him from touching the computer. You told his parents what he did and explained to your kids that he must not love his family anymore. When you make dinner, you make only enough for you and the kids. He's in the doghouse now.

Your objective is not to make him hurt as much as he made you hurt; that would be a negative form of distributive justice, making sure everyone has a fair share of what's bad. Your objective is to make him hurt more than you. You want retributive justice.

You could be even more punitive, petty, and vindictive. You know where his buttons are, so you could push them. You know where his skeletons are buried, so you can dig them up. You could get on Ashley Madison yourself and see how he likes it. You could derive satisfaction from not saying what you want and make him sweat. You want revenge.

When you want revenge, you've not interested in fair play; revenge is all about imposing your will on the person you're punishing. When you want revenge, you're not concerned with fair shares; you'll take greater than your share because you believe it's owed you in recompense. Retributive justice throws out the claims of distributive and procedural justice and pins its hopes on deterrence, incapacitation, and retaliation.

It's believed that retributive justice deters wrongdoing by increasing its cost. In our case, he'll think twice now before he cheats on you. Retributive justice is supposed to incapacitate criminals from committing any more crimes by throwing them in prison, executing them, or otherwise handicapping them. In this case, how can he go on Ashley Madison if he has no access by phone or Internet? Retribution feels good. It's said to remove your humiliation as you humiliate him. No one will blame you for retaliating, up to a point. Your girlfriends may even cheer you on.

But is this the relationship you want to have? Do you want to be so bitter? Deterrence sometimes works to prevent people from doing harm, but he had to know there would be hell to pay when he got caught, and he did it anyway. As for incapacitating him from doing it again by taking away his cell phone and computer: Who are you kidding? Do you know how easy it is to get a cell phone and access to a computer?

Retributive justice is like scratching an itch when you've been touched by poison ivy. It feels good, but it not only doesn't solve the problem; it makes it worse.

Restorative justice

So, you see, all the types of justice fall short to some degree when used in their unadulterated form. However, I believe it's possible to combine elements of all three in a mindful, deliberate, and, shall we say, judicious manner that fulfills most of their virtues while avoiding their shortcomings. This is called restorative justice.[19] If your main concern is to fix what's broken, then you're concerned with restorative justice.

If restorative justice had a sound, it would be the sound of a door opening, not a jail cell slamming. It smells like spring, not death. It looks like someone who's done the wrong thing, now doing the right thing and holding his head up high, not cowering in a corner. It's an open hand, not a closed fist. It's a new contract, not a death sentence or a pronouncement of guilt. Repairs make the world a better place, not a worse one; they spread around goodness, not more heartache.

If you ask me, I think restorative justice should really be called renovative justice. You're not restoring a relationship to what existed before the problem came along. You're renovating it to be better than ever. Chances are, your relationship was not that good before he went on Ashley Madison. Chances are, it could be better.

Let's look closer at restorative, or renovative, justice in the next part.

Restorative Justice in Your Relationship

Something called restorative justice is beginning to appear in the court system. It also has a place in personal relationships when there has been an injury and trust needs to be repaired.

This is how restorative justice works in the court system: A kid gets caught with a can of paint, spraying a swastika on a synagogue parking lot. The congregation is outraged. Intense fears and memories of the Holocaust get activated. The kid appears before a judge and admits he's guilty.

The judge could sentence him to jail, but how would that help? In jail, the kid might likely fall in with a gang of skinheads who would further radicalize him, casting him as the victim, not the perpetrator of injustice. His schooling would be interrupted, his friendships disrupted, his time wasted, all at great cost to the taxpayers. The congregation might enjoy some small satisfaction that the power of the state is being used to punish the kid, but there would be no true healing, only retribution.

The judge might give the kid probation or a suspended sentence and say don't get in trouble again. Many, including the congregation and the kid, might think he got off easy.

Many judges, wanting to avoid these unproductive options, might send the kid to someone like me to arrange a restorative justice conference.

The first time I met with the kid, I'd check to see if he was ready to take responsibility for his actions. I'd ask him if he could imagine how spray painting a swastika on a synagogue parking lot might affect the congregation. I'd invite him to consider how he could make amends. If he couldn't do any of these or wasn't willing to make amends, I'd send him back to the judge.

If he was able and willing, then next I'd meet with representatives of the congregation. I'd tell them about restorative justice. I'd ask if they're willing to participate. I'd invite them to consider how the kid could make amends. If they can't deal with meeting him, or if there is nothing he could do to make amends, then I'd tell the judge that restorative justice is not right in this case.

But if we have a go on both ends, then we arrange a conference with everyone. The kid speaks first, taking responsibility, acknowledging the harm he's done. The congregation then speaks, filling in details the kid might have missed. If the apology is accepted, we move on to construct a plan to make amends. The kid and the representatives work toward an agreement on what he'll do to make it right. Maybe he'll scrub the parking lot, rake leaves, speak to the whole congregation, or whatever. A time limit is placed, and everyone shakes hands.

If the kid follows through with his promises, then the judge dismisses the charges, the congregation forgives him, and everyone moves on. The taxpayers keep their money. The skinheads look for other recruits. The world is a better place.

You can do the same thing in your personal relationships. If you need it, someone like me can help you.

You walked in and found your wife having sex with another man. You could pull out a gun and shoot them both, but that would just get you in trouble. You could just get a divorce, but how do you get that image out of your head and move on? You could just tell her not to do it again, but that seems too mild. Your wife is remorseful. She's ended the affair. She wants you back. She wants you to forgive her. You need to be able to trust her for any forgiveness to be real. You could have a restorative justice conference.

Restorative justice is possible only if your wife is ready to take responsibility for the affair. She may want to point to things you did that "made" her have an affair, but for restorative justice to work, she'll have to lay those points aside so you both can get past the incident. She should be able to say how you might have been affected by seeing her having sex with her lover in your marital bed. She should consider how she could make amends. If she can't do any of these or is not willing to make amends, then skip the restorative justice conference and head right to the divorce attorney.

Even if she is able and willing, you need to be too. You have to be willing to meet with your estranged wife and work with her to develop a plan for making amends. You have to be open to her repairing things and not be stuck in retaliation mode. If you can't deal with meeting her, or if there's nothing she could do to make amends, then you need a divorce attorney more than a restorative justice conference.

But if it's a go on both ends, then you have a conference. Your wife speaks first, taking responsibility, acknowledging the harm she's done. Then you speak, filling in details your wife might have missed. If you have questions about the affair, you ask them. If she answers them fully and if the apology is accepted, you move on to construct a plan to make amends. You both work toward an agreement on what your wife will do to make it right. Maybe she'll never talk with him again; maybe she'll go to therapy and change factors that led to her affair; maybe she'll paint the bedroom, burn the sheets, buy a new bed, and let you use that position you saw her in with her lover but she never lets you try. Whatever floats your boat.

Coming up with ways to make amends is often the hardest part. Your wife would do well to not agree to tasks that degrade her or that are impossible or vague. She can't promise to never talk to another man. She may promise to love you, but what does that mean? You would do well to make them hard enough to be meaningful and related to the wrongdoing. The best amends are measurable, attainable, and concrete.

A time limit is placed, and everyone shakes hands. If she follows through with her promises, then you let it go. That's your promise. If you still have mistrustful feelings, dismiss them. That's called forgiveness. Everyone moves on. The world is a better place.

For you, as a victim, the key to making all this work is knowing what you want for her to make amends.

Using the Rupture Ratio to Decide What You Want

Hurting sucks. You'll want to move on. Before you can, you'll need to know where to go. What is it that you want, exactly?

If your wife has been sleeping with another man, you might not know how to heal. It's not like she can undo what she did or that you can unknow it. What's done is done. You find it hard to trust, and a persistent image keeps popping into your mind whenever you go to kiss her. You try to imagine feeling the same about her as you once did, but you can't get there from here. It seems like the roads have all been closed and a confusing array of detour signs are sending you every which way.

The rupture ratio

Pick a number from zero to ten that expresses your interest in staying in the relationship, versus the desire to leave. *Zero* means you're certain you never want to see your wife again. We're not only talking divorce; we're talking a scorched-earth annihilation of affection here. If there are kids involved, or an equally cherished Doberman, you'll even walk out on them so you don't have to see her again.

You're at a *one* if a bitter, no-nonsense divorce is what you want—angry enough that she keeps her distance but not so contentious that you lose the kids and the Doberman. *Two* is your number if you'd like it to be amiable; *three* means a trial separation.

The middle range, *four to seven*, represents a particular kind of hell of indecision and vacillation. You might even find the needle moving wildly throughout the day, depending on what you're thinking about at that moment. There are many factors to consider and it's all very complicated. The fact is, from *four* to *seven*, you don't really know how you feel or what you want to do. You may be sitting on the fence, keeping your options open, waiting to see which way the wind will blow. What your partner will do next will determine which way you go.

Eight is a grim decision to stay together for the kids, the Doberman, or finances because there are some benefits to the relationship, but you're not feeling so lovey-dovey about your wife herself. *Nine* is reserved for people committed to the relationship for religious reasons, or those who believe that a vow is a vow. You hurt like hell but are not going to let a little thing like suffering get in the way of doing the right thing. You're willing to extend grace, even though you don't feel like it, because we all need forgiveness for something.

If you're a *ten*, you're in the kind of love where nothing she could do could change how you feel about her. You want to stay together, no matter what. Divorce is off the table. No matter what she does, there's no need for reconciliation.

You can apply this scale and these questions to ruptures in other kinds of relationship. If you were hurt by an abusive father, you may want to consider how close you want to be with him today. Would you invite him to live with you and your family? That would be a *ten*. Live in the same town and see him regularly? *Nine*, or so. Or are you at the filial equivalent to a *one* and do no more than send Christmas cards, or a *zero* and never want to see or hear from him again? Or are you somewhere in the middle?

You might be surprised to hear that I, speaking as a certified shrinker of heads, am most suspect of the people at *zero* or *ten*. They need to have their heads examined more than the ambivalent do. While indecisiveness is torture, it's also the normal, and even adaptive, state of affairs, especially in the beginning, when the news is fresh and you don't know how it'll all play out. While we would all like to feel certain, certainty is an almost psychotic level of denial.

What moves you?

What matters more than where you are on the scale is what way you are heading and the direction you are moving. To get you going somewhere, whether it be toward *zero* or *ten*, I have two questions for you, in no particular order:

1. What gets you going toward *ten*, in the direction of reconciliation?
2. What actions move you toward *zero*, meaning dissolution of the relationship?

If you're in the middle range and your numbers are vacillating wildly from day to day, then you have a lot more information about what gets you going in one direction or another. You're feeling warmer toward her when she asks you about your day, colder the more time she's on her phone. You really felt hopeful when she made that appointment with a therapist, but you were discouraged the time she stayed out late. These observations tell you what you want and what to ask for.

In a like manner, your own actions can move you up and down that scale. Notice how you feel after you start a fight versus after you make a confession. When you engage in retaliation, does it bring you closer together? When you snoop, does it drive you apart? The answers to these questions tell you how to heal.

Asking for What You Want Without Asking for Trouble

All too often, people who know what they want fail to get it, not because their partner is unwilling but because they ask for it in a manner that starts a fight. If you've been following along as I've describe the Road to Reconciliation and dealt with your own shortcomings before correcting the faults of others, you can avoid a lot of these unnecessary fights, but not all. Manners still matter. The way you talk about things matters as much as the things you say.

If you want to ask for what you want and actually have a chance of getting it, there are certain rules to follow, regulations to adhere to, guidelines that increase your chance of success. I wrote about all of these in detail in an earlier book, *Constructive Conflict*,[20] but let me summarize some of these regulations for you here.

Pay no attention to the alarm going off in your head

When you're upset about something it's like there's this alarm going off inside your head, telling you it's an emergency. Unfortunately, you can't start a thoughtful, considerate, patient conversation in the middle of an emergency. Whatever way you do it, you have to calm down first.

Pick the right time and place

Don't start a difficult conversation just anywhere or at any time. Do it in a thoughtful and considerate way so that all extraneous factors can contribute to success.

Start with the easy stuff

Don't go into your conversation loaded for bear and begin with guns blazing. That'll put him immediately on the defensive. Start with things that you already agree on first.

Stay relevant

Don't expect your partner to change the past. She can't do it. All she can do is change what she does in the future.

Know what you're asking for

Work out what you're asking for beforehand. Know what you want or what you get may fail to satisfy.

Learn something

If your partner has something to say, summarize it aloud before you think you understand it. You may be getting it wrong. Ask your partner to summarize any important points you have to make, so you can be sure he gets it.

Acknowledge feelings

In a similar manner, summarize any strong feelings, as well as thoughts, that your partner expresses—just to be sure you're getting it right.

Avoid defamation, defensiveness, stonewalling, and contempt

These are the four fouls that never fail to start a fight.

Defamation is a false statement that disfigures the character of your partner. It occurs when you take normal complaints and turn them into pronouncements about your partner's personality.

To spot defensiveness, listen for when you are more concerned with blame than solutions.

Stonewalling is otherwise known as the silent treatment.

You're showing contempt when you engage in eye rolling, sneering, sarcasm, or an exasperated sigh. And then there's name calling, mockery, scorn, and the pulling out of all the dirty laundry. Contempt is implicit in domestic violence, backstabbing, betrayal, and alienating him from his children.

Don't be evil

If you are trying to ask for what you want, ask for what you want; don't use the occasion to inflict punishment or retribution.

Repair injuries

You probably can tell the split second when things start to go south in a conversation with your partner, when you say the wrong thing or she takes it the wrong way. When that happens, don't keep hammering away at the point you were trying to make. Stop, repair the injury, and then get back on track.

Detect dreams

If you find yourself grid locked, step back and be a dream detector. Behind every seemingly inflexible position, is a dream or a value that you and your partner find essential. Acknowledging and respecting these deepest, most personal hopes and dreams is the key to getting past the impasse.

Compromise

You don't have to have everything done your way, even when you're right.

Follow these rules and you will be more likely to get what you're asking for, and not trouble.

Don't Force It

My father was a car mechanic. When I was a kid, he tried to teach me all about cars, but I wasn't very interested. After a while, he might have thought he was wasting his time, but one of his lessons stuck with me. I think about it every day.

"Don't force it," he often said.

He was troubled by the way I was so hell-bent on getting those bolts loosened that I would stand on the wrench, extend it with a pipe, or perform any number of crazy stunts to get it to turn. A couple times, I snapped the bolt or rounded it off. Then we had had real problems. That's why he kept repeating, "Don't force it."

"How am I supposed to get the bolt off, if I don't force it?" I asked. "It won't go."

He answered, "Look at it from the bolt's point of view and work with it. What's keeping it from turning? Is it rust? Then WD-40 would help. Is it in too tight? Heating it up, then cooling it down will loosen it. Is there a nut you have to hold at the other end? Do you even have the right sized wrench?"

I thought he was crazy, trying to understand the problem from the bolt's point of view, but his advice prepared me for working with people.

Every day, I sit with people who won't change. They stubbornly persist with the same habits that get them in trouble. Strategies they've adopted don't work, so they try them again. I often have ideas of what could help, but my father's words come to me from beyond the grave.

"Don't force it."

So, I try to understand the issue from the client's point of view. What do they need to be able to see things clearly, to do something differently, to change? Then I work with them. I don't force it; I collaborate.

You might have a loved one whom you believe needs to change: a husband who leaves the toilet seat up; a wife who won't go down; an old mother who says whatever she thinks; a young adult son into drugs; anyone with a gambling problem using your money; anyone who, when you tell them something they don't want to hear, could respond in completely unpredictable ways. These are all bolts you're trying to turn.

Don't force it.

When you're using violence, you're forcing it, of course. But, when you bring up serious things at a bad time, you're also forcing it. When you complain about her when she complains about you, you're forcing it. When you find yourself in an argument and, instead of patching things up, you hammer away at whatever point you're trying to make, you're forcing it. When you don't let your partner come up with his own solutions, you're forcing it. When you lecture, when you accuse, when you shame, you're forcing it.

Don't force it.

How can you tell when you're forcing it?

When there's resistance.

The more you try to force the issue, the more resistance you're going to get. Are you getting an argument? Is he defensive? Does she agree with you but go on doing what she wants? Does he have a million excuses? Does it seem like you are working harder at change than she is? Then you're forcing it.

Don't force it.

What should you be doing instead?

Take a look at the problem from your loved one's point of view. Why is leaving the toilet seat up important to him; why is not going down on you important to her? Does your old mother feel she's not taken seriously? Does your young adult son believe he can do life on his own? What's the payout the gambler is looking for? What is the fear the angry guy is trying to avoid? Nobody does anything for no reason; what is their reason and is there another way to do what they want to do?

Don't force it; understand it. Your problem is their solution. Understand their problem before you offer another solution.

Then, work with your partner. Don't lecture; have a conversation. Put your heads together, don't knock them together. Don't confront; collaborate. Don't force it; just, like, relax man, and chill out.

Two Ways to Deliver a Message and Two Ways of Doing It Badly

If you have something to say to someone, there are two ways to deliver the message. You can go to the front door or the back door.

The front door and the back door

When you go to the front door, you're saying what you need to say clearly and directly. There's no mistaking what you want. You're being honest, sometimes brutally honest, and often presumptuous. This can be risky business if the person you are delivering the message to rejects you or takes offense. For that reason, many people prefer the back door.

When you go through the back door, you're subtle. You don't come right out and say what you want; you make allusions to it, hoping that they'll get the hint. You make a joke of it or pretend that it's no big deal.

Here are some examples:

Front Door: "When you blow your nose at the dinner table, it makes me want to gag. Could you please go to the other room when you need to do that?"

Back Door: "Did you hear a moose?"

There is no question about what the person in the front door example is asking for. He's being up front about what he wants. The nose blower cannot claim not to know how the other person feels. The nose blower is put on the spot. A line is drawn in the sand. There is an obvious confrontation. The front door approach can be effective, but depending on the sensitivities of the nose blower, it could cost you the relationship.

With the back door example, it's easy for the nose blower to miss the point or not even know that the moose refers to him. He may understand his nose blowing is loud but may not know it's disgusting. He may not know what to do and may go on making moose calls, thinking it's amusing. The nose blower might be embarrassed if he realizes he's being compared to a moose, but he's unlikely to feel put upon. He can easily save face. The back door approach is a light touch. It's easy to back down if it results in a confrontation, but it's unlikely to be effective.

You probably have an approach that you favor. If you're a front door kind of guy, you often get results, but people may perceive you as pushy, a bully, a whiner, a type-A personality, or a bitch. The results may not be worth the costs you accrue.

The back door person is a lot more fun to be with. Some will say you're easy going, but others will say you're passive-aggressive, the sneaky kind who never says how he feels. Therefore, you not only get fewer results; you may also earn contempt.

Maybe you're the kind who tries the back door a few times. If it works, great. When it doesn't, you have a choice.

You either try another back door approach, go in the front, or give up the whole project. What you don't get to do is pout that no one is listening. You haven't really tried to communicate in a clear fashion, so you can't blame people if they don't know what you're trying to say.

It's more difficult to try the front door first and change approaches if it doesn't go well. Once you go to the front door, you're committed.

I think there are times that call for either approach. It pays to be flexible, to be able to go through either door as the situation warrants: the front door for highly important matters and the back door for less essential messages. However, few people are flexible. They tend to favor one approach over another because they've had more practice with it and make blunders when they try the other.

Two ways to deliver a message badly

Here's a blunder that back door people make when they try to go through the front door. Rather than ringing the bell and waiting for someone to open the door, they conduct a home invasion.

Ringing the Bell: "Excuse me," you say, taking the nose blower aside. "Can I talk to you about something that's bothering me?" Then, after getting permission, "When you blow your nose at the dinner table, it makes me want to gag. Could you please go to the other room when you need to do that?"

Home Invasion: "That's disgusting!" you interject. "Go blow your nose somewhere else!" Everyone at the dinner table looks up in shock. The nose blower turns red. So do you when you realize what you've done. You have succeeded in being clear and direct, but you've embarrassed the nose blower, and yourself, in the process.

You see the difference between ringing the bell and conducting a home invasion? When you ring the bell, you wait for permission first. When you conduct a home invasion, you just barge right in. Now that you see the difference, maybe you'll find it easier to go in the front door as long as you ring the bell first.

Similarly, front door people have trouble trying the back door. They're concerned they won't be taken seriously, that they won't be heard. There are two ways of delivering a message at the back door. You can leave a message on the step and run away or you can hand it over and wait to get a receipt.

This is the difference:

Leaving a message on the step and running away: "Was that a moose?"

Handing over a message and getting a receipt: "Okay, who let in the moose? Can you please keep the moose away from the table?"

You see the difference between leaving a message on the step and running away and handing it over and getting a receipt? When you leave a message on the step and run away, you're leaving your delivery entirely up to chance. When you hand over the message and wait for a receipt, you're ensuring the message is delivered, albeit in a humorous, understated kind of way.

Front door or back door, it doesn't matter which, so long as the message gets delivered safely and they let you come to the house again.

The Broken Window Theory of Personal Relationships

Go to any down-in-the-heels, crime-ridden, poverty-stricken inner city and you're certain to find one thing. Lots and lots of broken windows.[21] Most of these broken windows will be in abandoned buildings, where no one appears to care and no one seems to be affected. Windows don't break on their own; someone picked up a rock and winged it. It's fun. If you've never done it, try it. Try it on your own window. Please don't do it on an abandoned building. Even though it may appear that no one is affected, people are.

Broken windows, besides just looking bad and being a safety hazard with all that shattered glass around, signal that no one cares about the neighborhood. They advertise that minor laws can be broken with impunity. You can damage someone's property and no one will stop you, they say. Broken windows proclaim you can do what you want, whatever feels good, because the consequences don't matter. There are no consequences. There's no reason to be restrained, no cause for self-discipline, no rationale for the delay of gratification. Pick up whatever rock you want and chuck it. It's fun.

The presence of broken windows can have a profound impact on the psychological health and social functioning of everyone in the area, but you would never know that if you looked at the priorities of many police departments in many cities. They're interested in going after the big crimes—murder, grand larceny, kidnapping, rape—not hassling kids chucking stones.

However, it is those very kids chucking stones who grow up to be murderers, thieves, kidnappers, and rapists when no one intervenes when they commit the petty crimes. It is for that reason that many of the smartest police departments have chosen to focus on quality-of-life issues like vandalism, littering, fare-dodging, and loud music, as well as major crimes. There is some evidence that it makes a big difference.

Some people have credited the broken window theory of community policing for the dramatic turnaround that occurred in crime statistics over the past few years.[22] Some others have blamed it for the poor relations that police departments have with the people they serve, people who are sick of being hassled and criminalized over trivial stuff.[23]

The broken window theory has fallen into some disrepute as it's used to justify *stop and frisk* police tactics and vigilantism and is used as a cover for the blatant harvesting of fines. Then there are the critics who question the methodology of the studies that draw a link between broken window policing and the drop in crime.[24] Nonetheless, I believe we can learn from the broken window theory, both in its application and misapplication, even if we are only people in personal relationships, and not people charged with the law and order of great cities.

If you were to apply the broken window theory to your personal relationships, you would pay attention to the small annoyances before they get a chance to fester and corrode. If you let the little things go and then become enraged by the big things, then you can learn from the broken window theory. Learn to intervene earlier before you lose it. Talk to your partner about what bothers you.

However, if you go after the small annoyances with the same assertiveness with which you address the larger issues, then you're doing it wrong. In the same way that a police officer must deal with a murderer differently than a vandal, you should complain about infidelity differently than, say, the toilet seat. One requires decisive action. The other, nuance, discretion, forgiveness, and mercy. If the police are perceived as coming down too hard on the vandal, or you're perceived as complaining too much about the toilet seat, you both alienate the very people you are trying to enlist.

There is a second misapplication of the broken window theory to look out for. It's not the kid chucking rocks through windows that starts a neighborhood on its decline. He is only creating the symbol of that decline. The decline started when the building became abandoned in the first place, when the business relocated, when landlords stopped making repairs.[25] Is anyone intervening then? Does anyone stop and frisk people in business suits? If not, then why go all fascist when a kid picks up a stone? Why does the kid get probation when the board of directors gets a raise?

Similarly, in your personal relationships, that thing you are so annoyed about is seldom the beginning of the annoying chain of events. If you are angry that he doesn't put the toilet seat down for you, do you put it up for him? You do stuff too. If you're wondering if there are things you do that are part of the problem, there are. If you're still wondering what they are, ask your partner. He or she will know better than you.

The broken window theory teaches us that small things matter, that there are consequences to our actions—both when we break a window and when we make a complaint.

Sharpening the Point Until You Miss It

There are two ways of asking for what you want: you can be broad or you can be precise. It's possible to be too broad or too precise.

Let's say you've been together for years and you have become vaguely dissatisfied. Nothing really bad has happened between you, but nothing exciting has happened either. One year goes by after another and it's the same thing. The fire's gone out; the passion is quenched. You're feeling taken for granted. You could complain, but what could you say? He may not know what you're talking about. He may not know what to do about it. Your dissatisfaction is pretty vague.

So, you sharpen your point and be specific. You use the rupture ratio in an earlier section and identify what could make you feel warmer toward your partner and what makes you go cold. You come up with some specific things and complain about them directly. "You never bring me flowers, anymore… You never talk about how you feel… You never thank me for all the things I do for you…" And so on.

That's getting pretty specific. It gives him something to work on, some concrete examples; it also gives you a solid standard so that you can measure progress or stagnation. If you have never operationalized your dissatisfaction in this way, you should do so, if only so you can clarify what it is you want. But don't confuse bringing flowers, talking about his feelings, and expressing gratitude with what you want.[26] They are the symbols of what you want, not the actual thing.

Chances are, if he dutifully starts bringing you flowers, talks about his feelings, and thanks you for everything, you'll be very happy that he listened to you. You'll enjoy the flowers, learn a lot about his feelings, and know that he notices all the little favors you do for him. But there will be something missing. For one thing, you had to ask for those flowers, those feelings, and that gratitude. It's not the same thing as when they come unexpected. But furthermore: all the things you ask for don't quite cover the dissatisfaction you feel. They are examples of your dissatisfaction, not the totality of it.

To better understand the phenomenon of dissatisfaction or wanting, let's say you're hungry.[27] Before you can actually eat, you have to take this hunger and be more precise. What are you hungry for? When you have an image of just the thing that would satisfy your hunger, you know what to do. You go to your kitchen and make it. You must first transform a vague hunger into a concrete hunger for something in particular. This is why taking your broad complaint of dissatisfaction and turning it into a specific complaint of no flowers, no talking, and no gratitude is helpful.

But let's say you're hungry and you start to imagine how beef bourguignon would be great right now. That's pretty specific. The specificity directs you to find your recipe and assemble the necessary ingredients. If you don't have any burgundy in your wine rack and you can be flexible, you settle for beef stew. But to the extent that you crave beef bourguignon, nothing else will do.

When you cling to a specific solution to your problem— have a craving, in other words—you start to lose touch with reality. As you form a picture of yourself eating beef bourguignon, the rich browns, the pungent smells, the complex tastes become almost real to you. Your mouth waters. As you imagine yourself eating it, you're an omnipotent, satiated hedonist. You leap over obstacles and evade frustration rather than settling for anything else. You replace uncertainty with certainty. You're triumphant. This triumph is a form of magic. The original hunger is still there; there is only an illusion of success over it. You enact a childish view of what it means to be satisfied. You seem to prevail over your need for food.

The problem is, the more you crave beef bourguignon, the less you'll be satisfied with anything else. You may not even enjoy the bourguignon if you get it, because the actual dish can never compete with your fantasy of it, except for the fact that you can actually eat it.

Craving begins as a flight from wanting, but it makes the wanting all the more problematic. Craving steals your hunger and preempts it with a ready-made, uncompromisable solution. When the solution to hunger is a craving for something specific, it becomes more of a problem than hunger itself.

The same thing happens if you cling to the idea that, if only he will bring you flowers, you'll feel excited again. The flowers become greater than any actual flowers.

The point is, if you're hungry, go ahead and imagine what will be good to eat. Look in your cupboards and see what you can prepare. If you don't create a picture of what will satisfy your hunger, you could starve to death; but don't get too attached to that picture or you will waste away if you can't get exactly what you want. In the same way, make concrete what you want from your relationship, but don't get too attached to the forms of those wants. You can't always get what you want. But, if you try sometimes; well, you might find, you get what you need.[28]

Cultivating Change

If you hang around a therapist's office long enough, or around anyone who's seen a therapist, they're going to tell you that you can't change another person; you can only change yourself.

Basically, it's true; but as with many adages, there's more to it than that. It turns out, there's a lot you can do to change a person. If there wasn't, there would be no therapists. But once you reach a certain point, there's nothing more you can do, and the other person has to take over.

Cultivating change is a lot like cultivating a garden. With a garden, you prepare the soil, plant the seed, water, weed, and fertilize the plants, but the growing is up to nature. There's a lot you can do to help nature do its thing. If you ignore the needs of nature, fail to prepare the soil, never plant the seed, and forget all about watering, weeding, and fertilizing, then you can't blame nature for your bad crop of carrots.

Preparing the seedbed

If you're feeling victimized, you've got to see the part that you played in the problem and take steps to change yourself. Doing this changes you, of course, but it also changes your partner and opens up your relationship. It's analogous to plowing the garden and preparing the seedbed. If you're feeling like the victim, it might seem that looking at the part you played turns everything upside down. Taking some blame may feel like a harrowing experience, but it gets your relationship ready for when you plant the seed.

Planting the seed

Planting the seed is an apt metaphor for when you inform your partner of the problem, ask for an apology, and demand change. If you never plant your carrot seed, you're never going to get carrots—except maybe some volunteer carrots. If you never ask for what you want, the only way you'll ever get it is accidentally.

Gardeners know that to seed a garden effectively, you've got to do it at the right time of year, at the right depth and the right spacing. Powerful agents of change know that asking for change is also a delicate matter of tact and timing. People who just complain a lot without paying attention to how they do it are like gardeners who just scatter their seeds across the ground. It's a waste of seed and a waste of complaints.

Good gardeners know that some plants can be started by seed in the garden and others must be started indoors. Change is like that too. Some changes need closer attention than others.

Paying attention

Once you've made your complaint, there's still a lot you can do to be sure that the change you desire takes root and grows up big and strong. A good gardener walks through his garden frequently to look at what he planted and see how it's growing. Does it need some weeding, some watering, or some fertilizer? Effective agents of change review progress often and make adjustments as needed.

If you complain effectively, something potentially unexpected may happen. He may begin doing the very thing you asked him to. Change is sprouting. When that occurs, it's a good idea to notice. Don't be one of those people who ask for an apology and convince your partner to change but forget to follow up. Don't speak up only when there's a problem and fail to acknowledge when your partner is attempting a solution.

You might be skeptical that she's making a permanent change. You might expect that, as soon as the heat's off, she'll go back to doing it again. You may be averse to heaping on the praise for something she should have been doing all along; but when you're silent when the very thing you asked for occurs, you're neglecting the most powerful means you have available: your affirmation. Praise and gratitude are like water and fertilizer.

If you frequently review the change you wanted, you might notice it's not growing well at all. You asked him to stop gambling, but you're still finding lottery tickets in the garbage. When a gardener finds his plants aren't growing well, she investigates why that is. She doesn't just blame nature for not cooperating; she looks to see what she could do to help it. Maybe the plant is competing with weeds. It could be that bugs abound. She could have planted the seeds poorly, so they're crowding each other, and so on.

Effective agents of change know that if they make too many complaints, the person doesn't know what to work on. When change fails to grow, they look to see if they can do some thinning. They concentrate their efforts on the things that matter the most and reserve the rest for later. If you peppered your partner with complaints about his gambling, his good-for-nothing friends, his intrusive family, the weight he's gaining, and the times he spends money like there's no tomorrow, and weeks go by with him doing nothing about any of it, then you've asked him to do too much. Work with him to choose a single item to change, and he will gather the momentum to do something about the rest, eventually.

Just as gardeners know that plants need help to ward off pests and compete with weeds, effective agents of change know that sometimes people need help to achieve their goals. If your partner is still playing the lottery, then maybe he can't stop gambling by his will alone. He needs some help, maybe more help than you can give.

Paying attention is so effective that, when you work out what you're going to ask for, you might want to ask for the things your partner can easily do right away, just so you can more easily notice.

Let's say your wife has had two DWIs. You have told her that if it happens again, you're done. You're leaving, and she can have six DWI's, as far as you're concerned; you're not going to stick around and watch it happen. She could swear to you that she'll never do it again, but you know that even when it happens a lot, it still doesn't happen very often. Five years could go by and you won't know if she'll get another DWI tonight.

The things you ask her to do should be things she can do right away, or even every day, and be related to the offense. Rather than asking her to not have another DWI, ask her to give up drinking, for instance—or at least limit it to when she's already home. Ask her to find other things to do when she needs to cut loose. Suggest she see other friends who don't encourage her to tie one on. If she makes these changes, which can be enacted immediately and noticed daily, avoiding DWIs will take care of itself.

Harvesting change

If you've never grown carrots in your garden, then you've never known the wonder and delight of pulling a carrot from the ground and marveling at what you and nature accomplished together. When you serve your carrots to your family and acknowledge you grew them yourself, you're tapping into a healthy source of satisfaction and pride. A carrot you've grown tastes better than any you could buy in the store. If you have a garden and don't partake in any of these pleasures, and just pull and eat your carrots mindlessly, then you're missing out on the best part of the gardening experience. You're likely to give up gardening and go back to buying your produce at the supermarket. So, take some satisfaction in a job well done.

In the same way, it's important to commemorate change when it happens. Make a big deal out of it. Applaud what you accomplished together. Document the difference. Go out to dinner, take a vacation, or renew your vows in celebration of the change. Go to the hardware store, buy a hatchet, and take it out in the backyard and bury it. Create or designate some kind of symbol of the achievement: a work of art or a piece of furniture, some jewelry, a tree you plant in the backyard. Have something you can point to as a symbol of reconciliation, an emblem of the renewal of love.

What If Nothing Changes?

If you effectively ask for your loved one to right a wrong he committed, you might find that he's interested in what you have to say and will do everything he can to please you and become a better person in the process. He just might surprise you and change. If that happens, it'll be an easy matter to forgive once you can trust that it won't happen again. You might still have your moments of terror if something triggers you into believing the problem's back, but you'll be able to put those fears to rest after you alert him of the warning signs and he takes you seriously. The best route to reconciliation is through authentic change. Anything less than authentic change is a bad road, full of detours, that might not go where you're wanting to go.

There are many cases, though, where you ask for what you need but never seem to get what you're looking for. What could possibly have gone wrong? What more do you have to do?

The problem could be you, the problem could be him, or the problem could be the problem.

The problem could be you
You might have committed an error in the way you went about asking for an apology and cultivated change. Ask yourself the following questions to see if your methodology is wrong. See if you could be getting in your own way.

- Do I expect him to change when I won't?
- Did I accurately describe the harm he's doing?
- Am I looking for a kind of justice that doesn't satisfy me?
- Do I know what I want?
- Have I asked for what I want, or have I asked for trouble?
- Do I overlook the small violations that lead to the big ones? Do I pounce on the small violations like I pounce on the big ones?
- Am I so particular about what I want that I can't recognize a positive change that looks different from what I expect?
- Have I failed to give him credit when he did what I asked?

If you can say yes to any of those questions, or you're not sure of the answers, go back and try again.

The problem is your partner

I knew a woman who had a snake for a pet. It was a beautiful snake, but she complained it didn't bark when someone came to the house. She took her snake to the park and threw it a frisbee, but it failed to catch it. She cuddled with it on the couch while she watched television, but it wasn't soft, fuzzy, or nice to pet.

If it's not you, then you have to ask yourself: Is it him? Could your loved one be a snake when you want a dog? Was he a snake when you met him? If that's the case, true reconciliation is impossible. The best you can do is arrive at Personal Peace.

Those who can't change

There's a second category of people who are the problem. Dead people. You might have been hurt by someone who up and died before you could reconcile with them. They're incapable of hurting you anymore, except by what your memory of them does to you. You can't expect them to change, so you'll have to change the way you think about them.

You might have a similar problem with people who have hurt you in the past who are still alive, but you never see them anymore. Just like the dead people, they can't hurt you, except by what your memory of them does to you. You can't ask them to change either. They would have no reason to please you.

You can't complain to dead people or people you don't see and expect them to change. True reconciliation is impossible with them; but I think you can arrive at Personal Peace. We'll have a section on that later.

The problem is the problem

When a person is set in their ways, or is addicted, it can be hard for them to change. To understand what you're up against, remember the last time you took a walk in the woods.

You probably walked on a path when you walked in the woods. It's easier that way. Others have gone before and cleared a way for you. It takes you somewhere. It might even be marked.

Consider what makes a path. It starts off with small animals gathering nuts, seeking food, pursuing mates, and escaping danger. They begin to wear out a trail that the larger animals take advantage of because it makes their travel easier. The deer and the bear begin to travel the same way that the squirrels and raccoons went. Then the humans take the same path because they're chasing the deer or running away from the bear and they'd rather not have briars lashing their faces.

There's one final step. Plants will not grow on an established path. All those briars will grow somewhere else where they won't be disturbed. The more a path is established, the more the rest of the forest will be dense and impenetrable.

The brain is like the woods. When it thinks and acts, it takes a path. When it takes a path often enough, the path becomes well marked and easy to follow. It becomes automatic. You don't even have to think about it. Alternate thoughts and actions become more and more difficult to access.

If you look at anyone with a well-established addiction, their brain is like a superhighway straight to the drug. Are you having a good day? Let's celebrate and get high. Are you angry, sad, frustrated? Getting high is the cure. Did your doctor just tell you your liver's shot? Did your probation officer threaten to put you in jail? Your wife just left? Your daughter won't talk with you? Get high, get high, get high. The more the addict goes to the drug, the clearer and easier the path becomes.

At some point, the addict decides the path she made doesn't take her where she wants to go. Then she has to make like Lewis and Clark and blaze a new trail. For her to change, she has to step off the easy trail, right into where all the briars are, and hack a new way. It's bushwhacking: hard work during which you can easily get lost or tempted to return to the old trail.

The same is true with anybody with any habit, good or bad. When you finish dinner and can't rest until you've washed the dishes, that's the path you have established. When your husband takes it easy and doesn't help you, that's his path. Changing that pattern may take the perseverance of Stanley and Livingstone, for both of you.

The thing is though: the brain is like the woods. When you jump up to do the dishes, you take a path. When you let him do the dishes, or do anything other than the usual way, a new path becomes established. In time, the old path becomes overgrown and more difficult to find.

To sum things up, if you find that nothing changes, the problem could be you, the problem could be him, or the problem could be the problem. Some problems, by their very nature, are resistant to change.

In our next section, we'll deal with the tougher cases, the situations when change and reconciliation may well be impossible.

8

WHEN PROBLEMS TAKE OVER

Persistent Problems

Even when people are firing on all cylinders, relationships can
be tricky. When there's a persistent problem, like an illness or
an addiction in the mix, they can be impossible. Persistent
problems can be the source of much harm. The alcoholic you
can't rely on. The gambler you can't trust with money. The
depressive who won't do anything. The phobic who won't go
anywhere. The narcissist who makes everything about her.
The guy who can't seem to keep his dick in his pants. When
problems like alcoholism, compulsive gambling, depression,
phobias, narcissism, or compulsive sex take over, it takes hard
work to eradicate them and eternal vigilance to keep them
away. Relapse can be expected. When we're talking about
addiction, it takes an average of seven real attempts before
recovery feels solid, and even then, you won't know if he's
going to need eight. Mental illness also tends to be episodic,
and if nothing is done about it, each new episode is worse
than the last. People who have succumbed once to the allure
of violence, sexual recklessness, self-harm, suicide attempts,
or self-pity are more likely to do it again. Moreover, problems
will often go into hiding when they feel threatened, so what
appears to be recovery is really a more pernicious hidden
phase of the same problem that caused so much trouble
before.

If you've been on this Road to Reconciliation and haven't gotten anywhere, maybe the person you have been traveling with, who you thought was your partner, is an impostor. If you're looking at everything differently. If what's black to you is white to him, up is down, and in is out; if when you think you're heading toward reconciliation, he says you're pointing the other way. If it seems like you're working off two different maps, you've got to consider that maybe the person you thought was your loved one has been replaced by something else.

Problems, if they persist long enough, tend to take over people. First, the problem tricked your loved one into thinking it was a good thing. Then it took control and spun him around. The problem made itself the priority, the ultimate value, the meaning of his life. He's not who you thought he was. He's been replaced by the problem. The problem is now governing your relationship. Next, it's coming for you.

Your loved one may be very sincere when she says she wants to stop drinking, stop gambling, stop being depressed, not let fear rule her life. He's speaking from the heart when he says he knows he's been self-centered. When he says he wants to keep his dick in his pants, he really means what he says. But then another day comes, and it's like nothing has ever changed. What's different? Who's in charge now? The problem is in charge. It's calling the shots today.

Have you ever seen those ambiguous drawings: when you look at them one way, you see one thing, but you look at them a different way, you see another? One way it's a young woman; the other way, it's an old one. Both views are contained in the same drawing, but in each case, it's organized differently. That's the way it is for your loved one and the problem.

In the Young Woman/Old Woman drawing, you might start off seeing the young woman. For the life of you, you can't find the old woman in the drawing. Every feature contributes to the idea that this is a drawing of a young woman. Then something happens that causes you to reinterpret what you see. The young woman's necklace is now the old woman's mouth. Her ear is now an eye. As soon as you see the old woman, you can't find the young woman anymore. In order to switch back, you have to go to a significant feature—the old woman's ear, for instance—and say to yourself, no matter how absurd it seems, it's an eye. Then the young woman comes into view.

When a problem takes over a person, that person's frame of reference is altered. Everything is interpreted differently, in a way that supports the problem. It's just like in these ambiguous drawings. That can't possibly be an eye, you say, because it's on the side of the old woman's head. In order to switch back from problem to person, the person with a problem has to be willing to believe the impossible.

In the case of alcoholism, that's why the very things that seem to you to be reasons to stop drinking are, for the alcoholic in the grips of his alcoholism, reasons to drink. Lost your job? Your old lady's mad at you? Your kids don't want to see you anymore? Your liver's shot? Got a third DWI? These are all reason for an alcoholic to drink, while for the rest of the human race, they are reasons to stop. But if you say to them, stop drinking and you'll feel better, everything will be better, they'll think you're speaking nonsense. That can't possibly be true because when they stop drinking, they feel hungover.

As long as your loved one is under the spell of the problem and you're not, nothing you say will make any sense to him. Your voice might just as well sound like a quacking duck. The problem reinterprets everything to suit itself. Within its own little world, everything is perfectly logical. In order for the frame of reference to change, your loved one has to be willing to entertain the illogical and take a chance on something that seems crazy to him.

If you've been traveling this Road to Reconciliation and don't believe you're getting anywhere, look to see if your loved one has been taken over by the problem. The problem may try to tell you what you want to hear, but the only reconciliation it's interested in is you falling under the spell of the problem. Our kind of reconciliation threatens its existence. The problem wants to confuse you, get you lost, and have you give up, so it can feast on the soul of your loved one all by itself. Then, if you're still around, it's coming for you.

How Problems Get Power

Persistent problems like an addiction or a chronic illness can take a couple into a dangerous territory where clarity turns gray and selfishness rules the day. This is a place where individuals disappear and are replaced by need; where loved ones are objectified, resented, and manipulated; where wedding vows, conceived to guide people to be the best they can be, are subverted into an evil parody no one intended. They take you into madness. It all starts when a problem demands special accommodations.

People sometimes deserve accommodations. Reasonable compromise is at the heart of friendship, much less love. If you have the flu, your boyfriend shouldn't expect you to be as attentive to him as he is to you. If you have a broken leg, your girlfriend shouldn't pout if you didn't take her out dancing. Loving partners soothe the nerves of a phobic spouse and cheer up a depressed one. They get you to the doctor, remind you to take your medicine, and don't walk so fast if it's a struggle for you to keep up. Few partners begrudge such kindnesses; most are willing to sacrifice quite a lot. Even those who freely break other wedding vows take *in sickness and in health* quite seriously.

However, there's a danger that, if accommodations persist, they will change the character of both the person with the problem and the one taking care of him. It ain't pretty.

It starts like this. You have one person who needs accommodations because he possesses a problem. In time, as the person become possessed by the problem, the needs of the problem become so great that they push aside all other needs. Then there's the other partner, who's just trying to be caring. She does everything she can to accommodate the person but ends up accommodating the problem at the expense of the person. If someone says to her, you're doing too much, she ends up questioning the meaning of her life.

The person possessed by a problem believes the problem is all powerful, its demands insatiable, so she obeys. Obeying it gives it power. Problems are fed by the accommodations we make. The sick person who doesn't eat because food makes her throw up gets weak. The disabled who doesn't push himself in his physical therapy withers away. The anxious person who lets his fears control him puts his fears in control. The depressed person who doesn't open the blinds doesn't receive the healing properties of light. The alcoholic who believes she must drink will drink, and no one can stop her.

The person become possessed by the problem may not have given himself the problem. The paraplegic may not have made herself paralyzed. Anxiety, depression, or alcoholism may all have a genetic component, but when people make themselves more ill, the problem has taken over and is running things. My name for that is madness.

Having anxieties is not madness. It's very normal, even desirable in some cases, to have anxieties; but letting your fears run things is madness. Being depressed is not madness, but not getting up to start the day when you have things to do is madness. Having alcoholism is not madness, but drinking alcohol when you know you have alcoholism is madness.

Once the problem takes over, resulting in madness, the other partner, if he does not already find satisfaction in self-sacrifice, finds that's all he does anyway. The needs of the problem push aside all other needs. The other partner stops listening to his own desires. It makes little sense for him to acknowledge, for instance, that he needs to get out and see friends when he's not able to do it. He has to stay home with his sick wife. He becomes more attentive to the problem than to himself until, at last, the problem is in charge and there is no self left for him either.

It may look as though this couple is locked in a pattern from which there is no way out, but opportunities to change come up frequently. You can see them if you know what you're looking for. The pattern can easily be broken when it arises if it's recognized and the parties do the brave thing and intervene.

Who Owns the Problem?

When a persistent problem like an illness or an addiction comes between a couple, no one wants it. It's your problem, one says to the other. No, the other says, you brought it here; the problem belongs to you. The couple comes to marriage counseling and asks, who owns the problem?

No one owns the problem, I say. The problem owns you.

Problems take hostages

The more a problem takes over, the more the life of the problem-possessed person centers on it. The person with the problem discards all forms of recreation in favor of activities that satisfy the problem. All his friends become problem-centered friends. The others drift away, and the person is drawn to those who don't judge because they, themselves, have the same problem. Sometimes particular careers are chosen for their acceptance of the problem. Agoraphobics find a job that lets them work at home. Alcoholics become bartenders; potheads become musicians; drug users become drug dealers.

Intimate relationships are changed when feeding the problem is more important than taking care of the relationship. The only loved ones who stick around are either the type where the loved one picks up after the problem and helps the person escape the consequences, or the type where the relationship is all about the shared problem.

Things go like this until the person enters recovery; then he finds that all the things he loves are all connected in some way to the problem. He can't see his friends because all his friends use and are unlikely to support his recovery because it would challenge their own problem. The alcoholic bartender can't return to work without being tempted to drink; the marijuana smoking musician has to watch what she does on breaks; the addicted drug dealer has to sell something else. Otherwise innocent forms of recreation, hobbies, or art may put the recovering person at risk. A writer who cannot write without a bottle of scotch at hand is stuck; a painter who seeks inspiration in LSD has to find a new muse.

Even intimate relationships can be trouble if they were associated with the problem. The wife who drinks is an obvious threat to the recovering alcoholic's sobriety. But so is the wife who lovingly keeps the alcoholic's refrigerator stocked with the beer he likes, even though she hates his drinking. She's almost as much trouble as the beer itself. She is too accommodating to the problem.

The general principle is this: first the problem takes the person hostage, then it takes everything he loves hostage. Even if the person gets himself free, the problem still has the other hostages in its clutches. This is how the problem tempts the recovering person back. You've seen enough hostage movies to know it's dangerous to free the hostages. It's a good way to get captured, or recaptured.

The problem is coming for you

Even if you didn't start off as the person with a problem, you soon will be if you love a person with a problem. The problem will be so demanding of them that it will take priority over you. We see this clearly in the case of the addict who chooses their drug over their relationships, but it's also the case with other types of problems. A person possessed by anxiety, for instance, may regard her anxiety as the primary thing she's concerned with. She will do nothing or go nowhere if it might make her anxious. If she does get anxious, as her partner, it'll be your job to calm her down. At first, you'll gladly hold her when she's scared, validate her fears, and reassure her when she encounters her insecurities. After a while, you learn to anticipate the anxiety and shield her from the things that make her anxious. Now you've made the problem worse. How? Two ways. One, she has not learned to cope with the anxiety; you've done it for her. Two, you have made her problem your problem.

When I say the problem is coming for you, I don't mean you'll have the same problem your problem-possessed partner has: generalized anxiety, for instance. Maybe, but not necessarily. The problem changes shape on its way to you. When it takes you over, it looks like something else. You become resentful of her and her problem, so resentfulness becomes your problem. You feel injured by a person you are told you cannot blame because she has a problem out of her control. So, feeling like a victim becomes your problem. You grieve for all the things you might have done if you did not have to deal with this problem. So, grief is your problem now.

When you make her problem your problem, its needs are so great that it pushes aside all your other needs. Then you're easy prey to be picked off and possessed by some problem that is all your own. You get sick because you haven't been taking care of yourself. You get your own depression, perhaps, because you feel so hopeless. You get your own anxiety because you're on your last nerve. You get your own addiction because you're looking for some relief.

Pretty soon, you're not a partner; you're a hostage.

Are you a partner or a hostage?

How can you tell if you are you a partner or a hostage?

What's the difference between the two?

- Partners have choices. Hostages have to do what they're told.

- Partners can leave and speak. Hostages are captive and silenced.
- Partners share power. Hostages have no power.
- Partners compromise. Hostages adjust.
- Partners are trusted. Hostages are checked up on.
- Partners are loved. Hostages are blackmailed.
- Partners' boundaries are observed. Hostages' boundaries are violated.
- People take partners. Problems take hostages.

So, which is it? Are you a partner or a hostage? Which do you have? A partner or a hostage?

Where Problems Come From

Chances are, neither you nor your loved one asked for a persistent problem. Illnesses happen beyond anyone's control. Some diseases are inherited, like Huntington's; others are transmitted, like Ebola. Mental illness and addiction are thought to involve a multifactor genesis called the Diathesis-Stress Hypothesis.[29]

The Diathesis-Stress Hypothesis

According to the Diathesis-Stress Hypothesis, people are born with a genetic predisposition which is then activated by stress. (It's really more of a theory than a hypothesis, but I like saying Diathesis-Stress Hypothesis more than Diathesis-Stress Theory. Try it yourself.) You may have schizophrenia written into your genetic code, according to this theory, but it is not until you encounter a peculiar stress in adolescence or early adulthood that the symptoms of schizophrenia emerge. Everyone's got something they are susceptible to: psychosis, depression, anxiety, addiction, or whatever. You could be fine all your life, but if that decisive straw lands on your camel's back, it'll break one way or another.

We shouldn't think of these genetic tendencies as bugs in the system or hairline cracks that widen when enough tractor trailers go over the bridge. They're natural variations. Remember your evolutionary theory. It doesn't pay for every individual member of a species to be exactly like everyone else. Nature needs to build in variation so that if the environment changes, some will be prepared for it. Back when people thought they needed to be in touch with the spirit world, even schizophrenia, a condition that we regard as extremely disabling, was a prized quality. In the same way, there are circumstances where being depressed, anxious, OCD, or ADHD may be adaptive. You never know when you might need a touch of kleptomania.

Normal reactions to abnormal experiences

Other things that emerge as problems are normal reactions to abnormal experiences. Almost anyone who smokes enough tobacco will become addicted to it. Addiction is the result of ordinary biological processes whereby the body adjusts to a substance ingested or self-created, although the path toward addiction may be speeded up if you've got that susceptibility.

Post-traumatic stress is another normal reaction to an abnormal experience. It is true that not everyone who experiences a particular horrible event develops post-traumatic stress disorder.[30] However, we do believe that the accumulation of stressful events or experiencing a single event in early childhood, when you are particularly vulnerable, will lead to the development of the condition.[31]

Choice

All of these accounts miss the part that personal choice and responsibility play in the matter. These theories make it look as though madness is preordained. I don't think people choose schizophrenia, for instance, but the person with schizophrenia does choose whether to isolate himself, take his medication, and work with the people available to help him. The depressed person has a choice about whether to stay in bed all day or open the blinds to let the sun in. The anxious person can decide whether to avoid or face that which makes her anxious. The alcoholic chooses whether to drink.

When an alcoholic doesn't drink, he is still an alcoholic, but he is not choosing to activate the condition. Similarly, the depressed, anxious, or psychotic person can do a tremendous amount toward alleviating or even eliminating their symptoms. They do not have to be passive victims.

I am aware that people with mental illness are subject to extreme social prejudice. I know that they often get blamed and blame themselves for things that are out of their control. I work with them intimately, on a daily basis. However, as a counselor, it is my business to help people identify the ways that they contribute to the problems they face and the things they can do about them. It does them no good to tell them that they are only the unlucky recipients of flawed genes or a chemical imbalance or have too much stress in their lives if they do not also address how they unnecessarily add to that stress.

Your loved one may not be responsible for having a problem, but he is responsible for what he does with it. What's more, when you locate that sense of personal responsibility, you have just found what's left of the person that's not possessed by the problem. Then you can begin to tell the problem to go back to wherever it came from.

Create Problem-Free Zones

If you've been hurt, and the problem has taken over your relationship, there's plenty that you can do other than succumb to the problem yourself. Just because your boyfriend wants to get stinking drunk every time he goes out, doesn't mean you have to clean him up when he comes home. If your girlfriend picks fights with everyone, it doesn't mean you have to make excuses for her. If your husband choses to gamble away his paycheck, it doesn't mean he has to spend yours too. Get out a little, be healthy, let your partner clean up his or her own mess. Create a Problem-Free Zone.

Create a Problem-Free Zone even if your wife has a problem through no fault of her own. Do it for the sake of your own health and so you can be more effective in helping her with it.

You've been on airplanes when they go over the safety procedures. They always say put your own oxygen mask on before helping anyone else. I've never been in a situation in which the oxygen masks are needed, but I think it's good advice. It's even good advice when you're dealing with a problem.

There are lots of ways in which a problem takes over a relationship, but the surest way is when the caregiver forgets to take care of herself. She becomes entirely preoccupied with what the problem needs. For good reason. Problems scream the loudest. They're the squeaky wheel that gets the grease. Your needs can wait, you think.

No, they can't.

I'm not talking about emergencies, of course. If a carotid artery is severed, then, yes, forget that you need to go to the bathroom. Call the ambulance and apply pressure to the wound. You can pee later. You can pee in your pants. In fact, you might be peeing in your pants anyway if someone's carotid artery is severed in front of you. Other than carotid arteries, there may be a few other kinds of emergencies that require you to forget your needs completely, but not many. Not everything is an emergency. In fact, very few things are. I know, I used to work in an emergency department.

There are practically no true emergencies
When I worked in the emergency department, I was the guy who handled all the psychiatric emergencies. There were the suicidal people, just talked down from ledges, the homicidal people the police brought, the domestic violence people who wouldn't settle down, the psychotic people who were trying

to fly. Often the people who brought them in—the friends, the relatives, the Good Samaritans—were breathless with excitement and trepidation. People were anxious to help. I had just the thing that would make them all feel better. I had a waiting room.

We even had a name for what happened when they waited: waiting room therapy. Believe it or not, there's a change for the better that occurs when people don't do anything—provided they're safe, of course. When you don't do anything, your heart stops beating so fast, your adrenalin wears off. You have time to think, to talk, to reconsider options. When someone else doesn't rush to solve your problems for you, you often solve them yourself. You discover your own abilities. You learn that you can bear most things; they are tolerable. You develop endurance.
It's not like I purposely made people wait. Far from it. I was always gung-ho about seeing people in a timely fashion. Most of the time I was keen to learn about new cases, and even if I wasn't, it was in my interest to close them. Sometimes I would see the people when my bladder was bursting, when I needed to eat, when I should have taken a break. But all the waiting couldn't be helped. We were in an emergency department after all. It was busy. It was understaffed. There were a bazillion forms to fill out. That's what people did there—wait. Just like everyone else, I was forced to learn the therapeutic properties of the waiting room.

When you rush to take care of her problem while neglecting your own, you're doing a disservice to not only yourself but also her. You don't give her a chance to solve her own problem or, at least, to learn that it's not as big a problem as she thought. If you make her dependent on you, she'll resent you for it and the problem will get stronger. You'll hold all your sacrifices against her, especially the ones she never asked you to make. Furthermore, by neglecting your own needs, you decrease your own effectiveness. How good a listener do you think I was when I took a case when I really needed to pee, to eat, or take a break?

Where you can put a Problem-Free Zone

Look for places where you can create a Problem-Free Zone, no matter what the problem. If your wife is bedridden, the Problem-Free Zone can be the whole rest of the house. Remove all the machines, the medical supplies, the pills, all the stuff involved with the management of the problem and confine it to just the spot where it needs to be. Redecorate the Problem-Free Zone to be an area of vitality. Put pictures on the walls and things that are involved with your other interests, activities other than caring for your sick wife. More importantly, keep those other interests. Go to your yoga class, play softball with the guys, stay connected with family as you would cling to a lifeline if someone handed it to you. Even more importantly, confine the attitudes of the problem to the sick room. Close off the hopelessness, the irritability, the dependence and don't let them invade everywhere else; but don't close the door on the bedridden person.

If your sick, bedridden wife doesn't want to be alone with the problem, then you're very lucky. That's a sign of health on her part, an indication that her whole personality has not been taken over by the problem. In addition to the rest of the house, create a Problem-Free Zone in her sick room by removing all the medical objects you can off to the side so that what she mostly sees are things associated with health.

Problem-Free Zones can be created in time as well as space. Play chess with her, watch shows together, let her take care of you however she can. Restrict actions related to care to certain necessary times of the day. Ban complaints of pain, grumblings about the doctor, screams of anguish to particular times when you ask how she feels. Lock up the problem, shove it in the basement, wrap it up in duct tape, and free the person.

If your problem-possessed partner is not bedridden, you might have to be more inventive about establishing Problem-Free Zones. Alcoholic husbands and angry, paranoid adult children tend to make messes and spread their problems everywhere they go. In that case, go somewhere they don't go; somewhere they would never go. Most alcoholic husbands wouldn't be caught dead at a tea party, so acquire a taste for having tea with your friends. Paranoia dislikes therapists, so find a therapist and create a zone in that office where you can be yourself. If your husband drinks too much whenever you go out with him, don't go out with him. He can go himself while you go to your tea party. If your wife fights with your mother every time they get together, do something different for Thanksgiving.

People often ask me how I tolerate listening to people's problems all day, every day. I tolerate it very well, usually, because I know my limits. I've learned that if I try to have more than six sessions a day, I'm not as effective as when I see fewer people. I seldom get calls from people outside sessions, I guess because people know they have my full attention during the sessions. When I do, I keep them brief. Six hours a day of problems is about all I can handle. All the rest is a Problem-Free Zone. I can do a lot in six hours. The rest of the time is for me, my friends, and family and giving me time to do other things, like writing these books and reflecting on my experience.

Creating a Problem-Free Zone is really very easy, though it might take some imagination. It's all about knowing the difference between the problem and health and creating a boundary between the two. It might look like a selfish thing to do, but it makes you a better caregiver and a more loving spouse. A Problem-Free Zone will ground you and nourish you so that you can better defeat the problem and maintain your relationship with the person you love.

Feed the Person, Starve the Problem

One Halloween when I was a kid, I came home from trick-or-treating with a plastic pumpkin full of chocolate. My mouth had been watering ever since the second doorbell, but my costume prohibited taking an early snack. As soon as I got home, the mask came off, and I had my first piece of chocolate. The taste of that chocolate was so exquisite that I can still recall it. If I hadn't been a kid who didn't know anything about it, I would have said I was having an orgasm over that piece of chocolate. It was so good that I had another and another and another, until before I knew it, or my parents knew it, the entire pumpkin was gone, and I was so sick I barfed all the chocolate right back into the pumpkin where it came from.

The funny thing is this: no single piece of chocolate I had that night tasted as good as that first one. Each subsequent piece held the promise of the same pleasure I experienced in the first but, to an increasing degree, failed to deliver. As I worked my way through the pumpkin, the pleasure was replaced by a feeling of revulsion, but I kept eating anyway. Apparently, it wasn't enough revulsion to overcome the promise of pleasure.

I knew that my parents would make me stop and put the chocolate away for later, but I told myself I worked hard trick-or-treating and deserved to enjoy my chocolate without interference. They were always telling me what to do and never listened when I told them I didn't like Brussels sprouts or that I would go rake the leaves when my TV show was done. Because they didn't listen to me, I wouldn't listen to them.

I started feeling sick to my stomach before I finished the chocolate. Once I'd barfed it all up, my stomach felt better, but my mother heard, and she was all over me about how greedy I had been. She sent me to bed immediately after making me clean it up. As I lay there feeling sorry for myself, I thought about what might make me feel better. You guessed it; I thought of more chocolate.

How a problem is fed

I think you'll agree that I had a problem with chocolate that night. How was that problem fed? You might think that initial, exquisite piece of chocolate got me going. Ask any addict and she will tell you about how wonderful her first high was. A gambler will recount how once he hit it big. Someone hooked on shopping will tell you about the time she found a certain pair of shoes. I experienced something on a minor scale that night that addicts experience on a major scale every day. I was chasing the initial high. No high will ever approach the joy of the initial high, however, because the neurochemical pleasure receptors fill up. In advanced stages of addiction, the addict isn't using to even feel good anymore; he's shooting up just to feel normal.

We see the same pattern with people who get consumed by anxiety and compulsively seek reassurance. Each reassurance holds the promise of peace but fails to deliver. Depressed people crave the comfort of their bedsheets but, when actually in bed, get no enjoyment from them. With all due respect to the addicts who cherish their first high, anxious people who seek reassurance, and depressed people who crave bedsheets, I disagree that problems are fed by these experiences. I believe they're fed by fantasy. Imagination, anticipation, and desire are the soup, salad, and main course that sustain a problem. They are washed down with rationalizations, justifications, and self-righteousness. Then self-pity comes in to provide dessert.

I think you can see how fantasy fed my problem that night as I craved that first piece of chocolate while I was still trick-or-treating. Then the first piece gave me more material to work with, enough to sustain my imagination until the pumpkin was finished. I had plenty of rationalizations and justifications in how hard I worked, in how I should be rewarded for my costume, and in my resentment of parental control. Rationalizations and justifications are fantasies too, fantasies of righteousness. And self-pity? No child can barf into a plastic pumpkin, get yelled at by his mother, have to clean it up, and go to bed early without being subject to loads of self-pity. Self-pity then returns the person to the fantasies of comfort and righteousness.

Problems are fed by the fantasy of relief, more than the experience of relief. People are able to recover to the extent they are able to release those fantasies and embrace a reality that may be unappetizing at first but sustains life better than a fantasy ever could.

So, where does this leave the loved one of the problem-possessed person who's being hurt every day by his partner's devotion to her problem? What can you do to break the grip that the problem has on your partner?

Feed the person, starve the problem

I never could keep my grandmother's advice straight. Is it starve a cold and feed a fever or feed a cold and starve a fever?

It's just as well that I can't remember it; modern medicine discredits the practice of withholding nourishment from any sick person, regardless of whether they have a cold or a fever. Therefore, I propose that we modify the old saying to something that actually makes sense.

Feed the person and starve the problem.

Stop feeding the problem

If my mother had been feeding my problem that Halloween, she would have been out there trick-or-treating for me. She wouldn't have sent me to bed; she would have baked me a chocolate cake. She would have cleaned up my barf for me.

So, if you know what he's like when he drinks too much, why do you buy beer for him? She gets paranoid when you keep secrets from her and starts to imagine all kinds of wild things, so why do you withhold information? His doctor has told him that, at this point, it's detrimental to his recovery from back surgery for him to lay in bed all day, so why do you bring him things so he doesn't have to get up? She's been feeling sorry for herself ever since she lost her legs in that accident. She doesn't believe she can do anything, so why do you push her wheelchair?

You do it because the problem talked you into it even though it's counter to the best interests of both you and your loved one. You've got your own fantasy of peace, comfort, and righteousness going on. You've bought into the belief that *the* problem can solve your problems.

Tough love

Starving the problem is commonly referred to as tough love: showing love to the person by being hard on the problem that's destroying him. But people have trouble giving tough love; either they do it wrong, or they don't do it at all. They don't do it at all when they give in to the problem. They do it wrong when they're tough on the person as well as the problem and starve them both.

You see the result of misapplied tough love when you walk on city streets and look at who's living there. The streets abound with homeless, abandoned people, the recipients of what is called tough love. The dream is that if they hit bottom hard enough, they'll be motivated to renounce the problem.

I've seen it, I've tried it, and I can tell you: it doesn't work.[32] If the person ever does become motivated, he then lacks the hope and the resources to follow through with recovery. If you're thinking of kicking your loved one out of the house, leaving him homeless, because it's not safe to live with him, that's one thing. If you're doing it because you think it'll motivate him, that's different. It won't. The person needs certain essentials if he's ever going to fight the problem.

Feed the person

Not feeding the problem doesn't mean that you stop doing all nice things for your partner. Feed the person. Identify those actions that make her stronger and promote your bond. Continue to do those or resume them if you've stopped.

People need certain essentials if they are going to thrive. They need good food, clean water, a healthy environment, and a roof over their heads. They need to be safe and have access to health care. Because people are social creatures, they need to be surrounded by people who aren't afraid to connect with them. Because people are self-aware, they need to have a sense of dignity and purpose to their lives. Take away any of these, and you cripple their ability to change.

So, confront the fantasies that feed the problem and starve it, but feed the real needs of your loved one.

Don't Play the Problem's Game

There's no question about it; starving the problem is a brave thing to do, even if you're careful to not starve the person. Your partner certainly won't give you any credit for doing it. He, after all, has already been overcome by the problem and is thinking like it does. When he's suicidal, he's going to say he feels betrayed because you called 911. No problem likes it when the guys in the white coats come; but when he's in his right, true mind, he's going to be glad that you made that call.

You also should not expect to see any changes right away. Before anything sinks in, you'll get caught in the snags of an intermittent reinforcement schedule.

Intermittent reinforcement schedule

A lot of psychological studies are just plain silly. Do we really need experimental data to tell us that power corrupts, or that pain and sickness are depressing, or that people like to hear things that confirm their biases? However, there is one bit of experimental psychology called operant conditioning that causes people's faces to light up when I tell them about it. It informs them of something that ought to be obvious but isn't. It can explain how you get caught up in the madness of doing what you have always done despite mostly getting the crappy outcome you've always got. What is this result of experimental psychology that has so much explanatory power? We call it the intermittent reinforcement schedule.[33]

It's easy to train a pigeon to peck at a lever. All you need to do is give it a piece of birdseed whenever it does. After only a few times, it will get the hang of it. It's nearly as easy to train a pigeon, once it's learned to peck at a lever, to stop. All you need to do is stop giving it the birdseed. It will keep pecking at the lever for a few times, but eventually it'll learn that no birdseed is forthcoming and it'll go on to do other things, whatever it is that pigeons do when they're not pecking at levers.

But what happens if, when you are teaching the pigeon to peck at the lever, you give it birdseed only once in a while? That's what experimental psychologist BF Skinner discovered when he ran low on birdseed in the middle of training his pigeons. In an effort to conserve the birdseed, he tried rewarding them intermittently. Skinner found that it took the birds a bit longer to learn that he wanted them to peck the lever, but once they caught on, they were lever-pecking machines, obsessed with pecking levers, pecking them whenever they could, pecking them till the cows came home. Then, when he tried to get them to stop by withholding birdseed entirely whenever they pecked at the lever, they kept right on pecking. Skinner discovered that rewarding behavior intermittently was more powerful than doing it consistently.

You know what was going on in those pigeons' minds when Skinner was trying to teach them that no birdseed was forthcoming when they pecked the lever; they were thinking, *Maybe this time I'll get lucky.* It's the same thing that's going on in your mind when you feed quarters into a slot machine for the zillionth time. It's the same thing going through the mind of any addict when he shoots up, walks into a bar, clicks on porn, or cruises the personal ads on Craigslist. They're all looking for the big payout. The fact that they more frequently come up empty or worse, have adverse experiences is insignificant compared to the fact that occasionally they're rewarded.

It's also the same thing that's going through the mind of a partner of those addicts, or the battered spouse, or the abused child when he seeks love and affection from a person who mistreats him. Some of the time, they get what they're looking for—sometimes they get love and affection—but sometimes they don't. They are on an intermittent reinforcement schedule from hell, unable to escape because of their own expectations.

So, where does this leave you, or anyone who's trying to help a person change? It leaves you having to endure your partner testing your limits to see if you're serious. It leaves you saying she's incapable of change. But she's not incapable of change. She's actually in the middle of the process of change. It leaves you with having to be consistent and persistent.

Eventually, Skinner's pigeons did stop pecking at the lever, but it took a while. If Skinner ever messed up and gave his pigeons birdseed when they pecked at a lever, he got them going all over again. They were thinking they were still on that intermittent reinforcement schedule and would go on pecking. That's what you do when you mess up and feed the problem, even just once.

You know what he's like when he drinks too much, but you bought a beer for him. She gets paranoid when you keep secrets from her and starts to imagine all kinds of wild things, but you withheld information. His doctor has told him that, at this point, it's detrimental to his recovery from back surgery for him to lay in bed all day, but you brought him breakfast in bed. She's been feeling sorry for herself ever since she lost her legs in that accident, but you pushed her wheelchair.

Now the problem happily thinks that nothing has changed and will go on doing what it was doing before you tried to starve it. You're back to square one and it's not entirely your loved one's fault. You gave some mixed signals and reactivated an intermittent reinforcement schedule.

Positive reinforcement
If you're really clever, you may have already thought of

something. If Skinner really wanted to make his pigeons stop pecking at levers, you might be saying, he was going about it the hard way. All he had to do was to reward his pigeons whenever they pecked at something else. They would naturally stop pecking at levers if they got their birdseed from another source.

You learned that positive reinforcement is more effective than negative reinforcement. Therefore, you reason, all you have to do is reward your loved one when he does well. Give him love and praise when he spends time with his family, when he takes out the garbage, when he saves for a rainy day, when he racks up the clean time; then he'll naturally stop doing drugs, gambling at the casino, running up the credit card bill, and getting hammered every time you turn around. Honey catches more flies than vinegar.

That might work for the easy things; positive reinforcement is more effective than negative reinforcement most of the time. But if you've got a real problem on your hands, then your praise, your rewards, your love, your kindness, your convincing rationale, your unconditional positive regard are never, ever going to be enough. You're competing with crack cocaine, with crystal meth, with heroin, with hitting it big at the blackjack table, with a big sale at the shoe store, with passionate sex with a new conquest, with a good buzz. Do you know what you're up against? Do you think gold stars are better than that?

So, how about pain? Can pain challenge the reinforcement that problems provide?

Negative reinforcement
What if Skinner had hooked up an electric current to those levers so that the pigeons got zapped every time they pecked at them? That would make them stop. Similarly, if your loved one suffered enough negative reinforcement as a result of the problem, she would stop too, you'd think.

If it worked, there would be lots of ways you could use negative reinforcement to end your loved one's dependence on the problem. You could yell, scream, and carry on whenever you caught him doing whatever he does. You could leave him and get all his friends and family to reject him too. If all those methods seem too mean, you wouldn't have to provide the pain yourself. You could just step aside and stopped taking the natural consequences of the problem yourself. If the kids are too noisy for him when he's hung over, then too bad; there's a negative consequence that will make him stop.

Wrong again. Problems already provide plenty of pain and continue their merry way, despite it all. First, there's the withdrawal, the hangover, the remorse, the shame. Then there're the consequences of having poor judgment when problems make decisions. The money problems, work problems, legal problems, and health problems that often arise. Keep a problem long enough and there will be plenty of pain. Keep it a little longer, the problem will use the pain as an excuse to keep doing what it was doing.

Think about it from the pigeon's point of view. If it thinks that lever is its only source of birdseed, it'll continue pecking, despite the zap, rather than starve. Hey, it's a living. You probably put up with a lot too, for the sake of making your living.

Playing the problem's game
BF Skinner and other experimental psychologists like him have often been criticized for confusing pigeons with people. The critics are partly right. Of course, you and your loved ones aren't pigeons. Normally you're a whole lot brighter than that, but the problem isn't. Problems think like pigeons, and anyone who's under the influence of a problem thinks like a pigeon too.

Problems are like pool hustlers when it comes to operant conditioning. You're never going to get anywhere as long as you play the problem's game. They've got you coming and going. A problem will outlast you. It'll dismiss your negative consequences, laugh at your positive ones, and make your loved one think there's an intermittent reinforcement schedule long after you've given up and gone back home. That's how it lures you in and takes your lunch.

The key to escaping this situation, for both you and your loved one, is as easy and as hard as thinking about what you're doing. Exercise your freedom of choice. Don't be a bird brain, recognize when you're the chump in this game, and play something different.

Team Up With the Person Against the Problem

If you get the opportunity to work with your loved one to vanquish the problem, don't mistake this opportunity for the problem itself. You could blow your chance because of the presence of your own problem.

Let's say your husband has not been able to keep it in his pants. He's flirted with others, cheated on you, and generally made a mess of things. Now, you're sitting in a restaurant, having a nice meal, when he leans over to you and says, "See that woman over there? I'm going to have a hard time keeping my eyes off her."

Before you lose your lunch, be glad he's telling you this. He's telling on his problem. He's trying to enlist you in a fight against it. He's not just a hound dog who'll never change; what he's exhibiting is a sign of progress.

At the core of every problem is a piece that ain't ever going away, nor should it. There are people who are sex addicts because human beings are attracted to other human beings. That's also why we have passion. There are people who are compulsive gamblers because it's thrilling to take chances. That's also why there's bravery. There are people who are drug addicts because human beings want to escape ordinary life. That's also why there's fun. There are people who are verbally and physical aggressive because human beings want to make their ideas prevail. That's also why there's leadership. The problem should not be confused with these core qualities. The problem has taken these qualities hostage and made them it's slaves.

Getting back to our example. I left you at a restaurant, beginning to lose your appetite. The problem is not the attraction your husband has to other human beings who aren't you; the problem is what he's done with it. What he used to do with it was handle it on his own. Back then, he would see a beautiful woman and he'd be all over her; if you asked him, though, he would say he didn't notice she was there. He did this because he was ashamed. Maybe he also had a ridiculous desire to protect you. Feeling shame never helped anyone do better. Shame drives people underground. And trying to protect you by keeping secrets from you gave you the indigestion you're feeling now.

So, what should you do if he says he finds another woman attractive? Well, if you admire her, you should say you think she's beautiful too. If you don't, then in the most uncatty way possible, say why. The idea is to take this dangerous situation, this bomb that's about to go off, and defuse it. Turn it into an ordinary occurrence and it'll stop being something special.

You can also praise him for being aware and getting help for his triggers. This is what we counselor-types try to teach addicts to do all the time. We don't try to teach an alcoholic to pretend that they're not near a liquor store—that's not possible—but we do teach them to notice when they're walking toward a liquor store. The problem is not that they notice liquor stores; the problem is that they walk in them without thinking through what they're doing. The more aware of their preoccupations they are, the less preoccupied they will be. Then we teach them to get help. Never handle a trigger alone.

You might not be the best person for him to confess his triggers to. Hearing him say he finds another woman attractive, even if it's just a stranger across the room, may just be too much for you. That's what your upset stomach is trying to say to you. The hurt from what he did before is still too raw. The memory makes you want to puke. If that's the case, then this is how his problem possesses you and becomes your problem. You're being triggered when he says he's being triggered.

At the core of your problem is a piece that ain't ever going away, nor should it. You're jealous because relationships matter and can be threatened by bad choices. That's also why we have fidelity. Your problem should not be confused with this core quality. The problem has taken your fidelity hostage and made it its slave.

Don't try to pretend that you're not jealous—that's not possible—but do notice what you're doing when you're jealous. The problem is not that you're jealous; the problem is when your jealousy prevents you from teaming up with the person to fight the problem that's making you jealous. The more aware of your preoccupations you are, the less preoccupied you will be.

If you can't do this, get help. Your husband needs help because he won't be getting it from you. You need help because you're being triggered. Never handle a trigger alone.

Get Help to Defeat the Problem

When a problem takes over a relationship and hurts people, the people in the relationship disappear and the needs of the problem consume everything. If you're the person with the problem, your job is to recover and get your self back. If you're the other person, your job is to recognize the problematic portion of the relationship, starve it, stay connected with the healthy parts, feed them, and get help. Once a problem begins to take over, never try to take care of it yourself. It's too dangerous. It already took possession of your loved one. Now it's coming for you. You need someone objective, preferably someone who understands the problem and its effect on relationships. Someone who isn't afraid to tell the hard truth, but also someone who can say it delicately, so you can listen.

Problems hate doctors

It might be obvious that a sick person needs a doctor, but when a problem is in charge, sick people don't go. Problems don't like what doctors have to say. (Although there are some problems like hypochondria and addiction to prescription medication that try to enlist doctors in their pathology.) Problems would rather everyone be in denial so that they can work their evil in secret. You can tell how much your loved one has succumbed to the problem by how much he resists working with the people meant to help him. If it seems like he's always fighting with them, it's really the problem trying to defend itself.

If the problem-ridden person is working with a doctor, then the other partner needs to as well. You both need to understand the problem and treatment. The doctor may need information about the condition that only onlookers can provide. You, your partner, and the professionals need to form a team that works together, not in isolation from each other.

There are two factors that get in the way of a treatment team effectively working together.

Get out of the problem's spell

The first is when the people who are supposed to treat the problem fall under its spell. Anyone who has ever been around an anxious person knows that anxiety is contagious. People dealing with the depressed often fall into despair. It's easy to get inflexible when you try to cope with a rigid person. Parents of addicts have been known to score drugs for their darlings, to keep them safe. Wives will wait on a husband hand and foot when he is supposed to get up and be active. Divisions are created between the people who are attempting to treat the problem and the ones facilitating it.

Betray the problem

The second most common barrier is put up by partners who

attempt to protect the sanctity of their relationship. They believe it's a betrayal of their partner to get help, a violation of boundaries. To be sure, some partners will see it that way. He may be angry if you tell on him. However, the sanctity of the relationship has already been violated; that happened when the problem moved in and refused to leave. You're not telling on him; you are informing on the problem, and it's the problem that is doing the objecting. You're not betraying your loved one when you send him to the emergency room, suicidal; you're protecting him from a common enemy that has him bamboozled.

If your ill partner will get help to combat the problem, that's very good. If she won't, then that should not stop you from getting help yourself. Remember, you're next in line to succumb to the madness. Create Problem-Free Zones, meet your friend for coffee, unload to your family, make an appointment with that counselor, if only so you can keep things straight and stay in contact with a rational world.

Learn to Walk

Stand with your feet comfortably together. Take one foot and stick it out in the direction you want to go until you throw yourself off balance. Then, at the last instant, when you're about to fall on your face, bring the other foot forward to stop yourself from falling. Repeat this dangerous operation as long as it takes to get where you're going.

When you think about walking this way, it's a wonder anyone would try it. Why would you throw yourself off balance and risk injury when you could stand in one spot?

Because you want to get somewhere.

To get somewhere, you have to take chances and do things that you are unaccustomed to doing. Throughout the whole journey down the Road to Reconciliation, you must do things despite an uncertain outcome. When you love someone, it's not natural to see that she is hurting you. When you're feeling like a victim, it's not natural to see that you have power. When you're self-righteous, it's not natural to accept some blame. When you're indignant, it's not natural to be merciful. When you're ashamed, it's not natural to take responsibility. People who seek justice want it fast. It's not natural to be patient with change. None of this is natural, but it's also not natural to stay stuck and immobile.

What should you do if a problem has taken over your relationship?

Walk.

For starters, once you learn to tell the difference between the person you love and the problem, walk toward the person and away from the problem. If they're inseparable, create Problem-Free Zones and walk there. Walk to get help and then walk with the help.

Every step involves you taking a risk and doing what seems unnatural. When a problem takes over, it's natural to be taken hostage, unnatural to break free. It's unnatural to trust a stranger. It's unnatural to say that your loved one has become possessed by an alien being. It's unnatural to acknowledge that your partner is divided in two and you're only going to cook dinner for one of them.

What if your partner doesn't walk with you?

What if, when you walk away from the problem, you leave your loved one behind?

Being in a relationship means you walk together. You and your partner are like two feet. When you stand together, things are perfectly comfortable, but you can't stand there forever. You want to try different things, be someone different, do something with your life, develop, grow. It's inevitable. You'd feel stuck standing in one place too long. It's static, suffocating. The blood pools in your legs. It's bad for the heart. You must move or the whole world will leave you behind.

Healthy relationships cycle through two phases: comfort and growth, standing still and moving forward. When you first meet, you take great strides together as you get to know and accommodate one another. Then you get comfortable. The next thing that happens is one partner gets a wild hair to do something outrageous, uncharacteristic, and steps out into perilous space. In healthy relationships, they're not afraid to do so, because they know their partner will follow. The partner will come along, like your other foot, and they will soon be safely in balance.

Healthy parent-child relationships are the same way. Generally, it's the child who takes most of the first steps, wanting to be independent or to try some new thing. Good parents follow along, celebrate or adjust to the changes, and support their children. No one can be a good parent if they are not open to their child changing.

In unhealthy relationships, people are afraid to change. They wait around for the other to be ready before they take a step. They don't want to be the first one to propose something. They don't want to risk disconnection. Conditions must be perfect before they try.

Can you wait for your partner, your other foot, forever?

Sad to say, people do. It happens all the time. But, whoever takes the step, sets the direction and the pace. The other has to follow or be left behind.

When a problem enters a relationship, people get stuck waiting for their partner to change. If one of your feet is injured, the other foot takes the weight. You nurse the bad foot. You don't go anywhere. Standing on one foot for a long period of time is very hard—just as hard as taking care of a loved one subsumed by a problem—but you could do it for a very long time if you thought you had to. People have done it forever.

At some point, even a broken foot will be mended. The bone will fuse together, but the muscles will be weak, the tendons stiff, and the spirit uncertain. You'll put weight on it gingerly and there will be some pain even though the bone is fine. Your first steps will be tentative. You might not even try, but it's important that you do, because the other foot has been bearing the burden and is getting tired. When a problem takes a person over, he doesn't even try, even when he is able. He avoids pain, dodges uncertainty, and lets the other partner carry the weight, even when there's no need.

So, if you're the partner, in order to prevent the problem from taking over, you will have to take a step. Distinguishing the difference between your loved one and the problem, getting help, creating a Problem-Free Zone, and taking care of yourself are all important steps, but the most crucial is to grow. Don't let the problem prevent you from growing. When he sees you change, he'll have to change with you or be left behind.

If he does get left behind, it's as much his choice as yours. He's choosing to remain with his problem. He's picking his problem over you. When that happens, keep walking.

9

WHEN RECONCILIATION IS IMPOSSIBLE

Settling for Personal Peace

Not everyone makes it all the way to reconciliation. You can't get there alone. If your partner has not done his part, you'll have to settle for Personal Peace. Personal Peace is nice, but because it's personal, you can't share it.

If you have done your part to arrive at Reconciliation, you've already experienced much of Personal Peace. You assessed the injury and noted the part of you that can't be hurt. You put the damage in perspective and have not been carried away by your feelings. You acknowledged your role in the matter and have done what you can to make that part right. You've asked for the kind of justice you can get effectively and waited long enough for it to be delivered. If you have done all that and your partner has not, you won't have a true reconciliation, but it may not matter so much anymore; at least you are starting to have a sense of Personal Peace.

In Personal Peace, you can't change the past or undo what has happened. You're not going back to the way things were in the beginning. You're at peace with what happened. You haven't effected change or stopped her from harming anyone ever again, but you're making the best of a bad situation. You took a bushel of sour lemons and made gallons of delectable lemonade.

When reconciliation is impossible

Your father was abusive to you as a kid. He called you names and beat you on more than one occasion. He never seemed happy with anything you did. This affected you deeply and caused you to be more than a little screwed up. After you became an adult, whenever you tried to bring up his mistreatment of you, he said you were whining. Now he's so old and demented he doesn't know who you are. You can go to therapy, nurture your inner child, and do your darned best to not repeat his performance on your own children, but reconciliation between the two of you ain't happening. He's incapable of reconciliation.

You could say that you're reconciling yourself to what happened. You could forgive him for what he's done, act like a loyal child, and visit him in his nursing home every other day, but it's not reconciliation with him unless he does his part. You'd be doing something good—acting with generosity, forgiveness, and grace—but it's just you who'd be doing it. You'd be doing it for him as you would want someone to do it for you. All by yourself, you would have made an undeserved gift of healing and gave it to him. You could be proud of that.

What you did is analogous to giving money to a beggar on the street, versus giving him a job like raking your leaves so he earns his own money. It's better when he earns his own money—better for him that he can make a fair exchange, retain his dignity, and contribute to the tidiness of the world. It's better for you in that you get your leaves raked. When he doesn't earn his own money, he runs the risk of becoming dependent on your largess, and you run the risk of lording it over him.

However, not every beggar can earn his own money, and not every offender can do what needs to be done for reconciliation. Some beggars can't hold a rake, or you may not have leaves, or you may not want the beggar near your house. Some beggars have nothing they can do that you'd want. In the same way, not every offender is capable of reconciliation, and I think that an elderly father with Alzheimer's might be one of them. The best you can do is to give him the forgiveness he cannot earn. You can feel good for doing so.

In this case, granting forgiveness is worth more to you than it is to him anyway. It's not like he can beat you anymore. You're not going to have him babysit your kids or expect him to show up to your dance recital and not point out every mistake you made. You can visit him at his nursing home, as if the bad stuff never happened, because it makes you a better person for doing it, and he'll barely notice.

When to give up on reconciliation

A spouse who's so lost in addiction that you barely recognize her might be another example of when reconciliation is impossible. You can't even count the number of times she swore she would get clean but disappointed you. Every word out of her lips is a lie. She can't even take care of herself, much less take care of your hurt feelings. If you're expecting her to turn it all around, stop doing the dope, and make amends for all the harms she's caused you, then you may be expecting too much. She might be able to do it, but not anytime soon.

Whether reconciliation is possible in this example depends on how much time you have and what it costs you to bear with her. As you stick with her, she may be accruing a massive debt to you, digging a bigger hole that she will never be able to climb out of. Breaking up with her while she's doing harm to you may be the kindest thing you can do for her as well as for yourself. Reconciliation is a tough road. Those who try to do it while, at the same time, battling addiction don't make it. They have to learn to manage the addiction first before they can take care of the harm they have caused you.

There are many cases where reconciliation is impossible now but may be possible later. If it's impossible now, it's best to stop trying. Abandoning reconciliation temporarily means you have that much less aggravation to endure, one less fight you have to fight. You can turn your efforts to something that'll actually make a difference, like seeing your friends, volunteering at a soup kitchen, or trying a new recipe for veal saltimbocca. You can abandon reconciliation for twenty minutes while you take a walk to clear your head or for twenty years, which may be how long it takes for her to get serious about her addiction. You can abandon reconciliation for good or leave the door open for when she's ready to try.

Reconciliation is a worthy goal, but the Road to Reconciliation is a difficult road. Like every road, it needs a place to pull over for when you can't go on.

Have an Escape Plan

If a grizzly bear wandered into your home while you were asleep, slipped into bed beside you, and woke you up with its hot breath in your face, what would you do?

I think you would plan your escape.

You might not run right away. The bear might seem friendly at the moment. You might think it best not to disturb it. You might not want to leave it alone with your family. Even if you didn't take off right away, you would still plan your escape.

That's what you should do when a loved one has hurt you. Devise an exit strategy for getting out of range even if you don't think you'll use it.

When you escape, you can go far or stay close. You can leave in the middle of the night without telling anyone, travel to another state and change your name, or you can just say I can't be with you now, go for a walk, and come back in twenty minutes. Both are escapes that differ only in implication and degree.

Having an escape plan can do wonders for your ability to cope, giving you a feeling of safety and security. Paradoxically, it can make you more able to be present.

Being more present by having an escape plan works like this. If I have a client who needs to talk about something she's never told anyone before, something she doesn't think she can tell anyone, and is hesitant about it, we'll set up an escape plan for her. We agree that if she feels she can't go on talking about it, all she has to do is say the word and we'll stop. I encourage her to try it. When she knows she can use the escape plan, and that I'll honor it, she'll be more able to move forward.

It's also like this. When you're driving down the highway and you have an empty breakdown lane to your right, you're going to feel a whole lot safer than when there's no place to pull over. Having an out feels more secure.

An escape plan works in concert with the Problem-Free Zone. It does you no good to have a Problem-Free Zone if you're not willing to use it, to escape to it when necessary. If a grizzly bear invaded your bed, you might let the bear have the bedroom and go to the rest of the house. The rest of the house would be what we call the Problem-Free Zone. Ideally, the Problem-Free Zone should be large enough and secure enough so that, when you go there to escape from the problem, the problem can't get to you there. If the problem follows you out there, then you need a new Problem-Free Zone.

In the same way, if you had pulled into the breakdown lane on the highway only to look up and see a tractor-trailer barreling down on you in the breakdown lane, you'd jump out of the car into the weeds on the side of the road. You should always have an escape plan, even when you've already escaped and should be safe.

Your partner might think of the escape plan as a threat, but it doesn't need to be. If he's in the middle of making a point in an argument, it's inconvenient when you say you can't talk any more. He might think you're avoiding the issue. But believe me, it's worse when you stay. Similarly, if you move out and place an order of protection against him, it's really for his own good. If he respects it, it'll keep you both from doing something you'll regret.

As a matter of fact, having an escape plan is good even if you're the one who has committed the offense—if you're the one who is alcoholic, drug dependent, a gambling fiend, violent, or whatever. You should have a couple of escape plans. One for when those self-destructive impulses are triggered, so you can escape your own demons. The other for when you fail to escape it and your loved ones finally get fed up with you and what you do. It's only a matter of time before they are.

In the next part, we'll go over the escape plan checklist: the elements of an escape plan that make it a good one.

The Escape Plan Checklist

Every problematic situation needs an escape plan. Escapes that are not planned tend to go awry, so plot your exit strategy beforehand. These are the elements of an escape plan to consider when a loved one has hurt you.

What would trigger the escape?

The most important part of any exit strategy is figuring out when you might use it. What kind of event would put it into motion?

There are three kinds of triggering events and three corresponding exit strategies. The first kind of triggering event is when you just can't take it anymore—when you've become emotionally flooded, you're on your last nerve, and you're ready to scream. You and your partner start off having a discussion, it turns into an argument, and next it'll be a fight. You know that if you keep going, nothing good will come of it.

When this happens, you need to make a small escape. Take a walk, go for a drive, or even just go to separate rooms. It's best not to make big decisions when you're in this state, but little ones, like deciding to take a break, can make a big difference.

If your partner doesn't let you take this kind of break, that proves your need to take it. It shows that the problem may be much more serious than you thought. Then you're going to need more time apart and higher security measures.

The second kind of triggering event is when there's an escalation or a return of the harmful behavior. If your verbally abusive husband ever puts hands on you, you know that things aren't getting better; they're getting worse. Or if the recovering alcoholic starts drinking again: you know you're in for another round of the same. Get out now, if only for a while, for your own safety, or because you always said you would.

The third kind of triggering event is when you see no improvement over a period of time. There haven't been any dramatic scenes, only daily misery. He makes promises to take action against the problem but fails to do so. He hasn't gotten roaring drunk, or spent a thousand at the races, or thrown another chair through a wall, but if he hasn't gotten the counseling he promised, if he still studies the racing pages, or if he hasn't fixed the wall; then you may not want to hang around forever waiting for the next shit storm. I would recommend setting a sell-by date like grocery stores do with milk.

If you're going to use the sell-by date to motivate your partner to make changes, then it needs to be far enough in the future for her to make recognizable changes, but soon enough so she doesn't forget it's there. If you're going to use the sell-by date to motivate yourself, then it's helpful to put it at a natural turning point in your calendar like a birthday, New Year's, or an anniversary. Sometimes it's when the lease is up, when school gets out, when the children leave home, or at retirement. Women who want children may want to consult their biological clock when setting a sell-by date.

What's the level of security you need?

The more danger there is, the more protection you're going to need.

To determine the level of security, think about the worst your loved one has ever treated you. Just how controlling, insistent, intrusive, pestering, violent, and unable to take no for an answer can she be when you try to be independent? Imagine one click more. That's the amount of danger there will be and level of security you'll need if you try to escape.

Therefore, if your partner is pretty easy going, figure on him being more than just piqued. If she's given to verbal abuse, she'll be making threats. If he's already made threats, now you'll see displays of anger. If you've seen holes in the walls and thrown objects, the next target will be your body. If she has put hands on you before, this time she'll use weapons. If he's already used weapons on you, now he'll mean to kill.

The reason for this is the problem. Remember, the problem wants you involved. It ultimately wants to get its claws into you. If you're leaving, even if it's just to clear your head, it'll double its efforts to keep you near. The person possessed by the problem believes the problem's interests and his are the same, so he'll act in concert with the problem's promptings.

Next, assess the comfort you have for these kinds of risks. If you're a six-foot-four football player and your partner is a hundred pounds, soaking wet, then you can tolerate physical danger better than when it's the other way around. If you're the kind of person who can brush off insults, verbal abuse, and the mind games that are sometimes played, then it's different for you than if you believe everything everyone says about you. If your financial status can accommodate losses, you can tolerate more risk than when you live hand to mouth.

Also, think about others who might go with you or help you escape. How much drama can they handle? A young child, or an older one with a case of the nerves, is not very well equipped to handle tension. They might be better off further from the problem too. If you're staying with your mother and your mother is a nervous type who can't handle your husband stalking you, you'll need to take security measures you might not think necessary.

Will you tell him before you go?

Ideally, you should tell your loved one that you have to take a break before you do so. Not only is it common courtesy to keep her informed, but giving her a warning that you may leave could motivate her to turn against the problem and make changes. But the level of security will determine whether you can give her notice. If she's likely to go apeshit and there are real risks, then it's best if you leave a note and disappear when she's not around.

Where would you go?

The level of security determines the distance you should put between yourself and the person who harmed you. You should go to a place where you are safe.

It could be as easy as going for a drive, taking a walk, or even hanging out in another room. If you can go to these places without the person following you there, and can clear your head and return refreshed, then that's as far as you need to go.

But if she doesn't permit you even that little space, then you need more of a break. You can approach the question of how far to go in degrees if you want: first by trying the walks, then, if that doesn't work, by staying with your mother. If she follows you to your mother's, then you've got to go further underground.

How long should you be gone?

The further you go, the longer you need to be gone; sometimes you need to be gone for good. In milder cases, like when you go for a walk to interrupt an argument, then twenty minutes is enough as long as you don't spend those twenty minutes rehearsing zingers. If you do, then you're not ready to be back.

If you're escaping to stay with someone else, then remember that fish and houseguests go bad after three days. If three days is not enough of a break, you either need another couch to surf or your own place.

When planning how much time you'll need away, you should take into account the emotional reaction the loved one you're leaving is likely to have. The initial response is often rage. She'll feel betrayed by you. You won't want to walk back in the door while she's still steaming.

Next she may go through a period of self-pity and may do something self-destructive. If you come back then, you're going to be roped into taking care of her. Resist the temptation to do this. Instead, wait for the point when she's ready to take responsibility for her actions and has begun to make repairs. Notice I didn't say when she makes promises to make repairs, but when she actually starts making them.

Depending on the level of security you need, and the level of pathology at hand, you may need to prepare to be gone forever. If that's the case, this road doesn't go all the way to Reconciliation, but it can take you as far as Personal Peace.

What should you take?

If the level of security is low, all you need are the usual things you take when you go for a walk or a drive. If it's high, you should already have a bag with essentials packed. Keep it in the trunk of your car or at the place to where you might run. Put in that bag all the important things you're going to need: a burner phone (he can trace yours), phone numbers, copies of keys, identification, and important papers and keepsakes. Since credit card use leaves a trail, you should have some cash saved up and stashed aside where he can't find it. If there are items she might attempt to use as hostages like heirlooms, pets, or children, plan to take them too. You don't want to have any reason to go back unless you're ready.

If the level of security is in the middle range, you may still want to pack a bag. It signals that you are determined to protect yourself. It fortifies you to take that step if you need it.

Un-merge money
No one with a persistent problem in their relationship should have a joint checking or credit card account. In a sense, your money should escape his control before you do. Long before you leave your residence or end the relationship, if it comes to that, you should equitably split up assets and obligations. This is not only to facilitate your escape but also to define boundaries, head off future disputes, and keep the problem from feeding off your financial assets.

Loans and mortgages that you have in common are another impediment if you try to escape. If it's possible to terminate those obligations, then do so; but it's not always possible. At the very least, avoid getting into any new ones. All the more reason to separate your other assets.

Who can you count on?
Except for when the level of security is low, part of your escape plan should include notifying or, at least identifying, allies and supports. Take inventory of who your real friends are, who you can call on to spend the night or take the kids while you keep an appointment. Choose the people you can trust who do not have a conflict of interest between you and your partner.

Take inventory of the support you can get from the community. Do you need an order of protection? Is there a probation officer who'd be interested in what he's been doing? Do some research into the resources your region has in place for people in your predicament: homeless shelters, if it comes to that, women's shelters, father's rights organizations, and the like. Do you have a therapist you can bounce things off of? A church congregation that can deliver casseroles and send up prayers? If divorce is part of your escape plan, then see an attorney so you know your rights and obligations.

How will you control communication after the escape?
You won't want to go through all the trouble of leaving your home only to have her pestering you wherever you go. Think about what you'll need to do to control communication. Block his number or, if you need to be reminded of all the trouble that comes when you pick up the phone when she calls, change her name in your contact list to *Trouble*. If your security needs are high, this might involve getting a new phone, changing your number, and not leaving a forwarding address. If things get verbally ugly, think about getting out of social networking sites for the time being, just so nasty grams don't get exchanged there.

Part of devising a plan to control communication may be to give him a channel for communication. That's what lawyers can be for, or mediators, or saintly relatives, if they're willing to be put in the middle. Have your ex call them if he needs to get in touch with you. Set this up beforehand while you're formulating your plan. If your security level is lower, then you may not need to do this. In that case, set up regular times, places, or media to use to discuss matters.

How will you support yourself?
If you're financially dependent on your partner or parent, then a crucial part of your escape plan will involve finding a way to support yourself. This is the time to get a job if you don't have one and deposit your earnings into your own account. In addition to financing an escape, a job gets you out of the house, away from the problem, and gives you an opportunity to make new friends, who can be a support.

If you're not able to work or you can't find a job, then you'll need to arrange other forms of financial support. This is the time to apply for welfare or disability.

What will you tell people?

I've found that one of the major things that holds people back from making their escape is that they don't know what they would tell people who need to know. You don't know how much to tell. You don't know if you can tell it without breaking down. You've been saying everything is fine for so long, you don't know how to admit there have been problems. You're not even sure, yourself, if you have a good enough reason to leave.

It's best to tell the truth to everyone, but you're going to need at least two stories: a long version for the people you owe a full explanation and a short version for the others. You'll need to make firm distinctions in your mind between who really needs to know and the ones who are looking for gossip. If there are kids involved, you'll need developmentally appropriate versions to tell them that don't alienate them needlessly from their parent.

Having an exit strategy, and executing it, is just a prudent, responsible thing to do. It doesn't mean you don't love the person. It means you love him too much to let him keep doing things he'll regret.

Getting Closer by Separation

Look at the shoes you're wearing. Your two shoes go together; they match. No one can say that they don't. Even if you lose one and leave it behind in the road, they are still a pair of shoes.

Now tie them together, one to the other. Go ahead.

Now try to walk.

You'll be able to do it. You'll take short, mincing steps. If you had to walk that way, you could. If you lived in a world where everyone tied their shoes together that way and walked, you might not consider doing it differently. However, I think you'll agree it's not the best way to get around.

Go ahead and retie them the way they are supposed to be tied. This is the end of the demonstration.

Now think about your relationship with the person who hurt you. How tightly are you tied together?

Be careful how you answer; it's tricky. If you say, "We're not tied together at all, she seems to do whatever she wants," that might be just part of the story. What do you do when she seems to do whatever she wants? If you're still with her, then my guess is that you try to tie her up to you.

Every moment, you want to know where she's been, what she's done, and when she's going to come home. You say you do this because you can't trust her, but the result is that you're tied all that much closer to someone you say you can't trust. You can't tie her up without tying yourself up too. Then she tries to break free. Maybe she does whatever she wants because being tied that close together is just weird.

We therapist types call this enmeshment.[34] It's a standard feature in codependent, addictive, problem-ridden relationships. Anxious parents seem prone to it, which drives their children to do the very things that make their parents anxious.

What would you do if someone came after you to tie you up? You'd run away, which would, of course, give them all the more reason to want to tie you up.

But think about how you lose a shoe. You don't lose a shoe because it's not tied to its partner. You lose it when it's not tied to itself.

Therapeutic separation

If you believe that two shoes tied together is a good metaphor for your relationship, and an untied shoe a good metaphor for yourself, then I have a special kind of escape plan for you. You might not go for the standard escape plan where you just leave. You might need to escape each other together.

This kind of escape plan is called a therapeutic, or trial, separation. It's a deliberate, bilateral decision to part ways temporarily for the sake of cooling off and focusing on individual issues. When done well, it can make your bond stronger while, at the same time, permitting the individuals maximum autonomy.

A therapeutic separation may be more common than you think. In the case of parents and children overly involved with one another, when the child goes off to college, both he and his parents can experience a kind of therapeutic separation that gives the child a chance to experience life on his own and parents a chance to adjust to an empty nest. There are, of course, many instances of helicopter parents attempting to hover over their child while they are off to college, but the opportunity is there for all parties to individuate by being apart from one another.

Therapeutic separation is an integral part of rehab. If your husband goes off to rehab for his alcoholism, for example, he's going to be separated from you. In addition to all the other services provided by rehab, it should give you both an opportunity to clear your head and get in touch with yourselves.

Therapeutic separation works best when there is a contract. Spell out the terms beforehand so you both know what the rules are.

Here are a few things to deliberate:

Living arrangements
Who will move out and where will they go? Having a therapeutic separation in the same house is hard to pull off. Borders should be clearly drawn and mutually respected. You need to give each other some space to find out who you really are. You should be far enough apart that you have some privacy. There should be doors and walls and locks and keys involved, to establish some boundaries.

Contact with one another
How and when will you get in touch with one another? Think about which means of communication works best for both of you, whether in person, by phone, e-mail, letter, or text. You should be able to reach one another in a true emergency, but

casual check-ins should be discouraged. Check-ins are often really check-ups. It's best to have no contact at all for at least the first week or two. Then you can start to have regular dates together, like you did when you first met. On these dates, try to find something new to do together, something that neither one of you has done before, so that you're both on equal, uncertain footing. The idea is to recreate the excitement you once felt when you first got to know each other. Alternate fun dates with serious ones when you talk about serious issues.

It's best not to have sex with each other until the later stages of the therapeutic separation. This is because of the role that sex plays to bind you closer to one another or as part of a dysfunctional pattern. This is a good time to find other ways of relating to one another and developing other satisfactory types of touch.

Prohibited activities

What activities are permitted while you are separated? Is it okay to date or have sex with others? To me, if you're separating so that you can get in better touch with yourself, then it doesn't make sense to get involved in another relationship that's going to have its own set of demands.

Mandatory activities

What are you expecting each other to accomplish while you're separated? This is a good time to go on a retreat or a pilgrimage, to do some art or writing, or to travel places the other has never wanted to go. If you're having a therapeutic separation so your husband can go into rehab, then completing rehab would be an expectation. But even when no one is going into rehab, some form of counseling for each of you, individually or together, is strongly encouraged and should be stated explicitly.

Family and friends

Before you begin the therapeutic separation, talk about what you will say about it to your family and friends. Some may deserve an explanation; others, none at all. Some family and friends may take a position and try to tell you what to do, but what I said about not getting involved in romantic or sexual relationships applies here as well. If you're having a therapeutic separation to get to know yourself, you wouldn't want a friend or family member to exert a lot of influence over you either.

If there will be important holidays or events during the therapeutic separation, plan on how to handle them.

Children

If you have young children, then provisions will have to be made for both parties to see them. The younger a child is, the less time should go by without contact from a parent. A therapeutic separation can result in a deeper, more responsible relationship with your child because there is no third party to interfere.

Duration

Three to six months is considered the optimal length of a therapeutic separation; any shorter is too brief to stop the dysfunctional patterns, and any longer generally means you're going to split for good. To me, the important thing is that, if you come back together, it's because you want to, after giving it a good try on your own. You'll want to stay apart long enough to get used to it, so that you are not coming back together out of an infantile dependency

Because rehab is seldom longer than twenty-eight days, this means she may be released before the therapeutic separation is done. Just because she's done with rehab, it doesn't mean she has to come back home. If you can afford it, she can go to a halfway house or get her own place. If she has to come home, then talk about if you can continue the therapeutic separation while still living together.

Getting back together

A therapeutic separation can help you come to a decision about whether to stay together or split for good. If spending some time alone makes you realize how much you have been putting up with, you might decide to go off on your own, permanently. Or you could conclude that you get along better when you don't live with each other. Or when you remove the stresses and strains of daily contact, you could fall in love all over again and make another go of living under the same roof.

You don't know what will happen, so don't make any promises about getting back together.

If, toward the end of the therapeutic separation, you both decide to come back together, then start spending more time with one another. Have some overnights. Have some sex. This might be a good time to renew your vows. Or, rather, take the things you have learned about yourself and about each other when you went through this process, and write some new vows that mean something.

Calibrate Your Compass

When you escape the madness that your relationship has become, whether you are gone for the rest of your life or for twenty minutes, you have an opportunity to do something that can set the course of your life from that point on. You can calibrate your moral compass.

Moral compasses need calibrating just like ordinary ones do. Take a perfectly functional compass and put it in a room with an electromagnet and it'll forget which way is north. It'll point to the electromagnet because the electromagnet is exerting a force that it cannot ignore, far more powerful than that exercised by the distant magnetic pole.

Every problematic relationship exerts a force every bit as compelling on your moral compass as that electromagnet on an ordinary compass. It'll alter your attitude, change your course, and make you forget yourself and your values. You can't do anything without checking with the relationship first.

You must get free of that interference in order to calibrate your compass.

What this means is that, for the moral compass to work properly, you must forget the needs and requirements of the relationship for as long as it takes to connect with yourself and recognize what is important. It means escape. It means if you have lost yourself; you try to find yourself. You abandon thoughts of reconciliation, at least for now, and focus on personal peace.

Getting your bearings

If you've ever calibrated an ordinary compass, you'll know that, for a minute or two, the needle will spin around aimlessly until it finds magnetic north. You'll be lost if you try to use it and confused if you rely on it for direction.

When people free themselves of the effects of a relationship, for a minute they feel similarly lost and confused. When they escape, they often feel as though they've lost their bearings. They don't know what's important anymore because they've been separated from their own values for so long and lived someone else's. Many go back to having their lives dictated by the relationship. It's more familiar and comfortable.

To remain free of the effects of a dysfunctional relationship, it's important to stay with the process of calibration long enough to get your bearings straight. Reconnect with your values by finding them behind your emotions, renewing your religious faith, exploring spiritual practices, writing the story of your life, clarifying where you find meaning and purpose, and reminding yourself of the things you told yourself you would never do. Listen to that still, small voice inside you, the one that had been drowned out by the bombastic cares of the relationship and identify where it tells you to go.

Finding the path

Your moral compass can tell you the general direction of whatever is significant to you, but it can't tell you completely how to get there. If you want to head to a destination, you still must contend with the topographical features as you go. You can't head straight in that direction all the time if a mountain, or a river or an ocean gets in the way. The compass direction is one thing; the path you take is another.

When you choose your path, consider whether it takes you where you want to go, to the things that you find important, either directly or the long way. If you have more than one thing you value, the perfect path will take you to all of them. If there are people you want to go with, the path should include their destinations as well.

Remember one thing. Your moral compass points to a very particular direction, but there are infinite routes that you can take you there. Insist on your values, but don't get so hell-bent on which path you take that you overlook the alternatives.

An example of using a compass

Say you and your wife have been hurting each other for years. You decided to have a therapeutic separation, which revealed two things to you. Once you removed yourself from the day-to-day strife, you found that you really love your wife. The second revelation was that your unhappy marriage was caused by an unhappy life. You hate your job because you feel that designing widget parts for a widget manufacturer is meaningless.

So here you have two important compass readings, two values: the love for your wife and the desire for a meaningful job. With this in mind, you plot a course that takes you to both destinations. You meet with your wife and tell her that ending your marriage would not make you any happier, so you want to get back together. Then you'd like to do something that makes a real difference to the world, like teaching math to inner-city kids. You believe that if you had some meaningful work, then you wouldn't be so grumpy when you came home.

That sounds like a reasonable path, except that, meanwhile, your wife has been looking at her own compass. If you love her, you must take her values and desires into consideration. She tells you that her unhappiness was an unhappiness in the marriage. Since you began the therapeutic separation, she's been feeling liberated of having to take care of you. She's lost her love for you. Her compass is telling her that independence is important to her. She's had enough of bearing the burden of your grumpiness, and she's not willing to support you while you quit your job, go back to school, and take up a new career with an uncertain outcome.

So, your best laid plans have come to naught. You now have the challenge of finding a path that fulfills both your dreams: to love your wife and find a meaningful career. Luckily, there are infinite paths to particular destinations. You just have to be flexible enough to use them.

In this case, the best expression of love for your wife may be to give her the freedom she desires. The Road to Reconciliation doesn't always take you where you want to go. It is sometimes necessary to set a new course and renegotiate the terms that will make you happy.

The Renegotiated Relationship

Once you're in a relationship with someone, you'll always be in a relationship with that person. The only real question is this: What kind of relationship will it be?

Seizing the rope

Picture yourself having fallen off a cliff and hanging on to a bush. Just as the roots are beginning to give, someone lowers a rope down to you. It's the person you once loved, who hurt you, and whom you no longer trust.

Do you grab the rope?

I think, no matter what you might say, you would grab the rope, but maybe not until after the bush began to give way.

If, out of spite, you don't grab the rope—you don't want to give him the satisfaction of saving you—then you die.

If you do grab the rope, then you've demonstrated that, no matter how untrustworthy a person is, if the need is great enough, you'll trust him.

After he hauls you back up and you catch your breath, you might not fall into his arms and live happily ever after. The wounds of the past are still unhealed. He may have saved your life, but he's still a jerk. However, you have succeeded in setting aside your differences to work together toward an important goal. You briefly renegotiated your relationship.

I tell this story as a way of saying that sometimes, not only when you fall off a cliff, you still have a need that only your former loved one will satisfy. When that happens, you renegotiate your relationship.

The renegotiated relationship

Once a relationship is made for one purpose, it's possible to change that purpose to another. When you get together with someone to hang on Friday nights and end up having sex, you've renegotiated the relationship. When you decide to be exclusive, you've renegotiated it again; and again when you give her a ring. Before you know it, your relationship is all about raising kids and paying off a mortgage. Hopefully, you still enjoy each other's company on Friday nights. In long, vibrant marriages, purposes accumulate. In ailing ones, they die off.

If you have lost some purposes but others remain, then it may make sense to renegotiate the relationship. People do this all the time when they get a divorce but cooperate with each other to raise kids. They say their union is finished, but it's really not; it's been converted into another kind of union, working together toward a different purpose.

The couple might not achieve authentic reconciliation this way; they never go back to the fullness of their relationship as it existed before. You don't need to trust that your husband won't sleep with other women, for example; you just need to trust that he'll bring back the kids. These can be very satisfying and valuable relationships, nonetheless, for both of you and, especially, for the kids.

Renegotiating and growing up

You can see this process of renegotiation in any healthy relationship between parents and children. In early childhood, parents are responsible for everything and they can claim almost complete access to their child. When you were young, you crapped in your pants and your parents had to clean you up. When they did so, they would touch you in a private area. As you got older, you had to clean yourself up, and in doing so, you earned the right to set boundaries on your parents. As an adult, your parents can't touch your ass—they may even have to knock before they can come in your house—but you can have a very satisfying, valuable relationship with them nonetheless.

In cases where you have been harmed by a parent, you may need to renegotiate the relationship further. If your father can't say three words to you without being critical, then you may not want to play golf with him every weekend, because you can't trust him to go eighteen holes without getting on your nerves. On the other hand, you might not want to sever the relationship completely, because you don't think that would be right. Besides, you still want to see your mother. That's what Thanksgiving dinner is for, I guess. For the sake of peace, your relationship has been renegotiated into one where you have a meal once a year.

The long way to reconciliation

When someone has been harmed in a relationship and the relationship is renegotiated into something more limited, we can't really say the partners have achieved full reconciliation. It's not like they've gone back to the way things were before, but they have negotiated a peace, so to speak. They instituted a demilitarized zone that none can cross. Having this understanding is so much better than all-out war, but the partners still warily patrol the border for violations and incursions. In time, if the DMZ is respected, it can turn into an ordinary boundary that requires no special defense. Then you might say there's reconciliation, if only because the two parties simply don't need to fight.

It's hard to believe that two former British colonies, the United States and Canada, have on several occasions in their history fought wars against each other. The issues between them have long since passed away and only historians remember why they fought. You could say that the two countries have reached reconciliation without ever uniting. This is the long way to reconciliation, which is achieved not by the members working it out but by agreeing to leave each other alone.

Take Out the Garbage

I once facilitated a group for people recovering from severe mental illnesses. We met once a week, and they talked about how things were going for them. They tried to support each other. One day a member of the group came in and said his landlord was going to evict him if he failed to clean his apartment. Landlords can do that if the apartment is really bad. We knew that just talking about it and offering moral support was not going to help him much, so the next week, we all went to his place to help him clean. In the end, he got to keep his apartment, and I got a story about letting go.

As soon as we walked in, we could see that the landlord was right to threaten eviction and we were right to help him.

251

It was too much to overlook and too much for one man to clean. He was a major hoarder. I can't even begin to describe everything we saw, but what really got me was the pile of apple cores by his chair. This guy must've really liked apples, and every time he ate one, he would throw the core on the floor and never pick it up. The pile was, and I'm not exaggerating, as high as the arm of the chair. There were worms and flies and mold, and it stunk in a way you would never expect a pile of apples to smell.

We got right to work, and in a few hours, we had straightened and cleaned things to the point where he would not become homeless. As we cleared out the junk, and the apple cores, we discovered that, despite his hoarding, something important was missing. He didn't have a garbage can.

There was one more thing we knew we had to do before we were done helping this man. It was not enough just to help him clean. We knew we had to get him some garbage cans—three, in fact; one for every room in his apartment. I thought I was wise to put one by the chair where he dropped the apples.

A year later, I was still facilitating the same group, and we had many of the same members in it. In some ways they all had made progress, I thought, until the day the same man came in and said he was at risk of being evicted again.

"My landlord says my place is a mess. It's a health hazard," he said.

"But we cleaned your place. Have you been using the garbage cans?"

"Yes," he said.

I couldn't believe it. I had to see for myself.

When I got to his apartment, I encountered a familiar smell. The stench was the same as before. Indeed, he had been using the garbage cans. In fact, there was the one by his chair, right where I had placed it, filled to overflowing with apples. He had been using the garbage cans, just like he said. He just hadn't been emptying them.

It's easy to say that this man is not like you. I'm sure you would never let your apartment get in this condition. Well, maybe you wouldn't, but there are plenty of people who let their lives get to this point and they see nothing wrong in it.

For instance, some let their lives become unmanageable by hoarding grudges.

The last thing you will let go of

When you break up a relationship, there's a lot that you let go of. You often lose a house, a family, a set of in-laws, and some friends. You no longer have that person to laugh at your jokes or cry at your funeral. If you no longer visit your mother, she can't make you her soul-comforting macaroni and cheese. If you don't answer your brother's calls, you can't ask to borrow his truck when you need to move. When you break up a relationship, you chalk up all those losses as the price you pay for your freedom.

There's also a lot you gain. You no longer have to be hurt by the same person, in the same way, ever again. You can move on and develop a healthy relationship with someone else. While you forfeit your rights to a side of a bed, you get a whole other bed and all the covers to yourself. You can sleep all night without his snoring and not have to step around his dirty underwear when you get up.

If you end a relationship, there will be one thing you will hang on to longer than anything else. There's nothing they can do with this thing; it's useless. Unless you make a conscious effort to let go of it, you will have a persistent desire to change your former partner. The last thing you'll let go will be the impulse to convince her she's wrong.

When you elect not to travel that hard road to all the way to Reconciliation, and instead settle down in Personal Peace, you can take off your pack and unburden yourself of having something to prove. It doesn't matter anymore if she feels sorry for what she did, so you can stop wishing she would.

Grudges are so hard to maintain, you'd think they would be easy to give up, but they're not.

The thing is, you can't just, one day, say you're going to let go of all your grudges and be done with them. You can say that, but they come back. It's like cleaning your apartment. When you're done cleaning, make sure you have a metaphorical garbage can to contain the subsequent mess. As long as you generate angry and resentful feelings, use it.

The crock of shit

To illustrate what I mean by a garbage can for feeling, let me tell you about an object in my office that I use as a therapeutic tool. One client aptly named it Keith's Crock of Shit.

I think the crock originally came with some kind of cheese in it. Now it contains people's shit. By that I mean the things people need to let go of, lest they back them up and poison them. All the things they need to release: resentments, regrets, reproaches, and recriminations go in the crock. All that shit.

It works is like this. First, you identify the thing you want to let go of. Be specific. Write it down on a Post-It note. You don't have to write a book and the spelling doesn't have to be right, just as long as you know what you mean.

Next, say it out loud, that thing you want to let go of. Say, "I want to let go of…"

Now comes the tricky part. You've got to get your shit in the crock, so it'll stay there.

I put the cover back on and we check to see that no one's shit has snuck out, stuck to our clothing, or hid in a pocket. When all is safe, we unlock the door. When you leave, you leave your shit behind.

Do me a favor though. If you see your shit on the outside, when you're sitting at home or driving around, send it back. Tell it to go back to the crock where it belongs.

What's that? You want to know if this method works? It works if you send the shit back. I've done my part. You have to do yours. If you see the shit walking around, whatever you do, don't grab it and keep it all over again. What did you give it to me for if you were just going to keep it?

Do you have some shit you need to get rid of? You can make an appointment and leave it in my crock. If you can't make an appointment, you'll have to create your own crock for your shit. It's easy to do, now that you know how.

The People of the Mind

As if it wasn't hard enough to deal with the people who hurt you, you also have to deal with their representatives you carry around in your head. Actual people you can divorce, send to jail, move across the country and never see again; the people of the mind follow you, and they share your bed despite divorce. Regardless of orders of protection, they dog your footsteps, day and night. It's imperative you find a way to cope with these imaginary people or they will do you more harm than the real ones ever could.

You've heard the things these imaginary people say to you: *You're never going to amount to much… You're just a slut… You're a failure…. No one is ever going to want to be with you.* No, they weren't actual voices that you can hear. They're thoughts, but thoughts are as persuasive as voices. These words may have originally come directly from the actual person. It's like you have a tape somewhere, playing them over and over again. You worry that you might be going crazy, except that everyone has these inner critics.

You've tried to argue with these voices, prove them wrong. You've written positive affirmations, taped them to your bathroom mirror, and repeated them fourteen times a day. *Every day, in every way, I'm getting better and better… I will be successful… I'm a loving, committed partner… Everyone wants to be with me.* You think this will help, but it doesn't. The niggling nabobs of negativity natter all night, nonetheless.

At the risk of adding my voice to theirs, you're doing it wrong. This isn't the way you handle an inner critic. You'd be happier if you trained it to be better at its job.

We all need the capacity for self-criticism. A good inner critic can stop you from committing many foolish things. It'll halt you from saying that impolitic thing you were going to say. It'll make sure your fly is zipped when you leave the men's room. It'll help you pick out the perfect outfit. It'll hone your performance so that every day, whatever you do, you'll do it better and better—not because you say so but because you're learning from your mistakes. A good inner critic is like a personal trainer, a portable therapist, a life coach, and a father confessor all rolled into one. You should thank your stars you have an inner critic. It might save you from public humiliation. But you need a good one.

You can train your inner critic to get better at its job by replying to all its statements with a single word question: *Because...?*

Because...?

So, let's take the things inner critics say to people and try out this method on them.

"You're never going to amount to much."

"Because...?"

"You're just a slut."

"Because...?"

"You're a failure."

"Because...?"

"No one is ever going to want to be with you."

"Because...?"

If the inner critic is able to complete the sentence and tell you why you're never going to amount to much, etc., then you've got some information you can use. For instance, if it says you're never going to amount to much because you spend so much time playing video games, then that's an intelligent point of view you should consider. Maybe it's right. Maybe it's wrong, but at least you can reason with it. When the inner voice doesn't do anything more than pronounce that you're a loser, then it's no different from those bullies who called you names on the playground. Their words are hollow, their arguments specious. You can dismiss their claims because they have nothing to back them up.

When you challenge the inner critic to give evidence and it follows through, then you turn the critic into a trusted adviser who gives you something you can use. It becomes a consultant who is more than just a yes man. If the inner critic doesn't follow through and provide any evidence for its point of view, then it's not a true inner critic; it's an inner bully.

A simulated world

It's important to understand who these people of the mind are and what they are doing there. In the same way that a meteorologist will program a simulated climate into a computer, you set the people of the mind up to match the actual world. Then you run different scenarios. They're your creations. There should be a strong resemblance, but they are not the people they represent, and they are not you.[35]

For example, everyone who's had a father has an inner father. When you were a child, it was in your interest to be able to predict what your father would do in a given circumstance. If you thought about swiping a cookie, you needed to know whether he would smile, yell, or beat you with a leather strap. You constructed an imaginary character you called your father, based on your father. The more accurate a representation of him it was, the more useful this construct could be. This inner father is not your father; it's a simulation of your father, but if you are a good author, it would be a damn good simulation.

You would also have to give these simulations free will in the same way that you might program a computer to make its own decisions based on preordained factors. The inner person has to be able to operate on its own, without too much input from you. It does you no good to hand a script to your inner father and tell it how to respond when you swipe a cookie; you need to know how it would respond so it can tell you how your real father would. This is how come these people of the mind seem to have a will of their own. You give it to them, so their behavior can be like the free will behavior of actual people.

The simulations also have to go on running when the actual person is not around. Just because your father has left the room, it doesn't mean you don't need the simulation. You need to know how he would respond to the missing cookie when he returns. Just because you haven't seen the actual person in months, doesn't mean you won't see him again. Just because he's dead and buried, it doesn't mean you won't come across people like him someday. This is why it's often not good to dismiss a person of the mind. You might need it again.

These simulations get repurposed when we come across someone new who somehow resembles them. When you meet a new boss, for instance, you may use the model of your father upon which to construct a new model of your boss because they have something in common: they are important, powerful males in your life. This way, if something comes up in which you don't know how your boss will respond, you run the contingency through the father program, so at least you have something to go on. You may easily get confused about who you're dealing with. Many assumptions about your boss may come from what you have come to expect from your father.

You can see that you can easily get confused about who these people of the mind are. You may confuse the inner person with the actual person. You may think you know them when you don't. If you do confuse them, then that's because you're a good author and have developed rich, well-drawn characters who seem real.

A simulated self

These people of the mind do more than give you models for how actual other people may behave. They also help you work out how you will behave. They help you play with possibilities to see how they might turn out. Before you swiped that cookie, you imagined yourself swiping that cookie. You worked out how to move the chair and reach the top of the cupboard without your father hearing you. You debated whether you should drag the chair or pick it up. You told yourself that if you dragged the chair, it would rub on the floor and make a sound. That was an inner critic. It said, "Quiet, you'll be too noisy."

You can thank your inner critic for helping you steal that cookie.

The construction of inner representations of yourself has to follow the same rules that apply to constructions of other people. The simulation of yourself has to be an accurate representation of how you could be in the real world. It has to know whether you are strong enough to pick up the chair, for instance. The simulation of yourself also has to seem to have a will of its own so you can accurately project how it will behave. The simulation of yourself also has to persist over time so that you can build on past failures and successes. It can also be confused with your actual self so that you can't tell the difference.

You can hear this confusion when you talk. You say, "I keep telling myself I'm a loser, a slut, and no one will ever want to be with me."

No, that's not you talking; it's your inner critic: a character of your own creation set up to resemble you or an important person in your world. If you confuse this character with you, then you did a good job creating it, but it's not you. You are the creator. You are the person directing, watching, and listening to the show.

You are God to the people of the mind

In summary, it's important to remember that you are not God in the real world, but to the people of the mind—these simulations you have constructed—you are God, and they are your creation. You are the Almighty, and if you want, you can cast them into Hell where they will cry and gnash their teeth; or you can extend grace, mercy, and redemption to a broken inner world that matches the broken actual world.

What Personal Peace is Like and How to Get There

If you're one of those people who says you can't understand how you can forgive when you've been deeply hurt, how you can be silent when injustice abounds, or how you can rest when you must make amends, I would say you already know how if you know how to sleep.

Even if you sleep poorly, you know how to sleep. Even if you don't know how to get to the land of nod, you get there, almost every night, somehow.

To get to sleep, there are things you can do, but doing things only gets you so far. If you want to sleep, it's best to be active during the day. Exercise will help you sleep because it makes you tired. You can't be hungry when you go to sleep. It's best to have a comfortable place to doze off, one that's quiet, dark, and warm. The next thing you do to get to sleep is to follow a bedtime routine in which you wind down and cue your body to rest. Then, when your head hits the pillow, if you must think, it's better to think of just one thing rather than everything at once.

However, once you get to a certain point, you don't get to sleep by doing things. You're required to stop doing, and just be. Then, as far as your conscious mind is concerned, as you fall asleep, you cease to be. As scary as it sounds, when you remove your ego's defenses, sleep will take over.

So will peace.

As with sleep, there are certain things you can do to facilitate peace.

You can't still be in danger and have peace; you must do what it takes to convince your partner to stop hurting you or you must escape.

You can't expect to give away cheap pardon and have enduring peace; nor can you expect to have peace when you have an axe to grind, are swept away by your emotions, or are picking your sores. You have to wind down and cue your mind to accept peace, just as you cue your body to accept sleep.

You need to recognize the value of peace. Perhaps this comes when you are tired of warring with your loved one, or when you see what war can do. You get tired of war when war doesn't achieve the things you want; when the arguments, the reprisals, the revenge don't get you anything good.

Guilt is famous for keeping people up nights unless they do something to make amends. Just as the bumper stickers say: if you want peace, then do justice.

If these things you can do to facilitate peace look familiar, that's because you just read a whole book about doing them. If you have worked toward Reconciliation, then you've worked toward Personal Peace, even if you haven't made it all the way.

If you make it to Reconciliation, you get Personal Peace along with it. You can bed down beside your partner and sleep well for once.

If you don't make it to Reconciliation, at some point, you have to stop and settle for the personal variety of peace, as you would settle down to sleep, even when you have a lot to do.

Has he done nothing to deserve forgiveness? You don't have to forgive for all time. As long as you're safe, you can forgive for today and accept peace.

Does she still not understand what you're angry about? You've done all you can do now. Stop trying to convince her and accept peace.

Do you still have a debt you must pay, a wrong you must right, a transgression for which you must atone? Once you've done what you can do for one day, you can rest and be at peace, so you can do more tomorrow.

In the same spirit, this book must come to an end sometime. I've said as much on the subject of the Road to Reconciliation as I can say, for now. Maybe I'll have more to say later. If so, I'll write a second edition. I've done everything I can do, like a travel guide, to describe the Road to Reconciliation; the rest is up to you—to travel the road and see if what I have said is true for you.

That, too, is what Personal Peace is like. You do what you can do toward Reconciliation, but your loved one has to join you to make it all the way. If she does, then great. If she doesn't, then you can be at peace that you have done your part.

ACKNOWLEDGEMENTS

The first people I'd like to thank are the hundreds, if not thousands, of troubled people and relationships I've learned from during the more than thirty years I've been a psychotherapist. Every single client—whether they were an alcoholic, a drug addict, or a loved one of an alcoholic or addict; a sexual offender or the victim of a sexual offender; a person with a mental illness or someone affected by a loved one's mental illness—have all both experienced and perpetuated harms. These injuries and the need for reconciliation have been central to our work together. If I could mention you without violating confidentiality, I would. You know who you are.

Then there are the people I've hurt and been hurt by in the past. I have not reached reconciliation with all of you, but you have all taught me. It's probably better if I don't mention your names.

I've also read a few books on the subject. Some that have contributed to my understanding of forgiveness and reconciliation are listed below.

Ahrons, Constance (1998). *The Good Divorce: Keeping Your Family Together When Your Marriage Comes Apart.* New York: HarperCollins.
Bancroft, Lundy and Patrissi, JAC (2009). *Should I Stay or Should I Go?: A Guide to Knowing if Your Relationship Can—and Should—be Saved.* Black Swan.
Bass, Ellen, and Davis, Laura (1994). *The Courage to Heal: A Guide for Women Survivors of Child Sexual Abuse.* New York: HarperPerennial.
Baumeister, Roy F. (1997). *Evil: Inside Human Violence and Cruelty.* New York: Freeman.

Beck, Aaron T. (1976). *Prisoners of Hate: The Cognitive Basis of Anger, Hostility, and Violence*. New York: Perennial.

Casarjian, Robin (1992). *Forgiveness: A Bold Choice for a Peaceful Heart*. New York: Bantam.

Engel, Beverly. (2001). *The Power of Apology: Healing Steps to Transform All Your Relationships*. New York: Wiley.

Enright, Robert D., Rique, Julio, and Coyle, Catherine T. (2000, September). *The Enright Forgiveness Inventory User's Manual*. Madison, WI: International Forgiveness Institute.

Flanigan, Beverly (1992). *Forgiving the Unforgivable: Overcoming the Bitter Legacy of Intimate Wounds*. New York: Macmillan.

Flanigan, Beverly (1996). *Forgiving Yourself: A Step-by-Step Guide to Making Peace with Your Mistakes and Getting On with Your Life*. New York: Macmillan.

Fromm, Erich (1963). *The Art of Loving*. New York: Bantam.

Gottman, John (1994). *Why Marriages Succeed or Fail*. New York: Simon and Schuster.

Gottman, John M., and Nan Silver (1999). *The Seven Principles for Making Marriage Work*. New York: Crown/Three Rivers.

Guilmartin, Nance (2002). *Healing Conversations: What to Say When You Don't Know What to Say*. New York: Wiley/Jossey-Bass.

Karen, Robert (2001). *The Forgiving Self: The Road from Resentment to Connection*. New York: Doubleday.

Kushner, Harold S. (1997). *How Good Do We Have to Be? A New Understanding of Guilt and Forgiveness*. New York: Little, Brown.

Lerner, Harriet (1985). *The Dance of Anger: A Woman's Guide to Changing the Patterns of Intimate Relationships*. New York: HarperCollins.

Lerner, Harriet (2001). *The Dance of Connection: How to Talk to Someone When You're Mad, Hurt, Scared, Frustrated, Insulted, Betrayed, or Desperate*. New York: HarperCollins.

Lewis, Helen Block (ed.). (1987). *The Role of Shame in Symptom Formation*. Hillsdale, NJ:

Erlbaum. Love, Pat (2001). *The Truth about Love: The Highs, the Lows, and How You Can Make It Last Forever*. New York: Fireside.

Luskin, Fred (2002). *Forgive for Good: A PROVEN Prescription Prescription for Health and Happiness*. New York: Harper San Francisco.

Madanes, Cloe (1990). *Sex, Love, and Violence: Strategies for Transformation*. New York: Norton.

McCullough, M. E., Pargament, Kenneth I., and Thoresen, Carl E. (2000). *Forgiveness: Theory, Research, and Practice*. New York: Guilford.

McCullough, Michael E., Sandage, Steven, J., and Worthington, Everett L., Jr. (1997). *To Forgive Is Human: How to Put Your Past in the Past*. Downers Grove: InterVarsity.

Perel, Esther (2017) *The State of Affairs: Rethinking Infidelity*. Harper Collins

Pittman, Frank (1989). *Private Lies: Infidelity and the Betrayal of Intimacy*. New York: Norton.

Rosenberg, Ross (2013) *The Human Magnet Syndrome: Why We Love People Who Hurt Us*. Pesi

Safer, Jeanne (1999). *Forgiving and Not Forgiving: A New Approach to Resolving Intimate Betrayal*. New York: Avon.

Scarf, Maggie (1987). *Intimate Partners: Patterns in Love and Marriage*. New York: Random House.

Shafir, Rebecca Z. (2003). *Wounds Not Healed by Time: The Power of Repentance and Forgiveness*. New York: Oxford.

Sheinberg, Marcia, and Fraenkel, Peter (2001). *The Relational Trauma of Incest: A Family-Based Approach to Treatment*. New York: Guilford.

Simon, Sidney B., and Simon, Suzanne (1990). *Forgiveness: How to Make Peace with Your Past and Get on with Your Life*. New York: Warner.

Smedes, Lewis B. (1996). *The Art of Forgiving: When You Need to Forgive and Don't Know How*. New York: Ballantine.

Smedes, Lewis B. (1984). *Forgive and Forget: Healing the Hurts We Don't Deserve*. San Francisco: Harper and Row.

Spring, Janis A. (1997). *After the Affair: Healing the Pain and Rebuilding Trust When a Partner Has Been Unfaithful.* New York: HarperCollins.

Spring, Janis A. (2004). *How Can I Forgive You?: The Courage to Forgive, The Freedom Not To.* HarperCollins. Kindle Edition.

Stone, Douglas, Paton, Bruce, and Heen, Sheila (2010) *Difficult Conversations: How to Discuss What Matters Most.* Penguin.

Yancey, Philip (1997). *What's So Amazing about Grace?* Grand Rapids: Zondervan.

Young, Jeffrey E., and Klosko, Janet S. (1993). *Reinventing Your Life: How to Break Free from Negative Life Patterns.* New York: Dutton.

Then, of course, there's the Bible, which has something to say about forgiveness throughout.

Other shout outs

As I was writing *The Road to Reconciliation*, I posted chapters in my blog at keithwilsoncounseling.com. I got much encouragement from readers of the blog. I also assigned portions of the book to clients for whom they were relevant. Watching them struggle and profit from early drafts gave me further guidance. Thanks to you too.

My wife and first reader, Karen Rosenbloom, gave me invaluable editorial assistance. She has much better judgment than I and is a better speller.

Related Notes

[1] Readers who want scientific evidence of the connection between feeling like a victim and committing evil should read *Evil: Inside Human Violence and Cruelty* by Roy F. Baumeister

[2] The earliest use of the concept of *prohairesis* is in Aristotle's *Nicomachean Ethics*. The Stoic philosopher, and Roman slave, Epictetus, expanded the idea.

[3] I'm alluding to *The Charge of the Light Brigade* by Alfred Tennyson.

[4] Here, the allusion is to *If—* by Rudyard Kipling.

[5] The concept of codependency is, as far as I know, the invention of Melody Beattie in her book *Codependent No More: How to Stop Controlling Others and Start Caring for Yourself*. I have used this a book and concept for many years in my work with victims. My writing this book, and this section in particular, is largely motivated from a desire to get past that concept into something more nuanced and less pathologizing.

[6] To read more about learned helplessness go to *Helplessness: On Depression, Development, and Death* by Martin Seligman.

[7] Devout Christian readers who think that the commandment to forgive means to forgive easily should read Dietrich Bonhoeffer's book, *The Cost of Discipleship (English 1948)*. In it, he inveighed against cheap grace versus costly grace.

[8] Alcoholics Anonymous (1952) Twelve Steps and Twelve Traditions. Alcoholics Anonymous World Services

[9] The example of the waiter, and the existential term, bad faith, come from *Being and Nothingness* by Jean Paul Sartre.

[10] My ideas of what it means to be an adult is taken in part from David Schnarch's book, *Intimacy & Desire: Awaken the Passion in Your Relationship*. I added wisdom to Schnarch's list. He got his ideas from Murray Bowen's concept of differentiation.

[11] I am referring to studies taken in the wake of the famous Marshmallow Test, conducted by Walter Mischel. See *The Marshmallow Test: Mastering Self-Control* by Walter Mischel.

[12] Two books by the contemporary philosopher Martha Nussbaum contributed greatly to the section on emotions: *Upheavals of Thought: The Intelligence of Emotions* and *Anger and Forgiveness: Resentment, Generosity, and Justice*.

¹³ If you want to learn more about disgust, read *Anatomy of Disgust* by William Miller and the provocative *Unclean: Meditations on Purity, Hospitality, and Mortality* by Richard Beck.

¹⁴ This is another concept from Sartre. Sartre believed in the essential freedom of individuals, and with total freedom comes total responsibility. There's plenty who declare themselves not responsible for themselves or their actions, but they're making a conscious choice and are responsible for anything that happens as a consequence of their inaction.

¹⁵ Almost everything I know about shame and guilt, I have learned from making mistakes. Lots and lots of mistakes. Everything else, I learned from my clients. But the way I've made any sense of it all has been from the work of June Tangney, professor of psychology at George Mason University, the queen of shame and guilt. Together with Rhonda Dearing, Tangey wrote two books on the topic, *Shame and the Therapy Hour* and *Shame and Guilt*. She also has a very engaging lecture posted on YouTube, *Shame and Guilt: The Good, the Bad, and the Ugly*.

Somewhat more well known is Brené Brown, author of *Daring Greatly: How the Courage to Be Vulnerable Transforms the Way We Live, Love, Parent, and Lead* and *The Power of Vulnerability: Teachings of Authenticity, Connections and Courage*. She is also all over YouTube.

¹⁶ I believe when we are ashamed, we are committing the Fundamental Attribution Error. That's the mistake people make when they believe the cause of people's actions to be some internal characteristic or motivation, rather than an external factor. When an old lady ahead of you falls, you think she's too weak to get around without a walker until you trip over the same bad spot in the sidewalk.

It's easy to make the Fundamental Attribution Error when you're observing other people. There's stuff that affects the outcome you wouldn't know anything about. But you make the same mistake when you observe and judge yourself. Some things about yourself are more noticeable to you than other things.

I learned about the Fundamental Attribution Error from Kahneman, D., Slovic, P., & Tversky, A. (1982) *Judgment Under Uncertainty: Heuristics and Biases*. New York: Cambridge University Press.

[17] People familiar with Twelve Step programs will recognize that a lot of what I have to say in this part of the book is based on the methods of those programs. There's a reason for that. I got it there. Read the *AA Big Book* by A.A. Publishing if you want to see the source of it all. Unfortunately, in practice, I have found that this part of the program is often delayed and then rushed, to the detriment of the recovering person and his or her family.

[18] In 2009, the US government offered an official apology to Native peoples. It was done so quietly, with no ceremony, that it was practically a secret. What's the point then? This, and other apologies were explored by Layli Long Soldier in a book of poetry titled *Whereas.*

[19] Howard Zehr began the whole restorative justice movement with his book *Changing Lenses: A New Focus for Crime and Justice.* Gerry Johnstone continued it with *Restorative Justice.*

[20] The book I'm referring to is *Constructive Conflict: Building Something Good Out of All Those Arguments,* by yours truly.

[21] The Broken Window Theory belongs to George Kelling, from his 1998 book, *Fixing Broken Windows: Restoring Order and Reducing Crime in Our Communities.* The application to personal relationships is mine.

[22] Corman, Hope (Jun 2002), *Carrots, Sticks and Broken Windows*

[23] Sampson, Robert J.; Raudenbush, Stephen W *(1 November 1999).* "Systematic Social Observation of Public Spaces: A New Look at Disorder in Urban Neighborhoods"

[24] Sridhar, C.R. (13–19 May 2006). "Broken Windows and Zero Tolerance: Policing Urban Crimes". *Economic and Political Weekly. 41 (19): 1841–43.*

[25] Ralph B. Taylor. *Breaking Away from Broken Windows: Baltimore Neighborhoods and the Nationwide Fight Against Crime, Grime, Fear, and Decline.*

[26] We see this same point made by critics of educational testing, such as Jerry Z. Muller in *The Tyranny of Metrics.* Lawmakers, dissatisfied with the schools, attempt to quantify performance. What can and does get measured is not always worth measuring, may not be what we really want to know, and may draw effort away from the things we really care about.

[27] The general idea here comes from Adam Phillips, *Missing Out: In Praise of the Unlived Life.*

[28] Thank you, Rolling Stones. "You Can't Always Get What You Want" is a song by the Rolling Stones on their 1969 album *Let It Bleed*.

[29] B.L. Hankin & J. R. Z. Abela first made the Diathesis Stress Hypothesis in a book they edited, *Development of Psychopathology: A vulnerability stress perspective*.

[30] Wenjie Dai, Long Chen, Zhiwei Lai, Yan Li, Jieru Wang and Aizhong Liu. (2016) "The incidence of post-traumatic stress disorder among survivors after earthquakes: a systematic review and meta-analysis." *BMC Psychiatry*.

[31] Jonathan E. Sherin & Charles B. Nemeroff. (Sept. 2011) "Post-traumatic stress disorder: the neurobiological impact of psychological trauma." In *Dialogues in Clinical Neuroscience*.

[32] Maia Szalavitz (2016) *Unbroken Brain: A Revolutionary New Way of Understanding Addiction*. St. Martin's Press.

[33] Skinner, B. F (1938) "The Behavior of Organisms: An Experimental Analysis." Appleton-Century-Crofts

[34] Enmeshment is a concept introduced by Salvador Minuchin (1974) *Families and Family Therapy*. Harvard University Press

[35] The metaphor of the people of the mind being a simulated world is largely my own, but I arrived at it after reading *Internal Family Systems Therapy* by Richard C. Schwartz. I have to thank him for that.